Perestroika and International Law
Current Anglo–Soviet Approaches to International Law.

Perestroika
and
International Law

Current Anglo–Soviet
Approaches to International Law

Edited by
Anthony Carty
and
Gennady Danilenko

EDINBURGH UNIVERSITY PRESS

© Edinburgh University Press 1990
22 George Square, Edinburgh

Set in Digitek Plantin
by Jetset, Aberdeen, and
printed in Great Britain by
The Alden Press, Oxford.

British Library Cataloguing
   in Publication Data

Perestroika and international law:
   current Anglo-Soviet approaches to
   international law.
1. European Community. Law
I. Carty, Anthony   II. Danilenko,
   Gennady 341
ISBN 0 7486 0157 0
        0 7486 0187 2 pbk

Contents

Contributors

SOVIET CONTRIBUTORS

Mark M. Boguslavsky is Professor of Law, Head of Department of Private International Law at the Institute of State and Law, Soviet Academy of Sciences. He is the author of numerous monographs on international law, including *International Economic Law*, Moscow 1986. (in Russian), *Private International Law: The Soviet Approach*, Dordrecht, Boston Lancaster 1988, and *The Reorganisation of Soviet Foreign Trade: Legal Aspects*, New York and London 1989.

Gennady M. Danilenko is Doctor of Law, Senior Research Fellow, Institute of State and Law, Soviet Academy of Sciences. He is Deputy Editor (Theory), *Soviet Yearbook of International Law*, and author of *Custom in Modern International Law*, Moscow 1988 (in Russian).

Elena P. Kamenetskaya is Doctor of Law, Senior Research Fellow, Institute of State and Law, Soviet Academy of Sciences. She is author of *Outer Space and International Organisation: International Legal Problems*, Moscow 1980 (in Russian) and joint author of *Outer Space, Politics and Law*, Moscow 1987 (in English).

Rein A. Müllerson is Doctor Habilitated, Head of Department of General Theory of International Law, Institute of State and Law, Soviet Academy of Sciences. He is a Member of Human Rights Committee (UN Covenant, Civil and Political Rights), and author of *The Relationship between International and Domestic Law*, Moscow 1982 (in Russian).

Galina G. Shinkaretskaya is Doctor of Law, Senior Research Fellow, author of a number of articles on dispute settlement and of a forthcoming monograph, *The International Judicial Process*.

Bakhtiar R. Tuzmukhamedov is Doctor of Law, Senior Research Fellow of the Diplomatic Academy of the USSR Ministry of Foreign Affairs, and author of *The Zone of Peace*, Moscow 1986 (in Russian).

Vladlen S. Vereshchetin is Prof. of Law, Deputy Director, Institute of State and Law, Vice-President of the International Institute of Space Law, and author of numerous works on international law.

Elena E. Vilegjanina is Doctor of Law, and from 1977 to June 1989 was a legal adviser to the Ministry of Foreign Affairs, USSR. She is Senior Research Fellow at the Institute of World Economy and International Relations, USSR Academy of Sciences, and author of a thesis, 'International Consultations as a Means of Peaceful Settlement of Disputes', Moscow, 1983 (in Russian).

Sergei V. Vinogradov is Doctor of Law, Senior Research Fellow at the Institute of State and Law, Soviet Academy of Sciences, and author of *International Law and the Protection of the Air*, Moscow 1987 (in Russian).

Olga V. Vorobyova is Doctor of Law, Senior Research Fellow at the Institute of State and Law, Soviet Academy of Sciences, and author of numerous articles on private international law.

vii

BRITISH/IRISH CONTRIBUTORS

Anthony Carty is Lecturer in International Law, University of Glasgow, Ph.D. the University of Cambridge, author of *The Decay of International Law*, Manchester 1986, and of numerous articles on problems of interdisciplinarity in international law.

Alpha Connelly is Lecturer in Law, University College Dublin, D.C.L. University of Magill, Canada, author of articles on human rights, the history of international law, women in legal education and the legal profession, and of a forthcoming book on prisoners' rights.

Phillip Dann is a legal adviser with the International Maritime Satellite Organisation and the author of numerous articles on space law.

Vaughan Lowe is Doctor of Law, Fellow of Corpus Christi College, Cambridge. He is author, with R.Churchill, of *The Law of the Sea*, Manchester, 2nd ed. 1988; of *Extraterritorial Jurisdiction: An Annotated Collection of Legal Materials*, Cambridge 1983, and of a forthcoming study on technology licensing.

Geoffrey Marston is Doctor of Law, Fellow of Sidney Sussex College, Cambridge, editor of 'United Kingdom Materials on International Law' in the *British Year-book of International Law*, and author of *The Marginal Seabed: United Kingdom Legal Practice*, Oxford

Colin Warbrick is Senior Lecturer in Law at the University of Durham, author of numerous articles on the foreign relations law of the UK and on human rights.

John Woodliffe is Senior Lecturer in Law, University of Leicester, and has a special interest in environmental law with specific reference to nuclear pollution.

Preface

As editors of this collaborative venture we wish to express our thanks to a number of people. Firstly, our contributors have all responded enthusiastically and in a spirit of goodwill to our invitation to join with this project. Secondly, we would like to thank Prof. William Butler of University College, London for his wholehearted support and encouragement of our work. Dr. Carty would like to thank University College, London for the opportunity to spend a month in the Soviet Union under the protocol of co-operation between University College, London and the Institute of State and Law of the USSR Academy of Sciences. Thirdly, we would like to thank the University of Glasgow and the Institute of State and Law of the USSR Academy of Sciences, both of which hosted the editors in the course of the elaboration of the book. Finally, we would like to say how happy we are that this undertaking is being published by Edinburgh University Press.

ANTHONY CARTY AND GENNADY DANILENKO

Moscow, 10 June 1989

1.

Introduction:
Perestroika and International Law

ANTHONY CARTY AND GENNADY DANILENKO

As 'peaceful coexistence' in the 1950s marked the Soviet wish to end the extremes of the post-1945 Cold War, so Perestroika now marks the Soviet desire to reshape international society into one interdependent community. While 'peaceful coexistence' did not abandon the belief in the inevitability of class struggle on the world scale, new political thinking (Perestroika) affirms the primacy of human values shared by all people. These values find a most vigorous expression in the tradition of international law. So it is not surprising to find that there is a new Soviet emphasis upon the primacy of international law.

This movement presents a dramatic challenge to Western diplomatic and legal attitudes. Protracted conflicts through two cold wars have left the West unaccustomed to undertaking innovative and constructive dialogue. Therefore there is a strong need for critical reflection on the existing structures and practices of international society. International legal scholarship has a significant role to play as a catalyst in the reshaping of the parameters for this debate.

While Perestroika may mean different things to different people, it undoubtedly expresses a new spirit of dissatisfaction with entrenched ideological stand-offs in East–West relations. It invites an increased open-ness, flexibility and hence realism in the face of the immense complexity and dangers present in modern civilisation. It implies that the prevailing rigidity can be abandoned if there is sufficient confidence in a common ability to meet such growing challenges.

It is against this background that the idea of our book originated. This is a new forum for a genuine dialogue between Soviet and British inter-national lawyers. It is necessary to furnish the Western reader with an opportunity to become acquainted with contemporary Soviet approaches to and styles of international law scholarship. The idea was also to invite detailed British responses to the new parameters set by this work. This book is not just a collection of conference papers or even articles solicited around a theme. It is the result of a genuine exchange of views about chapters which have gone through various drafts and have been the

1

subject of extensive revision on both sides. From this perspective the book is unique, representing a close collaboration of lawyers having profoundly different ideological, cultural and legal backgrounds.

The book does not intend to cover all substantive areas of international law. Instead it provides a survey of the main methodological divisions of the field, namely elaboration of general principles, questions relating to effective implementation of international law, the strengthening of international institutions and the progressive development of the law in selected areas. The chapters have been written and edited both in Britain and in the Soviet Union. The authors have had the opportunity to comment on one another's work and the editors have had an opportunity to work on the draft together in Edinburgh, London and Moscow.

The central theme has been to study the impact of Perestroika on the development of international law from both international and domestic perspectives. The Soviet contributions focus on a number of themes relating to the restructuring of international law, such as: critical self-reflection on prevailing Soviet attitudes to the law; a balanced realism towards international law-making; the need for openness in respect of state conduct and practice in international affairs, and the issue of genuineness of international commitment, presented as a case-study of verification of disarmament. There is also an emphasis on the strengthening of respect for human rights, the importance of international adjudication, and the need for further development of the law. The British authors have undertaken to consider the implications of the challenge of Perestroika both in terms of the British practice of international law and in terms of specific responses to the Soviet approaches set out in this volume. At the same time the reader might bear in mind that the Soviet and British contributors inevitably reflect the actual state of legal scholarship in both countries, and, in particular, the actual point to which they have been able to come together into dialogue.

In the first section, the chapter on The Primacy of International Law in World Politics has been written by Vereshchetin and Müllerson. They have emerged as the most prominent spokesmen for Soviet international legal thinking in the Gorbachev era. They argue for a critical review of the previous Soviet attitudes and practice in a much more interdependent international community. They present a strong case for the primacy of international law over ideology. At the same time they insist upon the close connection between the observance of the rule of law at the domestic level and the willingness of a state to allow its international conduct to be governed by objective legal standards. This leads them directly to argue for an extended role for international adjudication. Then Danilenko offers, in contrast to the previously highly politicised Soviet approach to global law-making, a more realistic analysis of the relationship between state interests and legal techniques. In addressing the issue of openness in relation to British state practice, Marston provides a comprehensive model for the construction of state practice as a major element in the ascertainment of the law. Finally Tuzmukhamedov devotes his chapter to the study of what is for the West the most fundamental issue of East–West relations. His examination of the question of verification, particularly in relation to the recent US–USSR treaty on intermediate-range nuclear weapons, emphasises the emergence of new legal methods of ensuring compliance with international law. As this concerns armament treaties it can be said to touch upon the most political sphere of what have been regarded as matters of vital national interest, which have traditionally resisted any international legal control.

The second section deals with the effective implementation of international law covering two major areas. In the first place it deals with the more effective implementation of international human rights standards in the domestic sphere. Müllerson describes the changing attitude of the Soviet Union towards this question. In reassessing the previously often used and maybe misused reference to domestic jurisdiction in this area, he points out the importance of observance of human rights standards for the building of a state governed by the rule of law in the USSR. Warbrick shows, on a theoretical and a practical level, the importance of, and difficulties attaching to, judicial implementation of international law at a domestic level, especially with respect to human rights in the British experience. Connelly, in a case-study relating to human rights in the Northern Ireland conflict, provides a critical examination of British state practice concerning two areas of human rights, namely, freedom of expression and liberty of the person. These papers show a common concern for basic human values and shared anxieties about effective implementation of international standards in all societies, notwithstanding their political, legal and ideological differences.

In the second place this section contains three papers on international adjudication and the effectiveness of international law. They reflect a common desire to avoid states' self-definition of their obligations under international law. The main focus of this part is a review of Soviet attitudes to arbitration and to the ICJ. Shinkaretskaya examines the history of Soviet approaches to arbitration and demonstrates that the Stalin and post-Stalin period of hostility to it represent a hiatus in a tradition of positive support which goes back from the early Soviet state to Tsarist times. Vilegjanina offers a dramatic way of breaking the deadlock about the decline in the use of the optional clause compulsory jurisdiction of the ICJ. She argues that the ICJ has in fact played a significant role in recent years in developing specific sets of rules on international law and that leading states should now take the initiative to agree to submit to compulsory jurisdiction disputes in mutually agreed areas of law. These could be gradually extended, thereby giving a major role to the ICJ. Finally, Carty focuses upon the one permanent member of the Security Council which still adheres to the optional clause jurisdiction, i.e. the UK.

In a critical historical review of British experience of the optional clause, he evaluates the possibilities for the use of the ICJ as a means of settling issues of crucial importance affecting what are traditionally called the 'vital interests' of states.

The third section gives instructive examples of close exchanges of views between Soviet and British writers in three specialised and rapidly developing areas of the law. This dialogue has revealed stark differences in attitude, style of argumentation and methodology. The Boguslavsky-Vorobryova chapter describes the importance of East–West technology transfer at a time when the economy of the Soviet Union is opening up to the global economy. It stresses the importance of joint ventures in future technology transfers. By contrast, Lowe concentrates on the broader political–legal implications of 'sensitive' technology transfers from the West to the East. He also stresses the need for a rethinking of approaches to technology which goes beyond East–West relations to embrace the whole international community.

In submitting a case for reform in the area of space law Kamenetskaya argues for the creation of a world space organisation which should be, in her view, a main means for achieving closer co-operation between all states in the more effective exploration of the use of outer space. By contrast Dann provides a critical analysis of such an approach for closer co-operation. He argues for the more adequate use of existing mechanisms. Although this argument relates to a specific area it may illustrate typical divergences of approach to international co-operation in other areas.

In addressing issues of the environment the Soviet and British authors display radically different approaches. Reflecting the emergence of a dynamic Soviet interest in the protection of the environment, Vinogradov argues for the creation of a comprehensive system of environmental security which, in his opinion, is the best response of the world community to the growing danger of global environmental degradation. He insists on a systemic approach to the issues treating them integrally with issues of disarmament and economic development. Woodliffe, in contrast, provides a case-study of British state practice in relation to nuclear pollution which treats the practice itself as the essential foundation for the construction of, and illustration of the development of, the relevant standards in the area under discussion.

Underlying the debate on the substantive issues there is a marked difference in Soviet and British approaches to legal argument. In the Soviet approach there is a tendency towards a systematic or global treatment of issues, concepts and institutions which is probably a reflection of the prevailing attitude of the continental European school of international law. In the British contributions there is a strong preference for analysis of concrete and specific issues with a modest inclination to elaborate general principles or conclusions.

The book also provides the Western reader with the opportunity to observe the differences which exist within Soviet international legal scholarship. It illustrates that the longstanding belief among many Western scholars concerning the 'monolithic' character of Soviet thinking does not correspond to reality. While there may be differences about specific legal issues, there are also important differences concerning style of argument. There is a growing tendency towards more technical treatment of international legal issues, even if they appear to be highly political.

British contributors also display differences in a legal method which no longer focuses purely on the description of judicial decisions. Even where there is close reflection on judicial practice, as in the case of Warbrick, the British international lawyer is able to construct a critical conceptual framework for the law. The main thrust of the British contributions is that there is a role for the legal scholar in using law as an independent standard to reflect upon British state practice. It is also clear that some British scholars are quite willing to engage in close legal policy analysis and make concrete proposals for the improvement of international law and institutions.

In submitting this book the editors and the contributors hope to stimulate further fruitful collaborative work among international lawyers crossing over the divisions of Europe.

Part I
The Parameters of Perestroika:
Criticism, Realism, Openness and Verifiability

2.

The Primacy of International Law in World Politics

VLADLEN S. VERESHCHETIN AND REIN A. MÜLLERSON

The treatment of international law at different historical periods has varied from unjustified exaggeration of its potentialities to complete disregard. Hugo Grotius[1] maintained that a people that violate the natural law and the law of nations undermine forever the basis of their own future security. Many statesmen in the past (and not so distant too) have frequently held, like Bismarck, that the great issues of the time were to be resolved by blood and iron instead of declarations and resolutions, and have acted accordingly when they were strong enough. Nearly a century ago the famous German international lawyer Franz Listz[2] wrote that the provisions of international law have too often been trampled underfoot while states have been openly and solemnly acknowledging the binding force of international law in settling their disputes, even in wartime.

The present-day development of human civilisation has led many scholars, scientists, statesmen, lawyers and people of other trades, professions and occupations, to begin to realise that to save the world from destruction, civilised relations, i.e. the rules of international law and common human morals, must prevail in relations between states. It is not accidental, therefore, that along with common human values and interests, interdependence and integrity of the world, and a free choice of the ways of development, the concept of the primacy of international law in politics has been increasingly fixed in new political thinking. And although international law dates back to ancient times the changes in the world community and in the very nature of international law have given it an absolutely new meaning. What frequently used to be only an attribute of foreign policy, a medium to justify one's own actions or, on the contrary, to accuse one's political and ideological opponents, is becoming today an essential means to resolve major problems of our time.

What has changed in the world? Why has international law begun to play such an important role in it? To put it briefly, the main thing is that the world has been growing more interdependent and integral. Unilateral actions of states without regard for the interests of other countries and peoples no longer produce any long-term gains; on the contrary, they can jeopardise the very existence of human civilisation. Reliance solely on military strength risks general destruction or the abandonment of the hope of defending oneself. These are the historical alternatives to the new political thinking and its practical implementation.

The interdependence of the contemporary world is manifested, of course, not only through the threat to survival and the presence of other global problems whose solution requires the efforts of all countries and peoples. The world is also too confined for one state to benefit at the expense of another. Gone are the times when an empire could expand and thrive through the robbery of colonies. The more integral the world becomes, and the more tangibly the conduct of a state begins to affect the interests of other countries or the international community as a whole, the greater the need for mutual co-ordination and an orderly state of things in the world. Both gains and losses in an interrelated world may only be reciprocal, and so the actions of states in such a world call for mutual co-ordination. The most perfect and frequently the only means to achieve mutual co-ordination of actions in the world is modern international law, functioning as a code of rules of conduct resulting from the harmonising of states' wills, positions and interests.

Contemporary international law is neither bourgeois, nor socialist; it is a common human, general democratic normative system based on a common humanity. Its rules and standards based on the principles of the UN Charter express the balance of interests between individual states and the international community as a whole. It legalises many common human values. For instance, the bans on the use of force and on the interference in the internal affairs of states, the right of nations to self-determination and other fundamental principles of international law, are called upon to safeguard the values and interests common for the whole of mankind. Gradually, binding rules are evolved to ensure ecological safety for the human race (for example, the 1985 Vienna Convention on the Protection of the Ozone Layer and the 1987 Montreal Protocol to it). At the same time an international campaign is under way for the creation of principles of a new international economic order. Treaties are coming into existence effecting real disarmament.

All of these developments confirm the necessity for the establishment of a system of general law and order that would ensure the primacy of international law in politics.[3] It follows from the orientation of present-day international law towards the protection of common human values that the primacy of international law in politics is in fact a normative expression of the precedence of common human values and interests.

The UN Chapter is a most unique document in many respects. Its most striking feature is probably that all its basic ideas and provisions adopted more than forty years ago constitute the core of contemporary international law and are becoming ever more vital. The reason that the Charter of this organisation for the maintenance of international peace and security is so outstanding is that it was formulated at a period in world history when the international community of states joined hands in the struggle for survival in a united front against fascist enslavement.

The principles and rules of the Charter and the whole machinery of the United Nations began to misfire when the countries of the anti-Hitler coalition began to lose unity, when the policy of confrontation began to take the upper hand and the ideological struggle had as a matter of fact turned into psychological warfare. It stands to reason that against such a background the rule of force instead of law became the chief rule of the game on the international scene.

The 'cold war' which in some regions was turning into a 'hot war' could not help being accompanied by breaches of the major principles of international law. Regretfully, the Soviet Union is not blameless in its approach to international law. It is little consolation that the list of violations by Western countries and, in particular, the United States of America, is longer than ours. A 'free' treatment of law not only damages the interests of the international community of states as a whole; it brings no benefits to anyone over a longer-term period.

At the same time one must not let out of sight the fact that the Soviet state has made an important contribution to developing contemporary international law with a general democratic content, for example, concerning the principles of non-use of force and threat of force, the right of nations and peoples to self-determination and other progressive rules. Our diplomacy has contributed importantly to the development of the UN Charter which fixes the fundamental principles of the modern world law and order. The same is true of legal rules on restrictions of armaments, in outer space, ocean space and other fields of international law. The Soviet Union has not only initiated legal rules and standards; it has energetically helped to enforce the progressive principles and rules in international practices.

Often the resolute position of the Soviet Union alone has helped uphold the independence of former colonies and prevent extension of the hotbeds of tension. Suffice it to mention the consistent policy of our state in the Arab–Israeli conflict and the assistance to Vietnam at the time of US intervention there. Our protests against US interference in the domestic affairs of Latin American countries and against the use of force in the same area (Cuba, the Dominican Republic, Grenada and Nicaragua) have been both morally just and juridically sound.

The more so we cannot help resenting and regretting 'flies in the ointment' of our own doing that damaged international law and impaired our positions on other matters as well as our international prestige in general: for instance, Soviet interference in the affairs of communist and workers' parties in other countries, in Yugoslavian affairs in the late forties and the Finnish war of 1939 for which the USSR was expelled from the League of Nations.

The bringing of the troops of five socialist countries into Czechoslovakia in 1968 was supported by unconvincing legal arguments which gave rise to the so called 'Brezhnev' doctrine, meaning that socialist countries enjoyed only a limited sovereignty. The Soviet press claimed at that time that formal legal reasoning should not have precedence over the class approach. Those giving up the only true class criterion of legal rules were alleged to measure events in terms of bourgeois law. Abstract, non-class approaches to sovereignty and self-determination of nations were severely criticised.[4]

All of it was said in respect of the generally accepted rules of international law which can be neither bourgeois, nor socialist. A purely class-conscious interpretation by states of such principles as sovereignty or non-interference could make a complete wreck of the principles of international law that express common human values. International law can accomplish its mission and fulfil its main function only when it is general, when it is not artificially divided into capitalist international law, socialist international law and the international law of developing countries.

It does appear that such double-thinking towards international law (active participation in its progressive development and strengthening world law and order, on the one hand, and crippling one's own positions and interests by particular actions, on the other) reflected complicated and conflicting developments within Soviet society as a whole. This is why the potential of an advanced social system and the Leninist ideas of peaceful coexistence of states underlying the foreign policy of our state were sometimes unfortunately accompanied by distortions of the Leninist policy not only domestically, but also internationally. For these reasons the ongoing processes of broadening democracy, strengthening legality and creating a socialist state based on the rule of law in the Soviet Union are being accompanied by a changed attitude towards international law. The new political thinking relies on the existing fundamental principles and rules of international relations and calls for their continued progressive development.

What is concretely implied by the concept of primacy of law in international relations? It stands to reason that such primacy can be achieved only if all states strictly follow the principles and rules of international law, ensuring the priority of common human values and interest over narrow-minded national and class interests. And we specially emphasise that we mean narrow-minded class and national interests because, in the present-day world, true national interests and even the aims and tasks of confronting classes inside an individual country which may be sharply conflicting, are nonetheless not antagonistic to international common human values and interests.

As a matter of fact no nation, no class can achieve its purpose if its survival has not been assured, if the acute economic and ecological problems which threaten all humanity have not been solved. It is also contrary to the interests of humanity as a whole if there is armed interference with the aim of preventing a nation's choice of its own ways of social, economic and political development.

The primacy of international law in politics presupposes pre-dominance of law over force because the use or the threat to use force undermines world law and order. The supremacy of international law may be achieved only when states are conscious of their interest in secur-ing the priority of co-ordinated, multilateral actions, favouring long-term and principled goals over short-lived benefits.

The primacy of international law presupposes also a free choice by peoples of their own route to social, economic and political development. History indicates that international conflicts are more often than not caused by the attempts of states to make other states have a similar system and follow their image – by a refusal to accept differences in socio-economic and political systems.

The primacy of international law in politics also calls for co-ordination between the principles and rules of international law and those of national law. The provisions of the latter must be consistent with the international obligations of a state. The level of legality and democracy in a country is closely associated with the state's attitude towards international law. In this connection the following statement by M. S. Gorbachev at the United Nations acquires special significance: 'Our ideal, [he said] is a world community in which states, governed by the rule of law, subordinate their foreign political activity to law as well'.[5] For this reason the construction of a socialist state based on the rule of law in the USSR is very important not only for the internal life of our society, but also for international relations.

Is a world order based on the rule of law realistic? (A) Is it not a Utopia when armed conflicts keep going on in various regions of the globe, when economic and ecological crises continue to deepen, while social injustice has not yet been ended and acts of international terrorism still flare up?

We would indeed seem idealists divorced from reality should we believe that a world based on the rule of law could emerge at once and everywhere. We would be Utopians should we think that the development of humanity as an integral whole were possible without the need to solve constantly-emerging differences, without continuing attempts to find a balance between the conflicting interests of states, groups of countries and even regions. It is also hard to imagine a world where violations of international law were non-existent. That would be an idyll, something unrealistic.

However, the existing tendencies of world development give the hope and reasonable belief in the possibility of securing the supremacy of inter-national law. For a long period of time there has been an awareness of the need for a movement towards a non-violent world among the best minds. For instance, many ideas in the new political thinking were anticipated in the famous Russell–Einstein manifesto written thirty years ago. Let us note that many an outstanding international lawyer underlined in his work the urgent need for states to obey international law and their real interest in doing so. For example, the famous American lawyer W. Friedman wrote that 'the common interest of mankind in survival in the nuclear age must by all means take precedence over the many traditional differences which are of a national, racial, ideological and other character'.[6]

A qualitative leap in understanding the reality of the nuclear and space age will come as soon as leaders of the largest nuclear powers realise the need for new thinking. The Soviet Union has made the most progressive ideas of contemporary public thinking the central principles of its practical policies.

Headway has begun to be made in the settlement of nearly all regional conflicts; ice has been broken even in the area of nuclear disarmament. The intention of the Soviet Union to reduce unilaterally its conventional armaments and armed forces is fresh proof of its new serious approach to international affairs.

Certainly, the primacy of law in international politics requires that a majority of states, especially the great powers, should realise the need for the predominance of law. Although certain positive changes are observed in the foreign policy of many countries, including those largely responsible for the international climate, the movement towards a nuclear-free and non-violent world, where law would rule over force, has not yet become irreversible. Much remains to be done.

The movement for the predominance of law in international relations is based on the political will of the peoples and various public organisations to secure a just and stable peace, but materialising this will require a series of steps both to develop international law as such and to improve the mechanisms and procedures of enforcing its principles and rules.

In our days probably no one state openly admits breaches of rules of international law. Any violator seeks to find or invent a more or less plausible legal excuse for its actions. Regretfully, because of their deficiencies, both the rules of international law and the procedure of their interpretation and application permit, to a certain measure, such behaviour.

It should be emphasised, however, that the said deficiencies follow largely from many states' lack of political will to remove them. Governments could easily find good rules to restrict the behaviour of other states, were not such rules binding on their own behaviour. This is why M. S. Gorbachev's saying that 'every state' should be interested 'in restricting itself by international law'[7] has made an impact on international lawyers.

Some major principles of international law – for example, refraining from the threat or use of force in international relations – are in a way ambiguous. At first glance everything seems clear; it is forbidden not only to use armed force, but also to threaten to use it. But there is an inalienable right to self-defence in the case of an armed attack. And that's where the ambiguities begin. What is an armed attack? Does the concept include, apart from acts of direct military aggression, also indirect forms of turning to force, such as the use of irregular forces or mercenaries; subversive actions against another state; acts of terrorism organised on its territory, or assistance to rebels or contras, etc.? More complications are involved when attempts are made by some states to pass off as self-defence operations to rescue hostages which involve full intervention in another country, or the use of force 'to restore democracy' either by a decision of regional organisations, or through the 'invitation of a lawful government', etc.

While it is, as a rule, more or less easy to identify the perpetrator of direct aggression on the grounds of who was the first to use force, it is very difficult to identify the indirect user of force, the more so that in the not-so-distant past, states made use of military provocations as a pretext for attack.

Two conclusions may be drawn from these experiences. Firstly, it is necessary to specify the content of very broad principles of international law and to remove the loopholes that make it possible to bypass them or, at least use them to justify, in the eyes of certain groups, breaches of the major rules of international law. Agreements on these points could be reached within the framework of the United Nations.

Secondly, a much wider use is required of the international mechanisms and procedures for settling disputes and conflicts, interpreting and applying the principles and rules of international law. The ancient roman maxim that no-one can sit in judgement on his own case applies just as well to international law. Hence, more extensive use should be made of the International Court of Justice for the settlement of specific conflicts between states, and for advisory opinions on the interpretation of the principles and rules of international law.

The states should recognise the overriding need for the existing control mechanisms and develop new ones. It is urgent that a mechanism be set up under the auspices of the United Nations for broad international control over the fulfilment of agreements to reduce international tension, to restrict armaments and to keep in check hostilities in areas of conflict. Such a mechanism could be an auxiliary organ of the Security Council (or, possibly, the General Assembly) of the United Nations and should have at its disposal space monitoring and verifications facilities. It should also be given the right to carry out inspections on the spot. The conclusions of such an organ should be brought to the notice of the UN political bodies and states and, if need be, the public at large. In appropriate cases such conclusions could be a guide for the International Court of Justice or other relevant arbitration tribunal.

In the nuclear and space age, when common human values and

interests have become uppermost, the international law of peaceful coexistence should be looked at afresh. The question whether this principle was a special form of class struggle was raised as far back as the 27th CPSU Congress. The need to reconsider was also elaborated in a series of later Soviet publications. New thinking about this principle is extremely important; international relations must not become an arena of class or ideological struggle.

Inadequate attention in our view is devoted to another aspect of this principle, that is, its sphere of application. Two wordings of the principle of peaceful coexistence are current in political and international law literature – 'of states with different social systems' and 'of states irrespective of their social system'. The first implies relations between socialist and capitalist countries; the second permits it to spread to socially homogeneous countries.

In his book *Perestroika and New Thinking for Our Country and the Entire World* M. S. Gorbachev speaks of the need for the assertion of peaceful coexistence as the supreme, general principle of relations between states. A similar thesis was set forth at the 43rd session of the United Nations General Assembly by Soviet Foreign Minister E. A. Shevardnadze. Indeed, all states should coexist peacefully with each other. The principle of peaceful coexistence presupposes respect for the sovereign equality of all states; it bans the use of force or any interference in internal affairs, and presupposes a free choice by the peoples of their own ways of social development. It goes without saying that all these democratic rules must be observed in relations between socialist countries, as well as in relations between capitalist countries.

At the same time observance of general democratic principles and rules does not exclude closer and friendlier ties between states if such ties are consistent with the said principles. For this reason the principle of socialist internationalism practised between socialist nations by no means rules out the binding principle of peaceful coexistence between them. It is self-evident that mutual or one-sided aid between two socialist countries cannot be accompanied, let us say, by interference in each other's internal affairs or other infringements on sovereignty.

Negation of the extension of the peaceful coexistence principle to relations between socialist countries gave rise to doctrines in the West of 'Brezhnev's' or the 'limited sovereignty' type. The reverse side of such doctrines, according to the famous American lawyer L. Henkin, was Reagan's doctrine licensing the use of armed force to spread 'democracy'.[8]

On the other hand, very close ties between some capitalist countries (for example, Common Market countries) in no way means that the principle of peaceful coexistence does not apply between them. As historical experience indicates, a homogeneity of social, economic and political systems of states as such is no guarantee of absolute harmony in relations between them. But no matter what are the differences or even conflicts, they should be settled in accordance with the generally accepted principles of international law. The aforesaid, naturally, is not denying the fact that the principle of peaceful coexistence plays an especially important role as a regulator of relations between states with different social systems. But here likewise accents should be shifted not only in words, but also in deeds. Instead of speaking of struggle and co-operation as we used to, we should speak above all of all-around, mutually profitable co-operation and of a peaceful competition between the systems; thus, not only are the advantages of either way of development demonstrated, but also there is mutual enrichment through the use of each other's achievements both in science and technology and in the social field.

These are just some reflections on the new role of international law in an interdependent world which begins to be aware of its integrity. To build a world based on the rule of law and common human values, vast joint endeavours of scholars, scientists, practical workers and specialists from many countries will be required.

Notes

1 *Hugo Grotius, On the Law of War and Peace*, Moscow, 1956, pp. 48–9 (in Russian).
2 Franz Listz, *International Law: A Systematic Outline*, Yuriev, 1909, p. 9 (in Russian).
3 Gorbachev, M. S., 'The Reality and Guarantees of a Safe World', *Pravda*, 17 September 1987 (in Russian).
4 *Pravda*, 26 September 1968.
5 Speech to General Assembly of the United Nations, November 1988.
6 W. Friedmann, *De l'éfficacité des Institutions Internationales*, Paris, 1970, p. 17.
7 *Pravda*, 8 December, 1988.
8 L. Henkin, 'International Law and National Interest', *Columbia Journal of Transnational Law*, 1986, 25, No. 1, p. 3.

Editorial Note

A. One of the main theses of perestroika is that a state which does not respect constitutional standards which it has accepted in relation to its own citizens will not respect international legal standards that it has accepted in relation to other states.

3.

International Law-Making: Issues of Law and Policy

GENNADY M. DANILENKO

Introduction

One of the principal propositions of the new political thinking is the emphasis on the fact that major problems facing the modern international community are of a global character. It asserts that planetary dimentions of global problems call for closer co-operation of all states in their solution irrespective of the political, ideological, economic or other differences among nations. Thus, mankind's common interest in survival requires the creation of a comprehensive system of international security. Continued degradation of the global environment increases the need for new rules aimed at its preservation. The entire international community has a strong interest in establishing a more equitable international economic order. Global concerns about the rational management of common resources, especially of the vast resources of the World Ocean and of Outer Space, provide the basis for continuous common efforts aimed at establishing a stable framework for their equitable use in the interests of mankind as a whole.

The increasing importance of global problems for the much more interdependent international community accentuates the need for early and effective development of new legal rules reflecting the universally shared concerns. However, although multilateral negotiations are conducted in a number of forums, the international community has discovered that it is extremely difficult to reach consensus on solutions acceptable to all. Multilateral treaty regimes have been established only in those areas most amenable to treaty regulation. Thus, there are a number of conventions establishing a broad legal framework for the uses of Outer Space and of Ocean Space. But even the successful adoption of these conventions does not mean that law-making efforts have resulted in lasting and effective legal regimes. The Moon Treaty[1] purporting to govern the exploration and exploitation of the resources of the Moon and other celestial bodies has failed to attract the support of states, especially of the major space powers.[2] The most ambitious legislative project for the Ocean Space – the 1982 UN Law of the Sea Convention[3] governing various uses of the sea, including the exploitation of the mineral resources of the international seabed areas, encountered serious difficulties in attracting the necessary number of ratifications, especially on the part of the developed states.

Experience indicates that while some of the problems of law-making on global issues may be caused by their complexity, major difficulties are determined by political factors. Global problems affect the interests of all states and of the international community as a whole. Consequently, the participation of all interested states in the relevant decision-making process has become a necessary condition for their effective solution. Claims to full participation of all members of the international community in law-making on global problems have resulted in the dramatic increase in membership of the negotiating bodies. In view of the highly divergent attitudes displayed by different states on the issues under discussion, the search for global consensus on new rules has become an extremely difficult task.

As the urgency of existing global problems intensifies there is no doubt that the international community is going to undertake new law-making projects in a number of fields. The time may have come for a reassessment of the existing legislative techniques in order to discover possible inadequacies which have impaired previous legislative efforts. In view of the fact that law-making on global problems is and will continue to be a particularly challenging task for the international community, serious efforts seem to be required to formulate proposals aimed at improving the existing law-making process. This paper will raise some of the issues relevant to the ongoing debate about the possible reform of law-making on problems affecting the entire international community.

Available sources

In assessing the available means of law-making, states have to rely on the established sources of international law. It is generally recognised that the hard legal rules necessary for the effective regulation of global problems may be produced only by custom and treaties. In this connection, of major importance is the realistic evaluation of the essential characteristics of these sources in order to discover which of them is most suitable to produce relevant rules. To understand properly the potential of custom and treaty it is necessary to take into account political, legal and technical factors.

Custom is traditionally based on the practice of states. Such practice may take various forms which include not only the behaviour of states but also their official statements. However, the development of the actual practice has always been considered as an essential element in customary law-making. In stressing this characteristic of custom the International Court of Justice (ICJ) pointed out that it is 'the actual practice of states which is expressive, or creative, of customary rules'.[4] From a political – legal perspective, this means that a principal factor in custom-formation is the practice of states which are in a position to carry out the relevant activities constituting the required actual practice. States lacking the necessary means to initiate the pertinent actual practice often find themselves in a situation in which they have to acquiesce in the already-established patterns of behaviour.

Another characteristic of custom, transforming it into an instrument directly reflecting the established power relationships within the international community, is the requirement according to which the custom-making practice must include the practice of those states whose interests are, as the ICJ put it, 'specially affected'.[5] The determination of the specially affected states depends on the subject-matter under discussion. Thus, the development of customary law governing the continental shelf is primarily influenced by the practice of states which are engaged in the exploration and exploitation of continental shelf areas.[6] On the other hand, in the case of the law on fisheries the most affected states may be different. It is asserted, for example, that 'the law on fishing limits has always been and must by its very essence be a compromise between the claims and counter-claims of coastal and distant-water fishing states'.[7]

While different states may have specific interests in specific areas of relations, the major powers with global interests and responsibilities tend to display strong interests in most areas amenable to normative regulation. As a rule they also possess the necessary technical and other means to initiatite new practice in new fields. As a result, these states have always played a leading role in the formation of general customary law. It is not surprising therefore that states lacking the effective power to influence the development of the pertinent practice tend to reject the customary process as 'undemocratic'.[8]

The developing states prefer multilateral negotiations operating on the principle of 'one state – one vote'.[9] Because of the structural changes in the international community these states have a majority in any negotiating forum. States whose actual practice has always been a major factor in the customary law-making have discovered that in a formal treaty process they are in a small minority. Such a situation provides the developing countries with an ideal opportunity to increase leverage over the decision-making process in the solution of global problems. Numerical strength at international conferences is used by this group of states to control the agenda and to press for solutions which satisfy their own interests. Thus, at the Third United Nations Conference on the Law of the Sea (UNCLOS) the developing countries maintained that 'because they were in the majority, the Conference gave the third-world countries the opportunity of imposing bold solutions in order to create a new law of the sea'.[10]

States having a numerical majority at international conferences have also developed an interest in using their numerical strength in the customary process. Serious efforts to reformulate the requirements of custom formation have been undertaken in order to free the customary process from naked power relationships. It is contended that a 'new custom' has emerged which differs from the traditional customary process in many respects.[11] In particular, it is asserted that simple statements and verbal expressions of consensus in international forums are sufficient for the creation of new customary law. Thus, the Group of 77 claims that 'a customary rule may be crystallized through the intermediary of a declaration of the United Nations'.[12] These claims are supported by some writers.[13] There are also assertions that multilateral treaties adopted in international forums may automatically produce general customary law.[14] If these claims were accepted, the majorities having no practical experience in the relevant activities would have acquired the authority to establish customary law. Specially affected states would lose their status, and instead of being the principal actors in shaping general rules, would find themselves acting as permanent persistent objectors. The customary process would reflect power relationships in international forums, rather than mirroring the discrepancies in effective power in the world at large.

There are grounds to believe, however, that the basic differences between customary and treaty law-making processes remain largely unchanged. As a source of law, custom continues to be based on real and concrete legal relationships which cannot be established by purely verbal claims. Verbal expressions of consensus at international conferences cannot in themselves produce general practice necessary for the emergence of customary rules. Actual state practice continues to serve as a principal test for determining whether the proposed rules have been accepted by states as general rules of conduct outside a particular treaty context.

Recent pronouncements of the ICJ fully support the traditional requirements of customary law-making. Thus, in the Nicaragua case the ICJ emphasised that in dealing with customary law it 'may not disregard the essential role played by general practice'.[15] The Court pointed out that an agreement to incorporate a particular rule in a treaty may be sufficient to produce a treaty rule binding on states' parties. In contrast, 'in the field of customary international law the shared views of the parties as to the content of what they regard as the rule is not enough'.[16] The ICJ stressed that in order to produce customary rules the 'shared views' should be 'confirmed by practice'.[17] In the North Sea Continental Shelf case the Court has also indicated that the passage of treaty rules into customary law requires the development of general state practice, which should include the practice of states whose interests are specially affected.[18] This means that whatever procedural rules have been used at an international conference which has produced a particular treaty norm, passage of this norm into general customary law is still governed by the traditional requirements of customary law-making.

While custom has resisted attempts to reformulate its essential characteristics, the treaty process has also proved not particularly useful as an instrument for 'imposing solutions' on dissenting states. Multilateral treaties reflecting only the preferences of numerical majorities may be rejected by the influential minority refusing to ratify them. In contrast to customary rules which always reflect the actual power relationships and therefore operate as effective guides for state conduct, treaties may be brought into operation by politically insignificant actors. If the proposed treaties are not supported by the most affected states they fail to exercise an effective control over the development of the actual state practice. There is a danger that the adopted rules could remain a dead letter.

This problem assumes a special significance in the case of global problems requiring global solutions based on normative instruments having a universally binding character. Attempts have been undertaken to overcome the structural difficulties of the treaty process by proposing a new notion of global treaty which may bind all states irrespective of their participation. The trend in this direction became particularly evident in connection with the adoption of the 1982 Law of the Sea Convention.[19] During a debate on the Convention a number of states have expressed the opinion that the Convention created the only valid law for the Ocean Space binding on all states irrespective of their participation. Many developing states claimed, in particular, that the Convention 'would be law for all states – even those that are outside its framework'.[20] This line of argument was also supported in legal writings, including the works of some Soviet authors.[21]

It is clear, however, that the existing international law relating to law-making cannot support such a far-reaching legislative claim. There is no evidence that the international community is ready to adopt legislative techniques based on majority law-making. On the contrary, states participating in the Third UNCLOS proceeded from the assumption that 'the conference was not a parliament, and a majority vote would not result in legislation'.[22]

There is also no evidence that the principles of the law of treaties, including those relating to the effect of treaties on third states, codified by the Vienna Convention on the Law of Treaties,[23] are not applicable to global conventions, including the controversial Law of the Sea Convention. Therefore, as a matter of law the conventional regime cannot be imposed on third states. The Law of the Sea Convention, like any other international treaty on global problems, may have the desired legal effects only between states which have expressed their consent to be bound by it.

Notwithstanding these clear limitations of the treaty process there are a number of factors which appear to favour the treaty as a most suitable instrument to deal with global problems. The customary process is essentially based on unilateral claims and counter-claims of different states, a process which involves an increased danger of conflicts. By contrast, the treaty process is generally regarded as more appropriate for deliberate and smooth accommodation of divergent attitudes. It should also be taken into account that, in contrast to a treaty, custom cannot generate anticipatory, forward-looking legal regimes. As a source of law it is always based on the existing state practice and in this respect, as Judge V. Kozetsky put it, it 'turns its face to the past'.[24] Global problems often call for the creation of effective legal mechanisms which could adequately address the relevant issues before they acquire significant practical proportions. Thus, in the field of environmental protection there is a strong need for effective preventive regulation before harmful activities may cause irreversible damage to the global environment. Rational management of the global commons also requires the establishment of a stable legal framework before actual exploitation of the common resources takes place.

One should also keep in mind that the establishment of a stable legal framework requires the adoption of both general principles and specific legal rules governing state conduct. While the treaty may produce rules of any degree of specificity, custom can, as the ICJ put it, 'of its nature provide only a few basic legal principles which lay down guidelines to be followed'.[25] Furthermore, since custom is based on isolated and uncoordinated instances of state practice it cannot produce a coherent and systematic body of law for relevant activities. In contrast to the treaty which usually introduces a system of norms governing a given matter, the customary process generates only individual rules. Such a method is not particularly suited to deal with complex issues posed by global problems. Finally, the effective solution of global problems may require not only the establishment of substantive legal rules but also the creation of relevant institutions to ensure implementation of the agreed standards of behaviour.[26] There is no doubt that only the treaty can be used by states for this purpose.

The search for a genuine consensus

In view of the foregoing considerations it appears that political, legal and technical factors favour the elaboration of treaties as the main device in the legal regulation of global issues. The major question in this connection is the determination of the most appropriate legislative method to deal with the world's problems. In particular, there is a choice between broad multilateral treaties and limited agreements elaborated in closed state groupings. The fact that global problems directly or indirectly affect the interests of all states provides a strong argument in favour of legislation based on a multilateral approach. New political and legal concepts developed in connection with some global problems, such as the concept of the common heritage of mankind, by their very nature require universal participation in the decision-making process. In view of these trends and tendencies it appears that viable legal regimes on global issues may be established only through multilateral negotiations leading to treaties of universal scope.

Attempts to legislate for global problems by limited groups of the most interested or powerful states may encounter serious opposition on the part of the majority of other states. The most prominent recent example in this connection is the agreement on the seabed[27] signed by eight Western states dissatisfied with the results of the Third UNCLOS. In view of the unsatisfactory results of the multilateral negotiations on the Moon, proposals have also been made that a commercially suitable legal regime for the exploitation of lunar resources should be elaborated outside the United Nations through an agreement of 'the space powers potentially capable of exploiting outer space natural resources'.[28]

There is no doubt that such schemes will be resisted by other states. In the modern international community characterised by increasing political and economic interdependence, an agreement contradicting the express wishes of the majority of its members cannot succeed. Effective implementation of these and similar legislative projects requires collaboration or at least tacit acceptance by other states. In the absense of the support on the part of other states the validity of limited agreements will always remain in doubt. Limited regimes denying the needs of the majority may eventually be rejected by states who will subsequently acquire the necessary technical and other expertise in a given area and therefore also qualify as new most affected states.

In a situation in which the successful accomplishment of treaties on global issues presupposes the agreement of all or almost all members of the international community, the accommodation of the divergent attitudes will require continuous negotiations in multilateral forums. This brings to the fore the question of what methods should be used to secure genuine general agreement on global issues facing the international community.

It is generally recognised that consensus is the most effecitve response to the problem of the discrepancy between the power of numerical majorities and the actual influence of the most affected states. Experience has indicated, however, that simple consensus is insufficient to bring into effect the proposed treaties. Indeed, in the framework of the negotiating procedure, consensus means no more than the absence of any formal objection to a particular decision. It does not imply positive support – which is necessary for the subsequent approval of the treaty by national bodies responsible for ratification. In the absence of such positive support, especially on the part of the most affected states, consensus may not pass the test of the ratification process where each state decides individually whether it is in its best interests to be bound by a particular treaty regime. The recent history of the ratification process of a number of multilateral conventions clearly demonstrates that treaties that are not based on genuine consensus may remain a dead letter. The most lucid illustration in this connection is the Moon Treaty[29] which came into force in 1984 but remains ineffective because it was not ratified by the major space powers.

It follows from the preceding observations that serious thought should be given to the need to secure the support of future legislation on global problems on the part of those states whose participation is indispensable for their effective implementation. Adequate international law-making would require the achievement of a consensus which presupposes the positive support of the proposed rules by the most affected states.

Realistic assessment of the situation should obviously proceed from the undeniable fact that not all states have the same level of interest in various global problems. While many members of the international community may not be directly affected by a proposed decision concerning a particular matter, states which are the most involved in the activities to be regulated have a very high level of interest in relevant issues. Therefore, it seems reasonable to suggest that the law-making process should reflect the balance of various levels of interests of the most affected states and all other states.

While treaty law-making should not necessarily parallel the customary process in this respect, consensus achieved in the treaty context should more clearly reflect the power relationships in the world community. In the light of this previous experience, states should consider the possibility of redefining consensus so that it would be given a more positive interpretation. In view of the political realities prevailing in the international community, it may be difficult to obtain acceptance of the idea that rules of procedure should overtly reflect the differences in power and importance of various states in the decision-making process relating to global problems. As a formal matter, however, states may carefully consider whether it would not be advisable to provide for a qualitative criterion of participation in the proposed treaties, in addition to the quantitative criterion normally used in clauses dealing with the entry of treaties into force. Such a qualitative criterion will ensure that an agreement will take effect only if supported by a sufficient number of the most affected states.

The major problem which will arise in this connection will be the identification of the most affected states. Of course, it is impossible to define the most affected states by a single standard. While politically, economically and militarily powerful states tend to display special interests in all major international matters, the precise determination of criteria of specially affected states will depend on the subject-matter to be regulated.

Argument in favour of the proposed approach may rely on existing precedents where states have expressly recognised that ratification of the negotiated treaties by specified states, whose participation is crucial for the implementation of the agreed rules, is a necessary precondition for the entry of a particular treaty into force. An overt recognition of the preponderant weight of the major powers who are the permanent members of the UN Security Council for the law-making or law-changing process on principal international issues is confirmed in the final clauses of the UN Charter (Articles 108; 110, Para. 3) Treaties governing specific areas may use different criteria to identify the necessary qualitative participation. Thus, the Outer Space Treaty[30] provides that it will enter into force only if it is ratified by three depository governments, namely the Soviet Union, the United Kingdom and the United States (Article XIV, Paras.2 and 3). The Partial Nuclear Test Ban Treaty[31] stipulates that it will take effect only if three leading nuclear powers, namely the USSR, the UK and the USA, ratify it (Article III). There is a well-established trend to require qualitative participation in treaties elaborated in the framework of the International Maritime Organisation. Thus, treaties relating to shipping[32] set requirements, not only in terms of a fixed number of states, but also in terms of the amount of shipping tonnage they must possess.

An analysis of recent legislative projects on global problems indicates that treaties which fail to provide for qualitative criteria of participation face serious problems in terms of their implementation. The Moon Treaty, which contains a clause that it will enter into force after only five ratifications (Article 19), has already been mentioned. The Law of the Sea Convention[33] may be another example, because it simply states that it will enter into force after sixty ratifications (Article 308). Proposals to set requirements for qualitative participation in this treaty which were contained in draft alternative texts on the final clauses prepared by the UN Secretary General[34] have not found support at the Third UNCLOS. The Conference has also had an opportunity to address the issue of qualitative participation with reference to the composition of the Council of the envisaged International Sea-Bed Authority. According to the Law of the Sea Convention, the Council has to be elected on the basis of the representation of special interest groups which includes the group of states which have the largest investments in the international seabed area (Article 161, Para. 1(a)). A number of states suggested that the Law of the Sea Convention should not enter into force until a balanced Council, reflecting all special interests, could be constituted from the parties to the Convention.[35] However, this proposal also failed to attract the necessary support. The Convention provides that if, due to the absence of state representation for special interests, Article 161 cannot be applied strictly when the first election of members of the Council takes place, the Council 'shall be constituted in a manner consistent with the purpose of Article 161' (Article 308, Para. 3) This loose wording provides no guarantee that the Convention will enter into force only if ratified by the most interested states possessing the financial and technical capabilities to undertake mining operations on the seabed.

To be truly effective, future law-making efforts on global problems should not repeat the mistakes of the past.It is submitted that one of the major mistakes was the disregard of the essential role of specially affected states in any law-making. Realisation of this fact will result in broader use of clauses requiring qualitative representation in order to bring the proposed treaties into effect. This approach will guarantee that after their entry into force, new treaties will have substantial control over the subject-matter covered by their provisions. Therefore, situations similar to the one created by the entry into force of the ineffective Moon Treaty will be ruled out. Moreover, the adoption of the proposed approach will also affect the negotiating process and the nature of consensus emerging from such negotiations. The tested consensus procedure will acquire a new quality leading to more realistic normative results and, therefore, more viable legal regimes in the future.

Conclusion

For a long period of time international law-making has been primarily based on the customary process ensuring the consensus of states most actively involved in activities to be regulated. The recent movement towards international legislature through a multilateral treaty process has dramatically increased the influence of many new members of the international community. Experience indicates, however, that treaties based on an excessive influence of the new numerical majority may not attract the support of states whose participation is often essential for the effective implementation of the proposed treaty rules.

The foregoing analysis suggests that the future of international law-making, especially of law-making on global problems, appears to depend on the ability of the international community to achieve a genuine consensus which would reflect both the legitimate common interests of all states in resolving these problems and the special interests and responsibilities of the most affected states. In a search for more rational and realistic methods of law-making, states will continue to experiment with consensus techniques in order to find solutions which will be able to reflect, not only the preferences of the numerical majority, but also the positive support of the most influential members of the international community. International democracy should learn, both from the earlier lessons of general consensus which has been traditionally required for the creation of a rule of international customary law, and from the failures of some of the recent treaty legislative projects which refused to take into account the existing power relationships in the world community.

Notes

1 Agreement Governing the Activities of States on the Moon and other Celestial Bodies, 1979. UN G.A. Res. 34/68 (1979) (hereinafter cited as Moon Treaty).

2. By 1987 the Moon Treaty has been ratified by Australia, Austria, Chile,

the Netherlands, Pakistan, the Philippines and Uruguay. See *Multilateral Treaties Deposited with the Secretary General, Status as of 31 December, 1987*, New York, 1988, p. 781.

3. UN Convention on the Law of the Sea, 1982. UN Doc A/Conf. 62/122 (1982) (hereinafter cited as Law of the Sea Convention).

4. ICJ Reports, 1982, p. 46. Compare also the statement of the Court in the judgement on the 1985 Continental Shelf: 'It is of course axiomatic that the material of customary international law is to be looked for primarily in the *actual practice* and *opinio juris* of States.' ICJ Reports (1985) 29 (emphasis added).

5. ICJ Reports, 1969, pp. 42, 43.

6. See the dissenting opinions of Judges Tanaka (ICJ Reports, 1969, p. 176) and Lachs (id., p. 227).

7. See the joint separate opinion of Judges Forster, Bengzon, Jimenez de Arechaga, Nagendra Singh and Ruda, ICJ Reports, 1974, p. 48.

8. Cf. M. Bedjaoui, *Towards a New International Economic Order*, Paris, 1979, p. 138.

9. Cf. J. Castaneda, 'The Law of Sea Convention and the Future of Multilateral Diplomacy' in *The 1982 Convention on the Law of the Sea*, Honolulu, 1984, p. 559. For new countries '... the preferred method for the creation of international law is the universal conference in which all States, old or new, big or small, participate on a plane of equality. Custom – i.e. practice mainly of great powers, particularly in the Law of the Sea – is not considered any more the dominant fact in the creation ...'

10. Statement of the representative of Columbia. Third UNCLOS. Official Records, v. II, p. 19.

11. See generally G. Abi-Saab, 'Le coutume dans tous ses états ou le dilemme du développement du droit international général dans un mond éclaté', in *Le droit international à l'heure de sa codification*, Étude en l'honneur de Roberto Ago, vol. I, Milano, 1987, pp. 53ff.

12. UN Doc. A/Conf. 62/106 (1980). Third UNCLOS. Official Records, v. XIV, p. 112.

13. See, e.g., E. Suy, 'Innovations in International Law-Making Processes', in R. St J. Macdonald *et al.* (eds.), *The International Law and Policy of Human Welfare*, Alphen aan den Reijn, 1978, p. 190.

14. See, e.g., A. D'Amato, *International Law: Process and Prospect*, New York, 1987, pp. 129, 145.

15. ICJ Reports, 1986, p. 98.

16. Id.

17. Id.

18. ICJ Reports, 1969, p. 43.

19. See *supra*, note 3.

20. The statement of the representative of Trinidad and Tobago. Third UNCLOS Official Records, v. XVII, p. 23. See also the statements of the representatives of Cameroon (id., p. 16), Peru (speaking on behalf of the Group of 77) (id., p. 22), Kenya (id., p. 47) and Chile (id., p. 67).

21. See e.g., Y. G. Barsegov, 'The Role of International Law in the Solution of Global Problems', in. *The Soviet Peace Programme and the Progressive Development of International Law*, Moscow, 1985, pp. 185ff (in Russian).

22. The statement of the representative of Bahamas. Third UNCLOS.

Official Records,v. I, p. 138. Cf. also the statement of the US delegation: 'Neither the Conference nor the states indicating an intention to become parties to the convention have been granted global legislative powers'. Third UNCLOS. Official Records,v. XVIII, p. 243.

23. The Vienna Convention on the Law of Treaties, 1969, UNTS, v. 1155, p. 331.
24. ICJ Reports,1969, p. 156.
25. ICJ Reports, 1984, p. 290.
26. Thus in the Nicaragua Case the ICJ stated: 'A State may make a rule contained in a treaty not simply because it favours the application of the rule itself, but also because the treaty establishes what that state regards as desirable institutions or mechanisms to ensure implementation of the rule . . .'. ICJ reports (1980), p. 95.
27. Provisional Understanding Regarding Deep Seabed Mining, 1984, *International Legal Materials*, 1984, v. 23, p. 1354.
28. See, e.g., M. L. Smith, 'The Commercial Exploitation of Mineral Resources in Outer Space', in T. L. Zwaan (ed.), *Space Law: Views of the Future*, Deventer, 1988, p. 54.
29. See *supra*, note 1.
30. Treaty on Principles Governing the Activities of States in the Exploration and use of Outer Space, including the Moon and other Celestial Bodies, 1967, v. 619.
31. Limited Nuclear Test Ban Treaty, 5 Aug 1963, UNTS 480 : 43.
32. See, e.g., The 1974 Convention on a Code of Conduct for Linear Conferences (*International Legal Materials*, 1974, v. 13, p. 910). The same approach was also adopted by the 1986 UN Convention on Conditions for Registration of Ships (Doc. TD/RS/Conf. 119/Add. I (1986)).
33. See *supra*, note 3.
34. See UN Doc. A/Conf. 62/L. 13. Third UNCLOS. Official Records, v. VI, pp. 125ff.
35. See especially, the statement of the representative of Britain. Third UNCLOS. Official Records, v. XIII, p. 26.

4.

The Evidences of British State Practice in the Field of International Law

GEOFFREY MARSTON

I State practice as source or evidence of international law.

Before examining British State practice, it is appropriate to assess to what extent State practice in general is important in the context of the sources of international law.

In 1905, Oppenheim asserted that 'since the Law of Nations is a law between States only and exclusively, States only and exclusively are subjects of the Law of Nations'.[1] As international organisations may have a personality in international law separate from those of their member States,[2] this assertion is no longer valid, but sovereign States still make up the basic category of those entities whose relationships with each other are governed by international law. Though the practice of international organisations themselves is of growing significance, it is evident that the practice of sovereign States still constitutes the basis for much, indeed most, of what Vattel called *le droit des gens positif*.[3]

This may be further demonstrated by referring to the principal sources of international law, one of which is international custom, once called by Oppenheim 'the original source of International Law'.[4] In a report to the International Law Commission in 1950, Manley Hudson, formerly a Judge of the Permanent Court of International Justice, considered that the following four elements must be present in order to constitute custom:[5]

(a) concordant practice by a number of States with reference to a type of situation falling within the domain of international relations;

(b) continuation or repetition of the practice over a considerable period of time;

(c) conception that the practice is required by, or consistent with, prevailing international law; and

(d) general acquiescence in the practice by other States.

Each of the above requirements implies the necessity for State activity of one kind or another. As the International Court of Justice stated in 1985: 'It is of course axiomatic that the material of customary international law is to be looked for primarily in the actual practice and *opinio juris* of States . . .'.[6]

Turning to the other sources set out in Article 38 (1) of the Statute of the International Court of Justice, treaties are another, and very particular, form of State practice. Similarly, the 'general principles of law', acknowledged as a source by Article 38 (1) (c), have to be 'recognized by civilized nations', which implies manifestations of State practice in their regard. A further type of law-creating act consisting by its very nature of State practice is the unilateral act, which although not included in the list of sources in Article 38 (1) may under certain circumstances create rights and duties for the State performing it.[7]

In view of the importance of State practice to the sources of international law, it might be thought that in an ideal world each State would take steps to make its own practice available for scrutiny so that, by reciprocity, it would gain access to the practice of other States; the wider the range of States with accessible practice, the greater the likelihood of authenticity in any customary rule deduced therefrom. In his preface to the first of the volumes of a series designed to publish in a co-ordinated manner the practice of several European States, Viktor Bruns wrote in relation to this point:[8]

> In the discussion of problems of international law it is very usual to argue on the basis of the practice of States. It is, however, very difficult to prove consistent practice on the part of all governments in any one field of international law, and it is only from such consistent practice that the existence of a generally recognized principle of international law may be concluded. It is, therefore, somewhat strange when the existence of a particular practice is said to be proved by reference to some assertion made by a government, i.e. to occasional allegations made by an interested party to an international dispute. To prove the existence of a principle of international law by means of State practice is by no means as easy as that.

In the real world, however, a variety of reasons, of which security and inertia are the most obvious, inhibit some States from making any disclosure of their internal practice and many other States, indeed all States, from making a full disclosure. Furthermore, where States have voluntarily disclosed some part of their practice to the outside world, it may not have been with the intention of adding to the range of academic knowledge, or of inspiring other States to do likewise, but for other and less altruistic reasons. Commenting upon the publication of diplomatic correspondence, a French writer observed:[9]

> Les *Livres jaunes* français et leurs similaires étrangers sont des recueils de documents diplomatiques destinés à donner, sur une affaire particulière, le point de vue officiel du gouvernement ou à publier le texte de négociations engagées, de traités ou conventions

conclus. Par définition, ces recueils ne contiennent que des pièces qu'on a intentionellement voulu rendre publiques; leur utilité est donc de livrer au public, sous la forme imprimeé, des pièces d'archives relatives à des affaires dont le dossier complet est encore très loin d'appartenir aux historiens.

He went on to consider that such partial disclosure might nevertheless have some utility:[10]

Tels quels, ils n'en rendront pas moins de grands services, précisement parce qu'ils font connaître ce qu'un gouvernement a desiré qu'on pensât sur telle affaire, et cela est souvent aussi important à connaître que sa vraie penseé puisque, par ce moyen, il s'est proposé de provoquer chez lui, chez ses amis et chez ses antagonistes, tel révirement ou telle réaction.

II *International attempts to make state practice available*

Although the diplomatic practice of some States, of which the United States of America is one, has been accessible to public inspection in substantial quantities from at least the early part of the nineteenth century, it was from within international organisations that initiatives arose to persuade States in general to adopt a positive and uniform attitude to the publication of their international law practice. Two of these initiatives, by organisations of which the United Kingdom is a member, will now be described.

(i) *The United Nations*

The United Nations Committee on the Progressive Development of International Law, meeting in May and June 1947, received a memorandum from the United Nations Secretariat entitled *Methods for encouraging the progressive development of international law and its eventual codification.*[10] This suggested that the General Assembly might recommend to Governments the preparation of digests of materials illustrating their point of view in questions of international law.

The deliberations of the Committee resulted in the inclusion in the Statute of the International Law Commission of Article 24:

The Commission shall consider ways and means for making the evidence of customary international law more readily available, such as the collection and publication of documents concerning State practice and of the decisions of national and international courts on questions of international law, and shall make a report to the General Assembly on this matter.

To assist the International Law Commission in its consideration of Article 24 at its first session which began in April 1949, the Secretariat of the UN submitted to it a substantial memorandum, dated 7 March 1949, entitled *Ways and Means of making the evidence of customary international law more readily available.*[11] The bulk of this memorandum con-

sisted of an account of 'the existing state of the evidence of customary
international law and suggestions hitherto made for its improvement'.
Having described the various collections and digests of treaties, judicial
decisions and State practice which had so far been published, both
officially and otherwise, in a number of countries the memorandum concluded: 'The foregoing survey reveals that a substantial body of evidence
of customary international law is available. But it is no less clear from it
that the existing state of documentation needs to be improved'.

It was then agreed by the Commission that one of its members should
submit a working paper on the subject to the second session of the Commission. That working paper, dated 3 March 1950, was presented by
Manley Hudson of the United States in which he reviewed the available
evidence of customary international law.[12] Having been discussed by the
Commission, the working paper, as amended, was incorporated as part of
the Commission's report to the General Assembly in July 1950. One of its
conclusions read:[13] 'The Commission recommends that the General
Assembly call to the attention of Governments the desirability of their
publishing digests of their diplomatic correspondence and other materials
relating to international law'.

The report of the International Law Commission to the General
Assembly, dated July 1950, was discussed by the General Assembly's
Sixth Committee where on 2 November 1950 a resolution, submitted by
the United States, the United Kingdom and Israel was adopted requesting
the Secretary-General to consider the recommendations in the report.[14]

(ii) The Council of Europe

On 28 April 1961, the Consultative Assembly of the Council of Europe
referred to its Legal Committee a motion for a recommendation to the
Committee of Ministers to the effect that it should study the possibility of
promoting the publication by member States of digests of their diplomatic
correspondence and other source material relating to international law.[15]
On 16 January 1962, the Legal Committee presented a draft recommendation, the preamble to which commenced:[16]

> Considering that it is from the consistent practice of States that the
> generally recognized principles of international law are derived and
> that it is therefore desirable that evidence of this practice be
> made available;
> Convinced that the publication by member States of their diplo-
> matic correspondence and other materials which constitute sour-
> ces of international law would substantially contribute to its
> clarification and development and, moreover, be of great assistance
> to government departments and international organisations in the
> conduct of their day-to-day business;
> Being of the opinion that the compilation of digests of national State
> practice is one of the most effective means of making the evidence of

customary international law more readily available,
Recommends that the Committee of Ministers
... should ... recommend to member Governments, which have not already done so, that they should facilitate the publication of digests of their diplomatic correspondence and other materials which constitute sources of international law ...

The above draft recommendation was based on a summary of conclusions agreed to by a group of independent experts (S. Bastid, P. Guggenheim, A. C. Kiss, Lord McNair, H. Mosler, C. Parry, H. Reichmann and M. Sørensen).[17]

The draft Recommendation was adopted by the Consultative Assembly on 16 January 1962.[18] By Resolution (64) 10, adopted on 6 October 1964, the Committee of Ministers having considered a report from a Committee of Experts, recommended to the Member States that they should publish digests concerning national practice in the field of public international law and should comply, as far as possible, in the planning and drafting of the digests, with certain uniform standards in order to make the digests readily accessible and comparable with each other.

The Committee of Experts carried out further work and, on 28 June 1968, the Committee of Ministers adopted Resolution (68)17 which recommended that national digests should be prepared according to an appended model plan and commentary thereon. A model index to national digests, designed as a complement to the annexed plan, was also prepared.[19]

III British State practice

(A) General observations

It is proposed to make a distinction for the purpose of analysis between on the one hand that part of British official practice which is accessible to public inspection at or shortly after the time of its creation, and on the other hand the totality of practice which becomes accessible in due course to those wishing to examine the history of past events. The former category will be called contemporary practice; the latter category will be called historical practice. With the passage of time, contemporary practice becomes part of historical practice. The difference between the material in the two categories consists substantially of archival material which is not made available until some period of years after its creation.

A further distinction adopted for the purpose of discussing each of the above two categories is that based on the separation of powers. By this doctrine, which is associated in particular with the French political theorist Montesquieu who based it on his observations of British institutions, it is meant that the legislative, executive and judicial functions of government are respectively allocated to a separate person or body, each independent of the other two functions. It is not proposed, however, to discuss to what extent such a strict separation of powers is observed in contemporary United Kingdom governmental practice.

(B) Contemporary practice

(a) Primary sources. *(1) The legislature.* The Parliaments of England and Scotland, and since their union in 1707 the Parliament of Great Britain and then of the United Kingdom, have enacted much legislation relating to international obligations undertaken or porposed to be undertaken. Most of these obligations are undertaken by treaty. It is a basic principle of English constitutional law that a treaty obligation cannot create a right or duty in domestic law unless it has been implemented by legislation. [20] Consequently legislation often precedes the treaty obligation, thus enabling the United Kingdom to beome a party to the treaty without the risk of falling later into breach by reason of failure to give effect to the treaty in domestic law. In recent years statutes of this kind have included the Diplomatic Privileges Act 1964, the State Immunity Act 1978 and the Channel Tunnel Act 1987. Although a statute which is intended to implement a treaty often contains a recital, usually in the preamble, that it is so intended, it is infrequent that a law will expressly state that it is enacted in order to conform to customary international law; the *opinio juris* is rarely made publicly evident.

Sometimes legislation is enacted, not to permit treaty implementation, but to declare a position in respect of a matter of international law in which the United Kingdom retains some discretion. Recent examples of this kind of legislation are the International Organisations Acts of 1968 and 1980 and the Territorial Sea Act 1987. All United Kingdom primary legislation, and the vast quantity of secondary legislation made pursuant to it, are made available to the public through Her Majesty's Stationery Office within a short time of its enactment.

(2) The judiciary. From time to time the higher courts in the jurisdictions comprising the United Kingdom, namely England and Wales, Scotland, and Northern Ireland, are called upon to deal with matters of public international law. The most common situation is the interpretation of legislation which is intended to implement treaties to which the United Kingdom is a party. In such cases the courts in certain circumstances may interpret the treaty itself by applying the interpretative rules of international law. [21] Other types of situation which raise issues of public international law include immunities of defendants, [22] the *locus standi* of parties, [23] and the justiciability of suits. [24]

The texts of the most important decisions of the higher judiciary in the United Kingdom become available within a short time in the several general and specialised series of law reports. Texts may sometimes be obtained more quickly and for a wider variety of cases through computer-based retrieval systems.

(3) The executive. Although, as will be explained below, much of the executive's involvement in matters of international law is not immediately made available to the public, there remains nevertheless a considerable amount of contemporary material which is so made available. Treaties form such a category. Treaty-making is the prerogative of the United Kingdom's chief executive, the Crown, although in practice it is exercised only on the advice of the Crown's Ministers in Parliament. Treaties to which the United Kingdom is a party are printed in the official Treaty Series a short time after their conclusion. Treaties which have been signed by the United Kingdom, though to which it is not yet a party, are published by Her Majesty's Stationery Office as Command Papers separate from the Treaty Series. Of additional importance are the regular publication in the Treaty Series of lists of reservations, declarations, etc., to multilateral treaties to which the United Kingdom is a party.

In addition to the legislation mentioned above, the proceedings in Parliament give rise to a large volume of published executive practice relevant to international law. Most substantial is the contribution made during the debates in the two Houses of Parliament, the elected House of Commons and the non-elected House of Lords (partly hereditary, partly appointed for life). These debates, published on a daily and weekly basis, contain relevant statements by Ministers particularly in the course of debates on proposed legislation (Bills) and in answer to oral questions. The Ministers of the Foreign and Commonwealth Office are the most fruitful in producing practice but those of other departments, including the Home Office, the Departments of Trade and Transport and the Defence Departments also supply relevant items from time to time. In addition, the published debates of the Houses contain an exceptionally fruitful source of State practice in the form of ministerial written answers to questions. These replies, it may be assumed, have been carefully prepared by the Minister's civil servant advisers and often contain material of great evidentiary weight.[25]

In addition to the parliamentary debates, a substantial amount of relevant material emerges from the evidence given by the executive to the various committees of Parliament and published shortly afterwards in the Parliamentary Papers. This material, which is submitted either by Ministers themselves or by their departments, takes the form of written memoranda or oral evidence, or both. Among the most significant committees for the receipt of such material are the Foreign Affairs and Defence Committees of the House of Commons and the Joint Committee on Statutory Instruments (secondary legislation). To give only one illustration, a particularly rich variety of material was produced when, following a fatal shooting outside the Libyan Mission in London in 1984, the Home Secretary, the Legal Adviser to the Foreign and Commonwealth Office and the Head of the Diplomatic Service were among officials who gave evidence to the Foreign Affairs Committee on the subject of diplomatic immunity.[26] The executive may also present to Parliament in the form of Command Papers its views on matters of international law. Thus after the Foreign Affairs Committee had rendered its report on the above Libyan Mission incident, the Government, through the Home Secretary, presented to Parliament in January 1985 a *Government Report on Review of the Vienna Convention on Diplomatic Relations*.[27]

Turning to governmental activity outside Parliament, statements made by virtue of the United Kingdom's membership of international organisations provide a further source of State practice. The United Nations, with its various Committees, is the most important forum, in particular the Sixth (Legal) Committee where the United Kingdom is often represented by the Legal Adviser to the Foreign and Commonwealth Office. Written material submitted to the International Law Commission is likely to be of high evidentiary value, e.g., the comments submitted in January 1988 in response to the Commission's draft articles on jurisdictional immunity of States and their property.[28] Statements by United Kingdom representatives in other international fora are also potentially relevant. These bodies include organisations of which the United Kingdom is a member, such as the Council of Europe and the European Communities, and *ad hoc* conferences such as the Vienna Conference on the Law of Treaties and the United Nations conferences on the law of the sea. Attention should also be given to statements made in the joint names of the member States of the European Community, whether or not the United Kingdom is its chairman. Public statements made by the executive government in the form of press releases, such as those issued regularly by the Foreign and Commonwealth Office, provide further source material.

The pleadings of the United Kingdom in international and domestic tribunals and even, in the form of *amicus curiae* briefs, in foreign tribunals produces a certain amount of material directly relevant to the United Kingdom's views on matters of international law. The evidential value of such pleadings needs to be examined critically, however, especially when the pleading itself is then rejected by the tribunal.

It is only rarely that advice tendered to the British Government by its legal advisers is contemporaneously released to the public.[29] There has for long been an unwritten convention that a Minister must take personal responsibility for his decisions and cannot excuse himself by sheltering behind the legal advice he has received. Similarly, the Cabinet (the committee of senior Ministers under the chairmanship of the Prime Minister which directs major Government policy) takes collective responsibility for its decisions and cannot transfer responsibility to its legal advisers.

(b) Secondary contemporary sources. The first attempt to make available contemporary United Kindom practice classified according to subject-matter began in July 1956 with the first instalment in the *International and Comparative Law Quarterly* of 'The Contemporary Practice of the United Kingdom in the Field of International Law – Survey and Comment'. The purpose of the survey was , in the words of its editor, E. Lauterpacht, 'to make more readily available materials and comment which may assist in ascertaining, by reference to current practice, both the views of the British Government on the content of the rules of international law and the manner in which the United Kingdom discharges her international obligations'.[30] The survey, which later appeared in the form of separate publications up to 1968, consisted mainly of statements in Parliament, legislation and treaties. It also contained detailed editorial commentary on the items of practice covered.

In 1978, a new initiative, 'United Kingdom Materials on International Law', edited by myself, commenced as an annual part of the *British Yearbook of International Law*. This volume is published normally towards the end of the year following that covered by the practice. On publication, therefore, the oldest material covered is less than two years old and the most recent less than one year. The classification of material is that recommended by the Council of Europe in its Resolution 68 (17). The publication sets out the original text of each item of practice together with the minimum amount of editorial explanation necessary to place the item in its context. The material is taken from a wide variety of sources, with parliamentary sources predominating. Only rarely, however, is material made available here which has not already been released to the public.[31] 'United Kingdom Materials on International Law', like 'British Practice' before it, is not produced by or under the direction of a government department. The Foreign and Commonwealth Office, however, renders valuable support in providing the texts of materials which otherwise might not be obtainable quickly.

(C) Historical practice.

(a) Primary sources. *(1.) The legislature.* The texts of British legislation as far back as the twelfth century are found in various collections of statutes, the most important of which is the official *Statutes of the Realm*. The original copies of statutes are preserved in the archives of Parliament located within the Palace of Westminster.

(2) The judiciary. The relevant official part of a judicial decision is the order of the Court. These orders are preserved in the Public Record Office with other official documents on the case. On the other hand, the reasons for the decision, which are of vital importance in the system of precedent applicable in the United Kingdom, are (with the exception of those of the House of Lords, the highest judicial tribunal) recorded only in a haphazard way, often as the result of private commercial enterprise. There are many thousands of volumes, available in specialist law libraries, which record these reasons in cases dating back to the sixteenth century and even earlier.

(3) The executive. (i) General observations. The contemporary sources

of executive practice surveyed above are all subject to a major limitation, namely that they are confined to materials which the government has expressly made public.[32] Documents and other sources of information belonging to the Government which have not been so published are potentially 'official secrets' and subject to the protection of the criminal law. The United Kingdom does not at present have any 'freedom of information' legislation such as exists in, for example, the United States of America and New Zealand. The release of official documents in a systematic manner in the United Kingdom is provided for in the Public Records Act 1958 as amended in 1967. The public records of England and Wales up to the union with Scotland in 1707 and of the United Kingdom since that date are deposited in the Public Record Office, London. The public records of Scotland prior to union and of departments concerned solely with Scotland after union are deposited in the Scottish Record Office in Edinburgh. There is a Public Record Office of Northern Ireland in which are deposited records relating exclusively or mainly to Northern Ireland.

There is probably no event relevant to British State practice for which some documents cannot be found in the Public Record Office, London, supplemented, in some instances, by certain private collections of papers, especially those of former Ministers or officials. Once again, the Foreign Office records are likely to be the most fertile for investigation, but the records of the Cabinet and its associated committees as well as those of the Home Office, the former Colonial Office, Lord Chancellor's Department and Treasury Solicitor's Department are also likely to contain items of State practice. But despite the more than 140 000 metres of documents shelved in the Public Record Office, it is not an easy task to obtain the full story on any particular item of past practice, and the more recent the practice the less easy the task is likely to be.

In principle, documents of the government departments are made available for public inspection when they have been in existence for thirty years. As the process of release occurs annually, this means that, for instance, the records for the year 1958 became available on 1 January 1989. It would be disingenuous to believe, however, that all the records created in a particular year become available for public scrutiny after thirty years. Certain procedures carried out after the records have been created and before the thirty-year period elapses ensure that this is not the case.

First, the records are examined within the departments and a decision is taken on which files are worthy of permanent preservation. Only these files are transferred to the Public Record Office. The residue, consisting of material of secondary or transient importance, is destroyed. This process, known as 'weeding', has been practised for over a century but it can be assumed that in recent years, when both the volume of records created and the cost of their storage and preservation have increased progressively, it has been carried out with more enthusiasm – though probably with less efficiency.

Secondly, the Public Records Act contains two major provisions which cause some files which survive the weeding process to be kept from public scrutiny even after the expiration of thirty years. In the first place, certain files or certain papers within files may be retained indefinitely in the government department of origin. This may be for administrative reasons or, more usually, because they contain matters of particular sensitivity. In the second place, certain files may be withheld from public scrutiny for periods longer than thirty years. The criteria for such extended periods of closure, which are normally 50, 75 or 100 years are:[33]

(i) Exceptionally sensitive papers, the disclosure of which would be contrary to the public interest whether on security or other grounds (including the need to protect the Revenue).

(ii) Documents containing information supplied in confidence the disclosure of which would or might constitute a breach of good faith.

(iii) Documents containing information about individuals, the disclosure of which would cause distress or danger to living persons or their immediate descendants.

Into the first category fall materials relating, for example, to unresolved international disputes to which the United Kingdom is, or has been, a party. So, to give two illustrations, the researcher investigating the territorial and boundary disputes between the United Kingdom (now Belize) and Guatemala, or between the United Kingdom and Argentina over the Falkland Islands would soon find him or herself frustrated by extended closure on some complete files and on some documents even within those files which are open to scrutiny. Extended closure is authorised by instruments signed by the Lord Chancellor under the 1958 and 1967 Acts and researchers are well advised to examine these instruments before beginning a search, particularly on matters occurring in the last 100 years, as they helpfully contain lists of the documents subjected therein to extended closure.[34]

In addition to the above categories of restrictions, it is understood that from time to time documents may be withheld at the request of other States, the reciprocal nature of such arrangements being obvious if a researcher tries to examine in a foreign State's archives the counterpart of documents closed in the United Kingdom, e.g., certain documents concerning the Suez Canal crisis held in the archives of Israel or the United States.

But quite apart from these formal restrictions on the availability of documentary evidence, though these are serious enough, the preserved written word is likely to give only a partial view of past events which, increasingly, are conducted in face-to-face discussions or in telephone conversations of which records may not have been kept. Furthermore, government officials, knowing that documents may become available in principle within a short period (in comparison with earlier periods of closure), and perhaps within their own lifetimes, may consider carefully what they put on paper; they may not always record matters which could prove embarrassing in retrospect. There is truth in Henry Kissinger's comment: 'Contemporary practices of unauthorised or liberated disclosure come close to ensuring that every document is written with an eye to self-preservation. The journalist's gain is the historian's loss.'[35]

Despite official proclamations about open government and the availability of records after a relatively short period of closure, the preservation of State security is another reason why the researcher of the future will find it more difficult rather than easier to discover the full story of a past item of State practice. Thus the main printed index to the political correspondence of the Foreign Office from 1920 to 1951 was not only made available for scrutiny at the Public Record Office, but has been reproduced commercially in 131 volumes and is now on the shelves of research libraries around the world.[36] This includes references to and brief descriptions of not only all the files but all the papers within the files handled by the Foreign Office, including those which have since either been weeded or retained in the Department or closed for periods of more than thirty years. Where a paper was of such sensitivity that even its subject-matter could not be made known, its entry in the index was simply erased on the relevant page, leaving a tell-tale gap in the list. Such instances were relatively few. But from the end of 1951 no more of this comprehensive index has been made available for public scrutiny at the Public Record Office. As the Public Record Office's lists contain the titles of only those files which have been transferred to it – and in the case of files retained or subject to extended closure periods, not even the titles – it is at present not possible to determine conclusively whether a particular matter after 1951 not expressly listed was ever the subject of Foreign Office consideration.

(ii) The confidential print. Until the invention of the typewriter towards the end of the nineteenth century, all communications to and from government departments and all internal minutes were in the normal course of events handwritten, either by their authors or by 'copyists' employed for the task. It is not surprising, therefore, that from the middle of the nineteenth century it became the practice, especially in the Foreign Office, to print important documents which required to be distributed to the Crown, Ministers, missions abroad and other government departments. This resulted in the Confidential Print, a series numbering in excess of 20 000 items, some a single paper, others a collection of documents on a particular topic consisting of many hundreds of pages. The Confidential Print, recently described as 'the product of a practice without parallel in the machinery of government of any other major power',[37] reproduced the text of material such as diplomatic exchanges, internal minutes and memoranda, draft legislation and the opinions of the Government's legal advisers. The Public Record Office has a nearly complete set of the Foreign Office Confidential Print and other, less complete, sets have found their way to other libraries, including the British Library, those of Oxford and Cambridge Universities and the National Library of Australia. Microfilms of some of the Prints are also available in some research libraries around the world. In addition to the Foreign Office, the Colonial Office produced a large quantity of Confidential Print. Although reduced in volume by the availability of other means of reproduction and distribution, the Confidential Print did not become totally extinct. An example of a Confidential Print made in the last year of open archives, 1958, is the comprehensive report by Sir Gerald Fitzmaurice on the proceedings of the United Nations Law of the Sea Conference in that year.[38] It must be emphasised that the decision to print was a selective one and that there is no substitute for examination of the original documents from which the Print was compiled. Errors in transcription occurred and sometimes certain documents, particularly internal minutes, were not printed. The Confidential Print, where it exists, is merely a convenient 'short-cut'.

(iii) Legal advice tendered to the British Government. Certain types of archival records are of particular interest to those seeking evidence of State practice. These include treaty negotiations, exchanges of diplomatic notes on matters of legal concern, protests to other States, and instructions to draftsmen prior to the preparation of legislative texts. For long the tendering of legal advice on such matters was the monopoly of the Law Officers of the Crown, namely the Attorney-General and the Solicitor-General. These two officers, who would normally be members of the House of Commons, were often assisted in matters of international law by a part-time officer called, until the abolition of his office in 1872, the Queen's Advocate. It was not until 1886 that a full-time legal adviser, W. E. Davidson, was appointed to serve within the Foreign Office. From that date until the end of the Second World War the substantial bulk of the successive legal advice tendered to the Foreign Office was given by a series of just six legal advisers – Davidson, Hurst, Malkin, Shearman, Beckett and Fitzmaurice. Since 1945, the number of professional staff in the legal adviser's department of the Foreign Office has increased considerably and the role of the Law Officers in this respect has correspondingly diminished.[39]

To the student of State practice in the area of international law, the legal advice tendered to a government must rank high in relevance. If the government acted on the advice, even though it made no reference to having been so advised, knowledge of that fact would be relevant in assessing whether the government's action was accompanied by *opinio juris*. It would equally be relevant to know whether the government acted otherwise than in accordance with the legal advice it received. Certainly there exists a view that the British Government normally accepts legal advice. Thus, in a draft letter written for perusal within the Foreign Office, probably in August 1956, Sir Gerald Fitzmaurice, the legal adviser, observed:[40] '. . . in the 27 years or so in which I have been a legal adviser in the Foreign Office, Her Majesty's Government have never (apart from one or two incidents in the heat of the War) committed a deliberate and premeditated illegality, or at any rate one not capable of some reasonable justification in legal terms.' However, in that particular context (the Suez Canal crisis), the United Kingdom then acted in a way considered by some commentators to have been contrary to international law.

It was considered at one time that that legal advice itself was particularly confidential and not suitable for release to public scrutiny even when the documents relating to the ministerial or Cabinet decision based on it were made publicly available in 'Blue Books' or at the end of a fixed period of closure. Thus in 1909, after the legal adviser, Davidson, had stated that he was sure 'that it is in the interest of the easy discharge of public business that the general public should know as little as may be about the advice itself on which the action of Her Majesty's Government in *international* matters is predicated',[41] the opinions of the Law Officers given to the Foreign Office between 1781 and 1870, estimated to number about 21 000 were bodily removed from the volumes of archival correspondence in which they had been bound, in order to prevent them becoming available for scrutiny when the archives for that period were opened.

The policy changed in 1924, when it was proposed to open the archives up to the end of 1878. Rather than support the removal of the Law Officers' opinions from the files, the legal adviser, Sir Cecil Hurst, wrote:[42]

> What makes international law is the practice of governments, and to know in any particular case not merely what the Government did but why it did it, i.e. the particular circumstances in the case on which its view was based, is what makes the precedent valuable as a guide for the future. Unless the papers which constitute these precedents are open to the public this source of knowledge is lost. It is really scarcely an exaggeration to say that international law is to a great extent being made now on the American continent because the United States' Government is so much more ready and willing to publish its proceedings than any other Government that it is usually the practice of the United States which alone is known to the writers on international law.

Consequently, not only were the Law Officers' Opinions in the volumes from 1870 onwards left undisturbed in their proper places in the files, but the opinions extracted in 1909 were returned to the Public Record Office. Since 1860, the Law Officers' opinions to the Foreign Office have been retained on the relevant files, as was always the case with other government departments which relied heavily on the Law Officers before they acquired specialist legal staff, such as the Home Office, the Colonial Office and the Treasury. Since 1860, Law Officers' Opinions given to the Foreign Office were reproduced in annual Confidential Prints, as were the Opinions given to the former Colonial Office.

(b) Governmentally published secondary sources of historical practice.

(1) Papers printed for Parliament (the 'Blue Books'). From the first half of the nineteenth century a vast amount of diplomatic correspondence was printed for the use of Parliament in the form known as 'Blue Books' from the colour of their covers.[43] The time elapsed between the date of the correspondence and the publication of the Blue Book was relatively short, sometimes a matter of months. Once again, it must be pointed out that not all the available documents on a particular matter were thus printed; internal minutes and in particular legal advice tendered to the Government were often excluded. The original files should always be perused to check on the completeness and accuracy of the Blue Books. The Blue Books and the Confidential Print often covered the same subject matter; sometimes a Confidential Print was not made the subject of a Blue Book and sometimes a Blue Book would be issued without there being a corresponding Confidential Print. The essential difference between the Confidential Print and the Blue Books is that the latter were part of the Parliamentary Papers and thus available for public scrutiny. Thus, until the publication of Blue Books declined following the First World War, the public had access to contemporary diplomatic correspondence of the British Government in a way which would be unthinkable today. The Blue Books, as part of the British Parliamentary Papers, are located in research libraries throughout the world. Since the 1870s, most of the Blue Books formed part of the Parliamentary Command Paper series.

(2) The British and foreign State papers. This series was begun by Lewis Hertslet, Librarian of the Foreign Office, in 1825 and continued by his son and successor in office, Sir Edward Hertslet.[44] Thereafter it was published officially until its demise after 170 volumes covering the period up to the end of 1968. As its title indicates, the series covered more than United Kingdom practice although the United Kingdom component was usually the most substantial. A considerable amount of diplomatic correspondence was reproduced in the series, though for reasons explained earlier, legal advice was rarely printed. With the withering away of the 'Blue Books' of diplomatic correspondence following the First World War, the content of the volumes became largely treaty and legislative materials. It was probably the relative accessibility of this material elsewhere, such as the *United Kingdom Treaty Series* and the *United Nations Treaty Series,* which caused the discontinuance of the series.

(3) The United Kingdom Treaty Series. This series commenced in 1891 and reproduces the text of every treaty to which the United Kingdom has become a party since that date.

(c) Non-governmentally published secondary sources of historical practice. The first attempt to publish a digest of British State practice using archival materials was the two-volume work *Great Britain and the Law of Nations* produced by Professor H. A. Smith of London University in 1932 (States) and 1935 (territory and territorial waters) respectively.[45] Smith relied heavily on the newly-released Law Officers' Opinions and on the Confidential Print. His aim was to present 'a documentary picture of the attitude officially adopted by Great Britain, chiefly through executive and diplomatic agencies, towards contemporary problems of international law'. The work set a pattern to be followed in the *British Digest* described below in supplementing the texts of the archival documents with a considerable amount of explanatory text.

In 1956, Lord McNair, recently retired from the International Court of Justice, produced a three-volume edition entitled *International Law Opinions,* which consist of an annotated analysis of the opinions given to the Foreign Office mainly between 1782 and the first years of the twentieth century.[46]

In the 1950s, proposals were made for the publication of a British Digest of practice. This was welcomed in particular by Sir Gerald Fitzmaurice, then legal adviser to the Foreign Office, who in a letter to the Foreign Office Librarian dated 20 January 1954 seeking for the compilers access to Foreign Office archives, including some still falling within the closed period, referred to the proposed Digest as a 'British *Hackworth*'.[47] He continued:[48]

> American ideas on many international law topics are very similar to ours, but on certain others they are different. Moreover, our practice in international law matters is no less rich and diversified than theirs but also goes back for a much longer period. It has therefore been felt that something corresponding to Hackworth ought to be produced in this country, and that such a publication would greatly assist to make the United Kingdom point of view better known and understood. The project was very dear to the heart of Sir Eric Beckett, who was prepared personally to supervise its realisation, and it is also strongly supported by such eminent authorities as Sir Arnold McNair (United Kingdom Judge on the International Court) and Professors Lauterpacht and Waldock.

The Digest which resulted from this, edited by Professor Clive Parry, was conceived on a grand scale, with two phases covering the periods 1865–1914 and 1914–60. At the time of the editor's death in 1982 only some of the volumes for the earlier phase had been published.[49] They consist not only of a reproduction of the texts of documents, but detailed narrative accounts of the background circumstances in which the documents played a part.

Parry also edited a nine-volume compilation, *British International Law Cases,* which contains the texts of over 1 000 cases in United Kingdom courts to the end of 1970 in which issues of public international law arose.[55] A further initiative of Parry was the publication, in ninety-three volumes of facsimile reproductions, of the opinions given to the Foreign Office by the Law Officers of the Crown between 1782 and 1860, and of the opinions for the period 1861 to 1939 on microfilm.[51].

As mentioned earlier, the Colonial Office had a considerable involvement in international legal problems. It, too, relied heavily on the Law Officers of the Crown for advice. Most of these opinions remain unpublished in the original archival papers and in the Colonial Office Confidential Print. Some of them have been reproduced with extensive analysis in O'Connell and Riordan, *Opinions on Imperial Constitutional Law*.[52]

In 1983, there commenced a new project which is of interest to a wider public than that of legal scholars, namely *British Documents on Foreign Affairs: Reports and Papers from the Foreign Office Confidential Print*.[53] When completed, this project will comprise 420 volumes reproducing in facsimile form a selection of the Confidential Print from the mid-nineteenth century to the Second World War classified according to area and subject-matter. Among the volumes already published are six volumes on Russia up to the Revolution and fifteen volumes on the Soviet Union thereafter.

IV Conclusion

The State practice of the United Kingdom is potentially the richest in the world by reason of the length of its diplomatic history, the global extent of its former imperialist activity, and the preservation almost intact of its archives. To some extent, this practice is now accessible in a systematic form. This has not come about through government initiative, but almost entirely through the work of scholars independent of government who in some considerable measure have subsidised the product by their labour. The diplomatic practice of the Soviet Union, including the Czarist epoch, is likely also to be rich though it is understood that little of it has been made accessible. The zeal of Soviet scholars to work on this source, once it is released, is not in doubt. It is hoped that they will be assisted by government interest and material support.[54]

Notes

1 Oppenheim, L. (1905) *International Law*, 1st ed., vol. 1, London: Longmans, p. 341.

2 See in particular *Reparation for injuries suffered in the service of the United Nations, Advisory Opinion:* I.C.J. Reports, 1949, p. 174, and in general Fassbender, B. (1986/87) 'Die völkerrechtssubjectivität internationaler Organisationen', *Österreichische Zeitschrift für öffentliches Recht und Völkerrecht* 37, 17–49.

3 Vattel, E. (1758) *Le droit des gens*, London; préliminaires, paragraph 27.

4   Oppenheim, L. (1905) op. cit., p. 22.

5   Yearbook of the International Law Commission, 1950, vol. II, p. 26 (U.N. Document A/CN.4/16). See also Ferrari Bravo, L. (1985) 'Méthodes de recherche de la coutume internationale dans la pratique des États', *Recueil des Cours de l'Academie de droit international* 192, 233-329.

6   *Continental Shelf (Libyan Arab Jamahiriya/Malta), Judgment*, I.C.J. Reports, 1985, pp. 13, 29. The same court in *Military and Paramilitary Activities in and against Nicaragua (Nicaragua v. United States of America) Merits, Judgment*, I.C.J. Reports, 1986, pp. 4, 108-9, stated that it 'has to emphasise that, as was observed in the *North Sea Continental Shelf* cases, for a new customary rule to be formed, not only must the acts concerned "amount to a settled practice" but they must be accompanied by the *opinio juris sive necessitatis'*.

7   See, e.g., Suy, E. (1962) *Les actes juridiques unilateraux en droit international public*, Paris: Librarie générale de droit et de jurisprudence.

8   *Fontes Juris Gentium*, Series B, vol. 1, part 1, Digest of the Diplomatic Correspondence of the European States, (1932) Berlin: Carl Heymanns, p. ix.

9   D[Ore] R. (1922) 'Bibliographie des 'Livres Jaunes' à la date du 1 janvier 1921', *Revue des Bibliotheques* 32, 109.

10 UN Document A/AC.10/7.

11 UN Document A/CN.4/6. The Secretariat also submitted a working paper entitled *Possible means of procuring the publication of more complete collections of evidence of customary international law* (Yearbook of the International Law Commission, 1949, p. 228, footnote 10 (UN Document A/CN.4/W.9)).

12 Yearbook of the International Law Commission, 1950, vol. II, pp. 24-25 (UN Document A/CN.4/16).

13 Ibid., p. 373.

14 UN Document A/C.6/SR. 231, p. 131.

15. Council of Europe, Consultative Committee, 13th Ordinary Session, 1st part, Documents, vol. 1, document 1300.

16 Council of Europe, Consultative Assembly, 13th Ordinary Session, 3rd part, Documents, vol. 6, document 1385, pp. 1-2.

17 Ibid., pp. 2-4.

18 Council of Europe, Consultative Assembly, 13th Ordinary Session, 3rd part, Texts adopted by the Assembly, 16-18 January 1962, Recommendation 309 (1962).

19 Council of Europe, Consultative Assembly, 20th Ordinary Session, 1st part, Documents, vol. 6, Document 2428, pp. 82-96.

20 See, e.g., *The Parlement Belge* (1879) L.R. 4 P.D. 129; *In re International Tin Council* [1987] 1 All E.R. 890, 901.

21 See, e.g., *Fothergill v. Monarch Airlines Ltd.* [1981] A.C. 251.

22 See, e.g., *Trendtex Trading Corporation v. Central Bank of Nigeria* [1977] Q.B. 529.

23. See, e.g., *Gur Corporation v. Trust Bank of Africa Ltd.* [1987] 1 Q.B. 509.

24 See, e.g., *Buttes Gas & Oil Co. v. Hammer* [1982] A.C. 888.

25. An example is the written reply by the Minister of State, Foreign and Commonwealth Office, on 4 December 1984, that '[t]he concept of the exclusive economic zone has developed into customary international

law' (Parliamentary Debates, House of Lords, vol. 457, col. 1301).

26 Parliamentary Papers, 1984–85, House of Commons, Paper 127, pp. 25–7.

27. Command Paper (Cmnd 9497), London: HMSO.

28 UN Document A/CN. 4/410, pp. 46–58.

29 An exception was the contemporaneous publication in December 1971 of the opinion of the Attorney-General (Rawlinson) and the Solicitor-General (Howe) on 'the extent of the existing legal obligations of Her Majesty's Government, arising under the Simonstown Agreement, to permit the export of arms to South Africa' (Command Paper (Cmnd 4589), London: HMSO.

30 (1956) *International and Comparative Law Quarterly* 5, 405.

31 One recent exception was the release of some of the papers in a private arbitration between the British Government and the Spanish shipping company over the salvage payable on a British 'Harrier' fighter plane which in 1983 had made an emergency landing on containers stowed on the deck of a Spanish merchant ship at sea. ((1985) *British Yearbook of International Law* 56, 462–7.)

32 It has been said that '[a]nterior to the Restoration of Charles the Second, the transactions between England and Foreign Princes were deemed to be of too secret a nature to be revealed to the public' (Hardy, T.D. (1869) *Syllabus of the Documents relating to England and Other Kingdoms contained in the Collection known as 'Rymer's Foedera'*, vol. 1, London: Longman's, p. i). The author is indebted to Mr. Jonathan Sumption QC for this reference. Publication of Rymer's *Foedera* itself began in 1704.

33 *Modern Public Records: the Government's Response to the Report of the Wilson Committee* (1982), Command Paper (Cmnd 8531), London: HMSO p. 59. See also *Committee on Departmental Records* (1954) Command Paper (Cmnd 9163), London: HMSO, and Public Record Office, London, Information Leaflet No. 37, 'Access to Public Records', 1986.

34 The periods of extended closure can be increased during the currency of an initial closure period. Thus the period of closure for some of the documents dealing with the territorial and boundary disputes between the United Kingdom (now Belize) and Guatemala, originally fifty years, were extended by Lord Chancellor's instrument to seventy-five years before the fifty-year period elapsed.

35 Kissinger, H.A. (1979) *The White House Years*, London: Weidenfeld and Nicholson, p. xxii.

36 *Index to the Correspondence of the Foreign Office, 1920–1951*, 131 vols., Liechtenstein: KTO Press. An additional volume indexes the 'Green' or secret papers, 1921–38, which were not indexed in the other volumes.

37 Bourne, K. and Cameron Watt, D. (1983–   ) *British Documents on Foreign Affairs: Reports and Papers from the Foreign Office Confidential Print*, Frederick, Maryland: University Publications of America, general introduction to each volume.

38 Public Record Office, London, reference F.O. 371/133746..

39 For an account of the arrangements for the provision of legal advice to the Foreign Office in the period before 1914, see Parry, C. (ed.) (1967) *A British Digest of International Law: compiled principally from the*

archives of the Foreign Office, Part 7, pp. 242–81. For the position in more recent years, See Fitzmaurice, Sir G. and Vallat, Sir F. (1968), 'Sir (William) Eric Beckett K.C.M.G., Q.C. (1896–1966): an Appreciation', *International and Comparative Quarterly* 17, at pp. 267–77; Sinclair, Sir I. (1982), 'The Practice of International Law', in Cheng, B. (ed.) *International Law: Teaching and Practice,* London: Stevens, pp. 123–34.

40 Public Record Office, London, reference F.O. 800/748. This was written in response to indications that the United Kingdom was prepared to intervene by force in the area of the Suez Canal (See Marston, G. 1988) 'Legal Advice tendered to the British Government in the Suez Canal Crisis', 1956, *International and Comparative Law Quarterly* 37, 773–817 at 815).

41 Public Record Office, London, reference F.O. 370/16 (Foreign Office file 40126). See also Marston, G. (1976), 'Law Officers' Opinions to the Foreign Office, 1782–1876: The Background to F.O. 83/2203–2404', *Journal of the Society of Archivists* 5, 302–6. The Chief Clerk in the Foreign Office, Eyre Crowe, wrote in an internal note on 30 November 1909 as follows:

> The Law Officers' reports made to the Foreign Office, chiefly on points of international law, stand on a somewhat different footing. Controversies with foreign governments often range over a wide period of time, the interpretation of ancient treaties remains even now a source of frequent disputes, and diplomatic representations addressed on behalf of private claimants to foreign governments constantly lead to grave international complications. Differences arising out of all such matters may at any stage become the subject of a reference to arbitration, and a published opinion of the Law Officers, given perhaps many years ago on a point of international law might easily prove an embarrassment in the conduct of diplomatic negotiations with a foreign government or of a case pending before an international tribunal, involving issues of the greatest moment in the interests of this country. (Public Record Office reference F.O. 370/23 (Foreign Office file 7526)).

42 Public Record Office, London, reference F.O. 370/203, folios 210–11 (Foreign Office file 4704); Marston 1976, op. cit., p. 305.

43 See generally Temperley, H. and Penson, L.M. (1966) *A Century of Diplomatic Blue Books,* London: Frank Cass & Co.

44 See Hertslet, E. (1901) *Recollections of the Old Foreign Office,* London: John Murray, p. 145.

45 Smith, H.A. (1932 and 1935) *Great Britain and the Law of Nations,* 2 vols., London: P.S. King & Son.

46 McNair, Lord (1956) *International Law Opinions,* 3 vols., Cambridge: Cambridge University Press.

47 This was a reference to Hackworth, G.H. (1940–44) *Digest of International Law,* 7 vols. and index vol., Washington: Government Printing Office.

48 Public Record Office reference F.O. 370/2403.

49 Parry, C. (ed.) (1965–   ) *British Digest of International Law: compiled principally from the archives of the Foreign Office,* 7 vols. to date, London: Stevens.

50 Parry, C. (ed.) (1967–73) *British International Law Cases*, 9 vols., London: Stevens.

51 Parry, C. (ed.) (1973) *Law Officers' Opinions to the Foreign Office 1793–1860*, 93 vols. and 2 vols. of indexes and summaries, Farnborough: Gregg International Publishers.

52 O'Connell, D.P. and Riordan, A. (1971) *Opinions on Imperial Constitutional Law*, Sydney: Law Book Co.

53 Bourne, K. and Cameron Watt, D. (general eds.) (1983–   ) *British Documents on Foreign Affairs: Reports and Papers from the Foreign Office Confidential Print*, Frederick, Maryland: University Publications of America.

54 As long ago as 1858, a Russian scholar called for the promotion of works on international jurisprudence in the countries of Europe including Russia and Britain (Katchenovsky, Professor D.I. (1858–63), 'On the present state of international jurisprudence', *Papers read before the Juridical Society* 2, 99–111, 553–76).

5.

Verification of Disarmament

BAKHTIAR R. TUZMUKHAMEDOV

The multi-million audience which witnessed the act of signing of the Soviet–American Treaty on the Elimination of Intermediate-Range and Shorter-Range Missiles (INF Treaty), heard a Russian proverb uttered by the American President: 'Trust but verify'.[1] This dramatic phrase contains the philosophy of disarmament verification: at the outset an agreement is already based on trust but the delicate nature of the sphere of regulation requires additional measures that augment the initial trust with precise facts, thus promoting it further.

The verification provisions have become part of international treaty practice since the nineteenth century[2] but they started to be included in arms limitation and reduction agreements in the 1950s – the years when the Antarctic Treaty was signed and nuclear test-ban talks were under way. Since then the problem of verification has undergone a complicated and contradictory evolution resulting by now in the general recognition of verification as a necessary element of any significant agreement on arms limitation and reduction, and more than that, in the establishment of 'comprehensive verification of the disarmament process as a norm of international relations'.[3]

The purpose of this article is to examine general principles of verification and the fundamentals of modern Soviet approaches to verification; to give a brief review of available experience and a more detailed analysis of a unique verification experiment under the INF Treaty, and, finally, to summarise an option of a multilateral approach to disarmament verification.[4]

I

In a broad sense verification may be defined as a system of methods for determining whether treaty provisions are observed, designed to provide each party with information about other parties' compliance with obligations, and to deter and uncover violations.[5] The significance of verification is not limited to arms reduction; verification provisions are introduced into 'civilian' treaties. For example, they have been included in a number of conventions concluded under the aegis of the International Labour Organisation and the International Maritime Organisation. Not attempting to belittle the significance of the treaties regulating various spheres of international relations, nonetheless it should be underscored that agreements designed to remove the threat of war; to limit, reduce and eliminate arms; to play a special role in the maintenance of international peace and security; to effect the dismantling of armaments, the disbanding of armed forces and other measures up to general and complete disarmament, are a complicated and protracted process. The implementation of such steps directly affects the security of states in their military dimension and the states undertaking such steps are entitled to certain guarantees. Verification is one such guarantee.[6] In this particular field verification is a major condition not only of compliance with, but also of the very conclusion of the agreements. It is obvious that although any international accord should build on mutual interest of the parties, the agreements on limitation, all the more on reduction of military potentials, cannot be based exclusively on mutual trust. Verification supports trust between the parties which is present in the very fact of their entering into an agreement by providing impartial information about the real state of compliance.

Thus, verification creates the necessary confidence for treaty compliance and by doing so it promotes trust between states. It enhances their confidence in their security, in the expediency of arms limitation and reduction, in the effectiveness of agreements in force and in the necessity of their preservation, as well as in the achievement of new accords.

The main requirement of verification is to guarantee to a maximum degree the strict observance of an agreement by all its parties. This requirement determines the general principles to be met by verification measures and mechanisms.[7] The authoritative and the most consensual source of these principles is the Final Document of the First Special Session of the UN General Assembly on Disarmament of 1978.[8] The following list is based on paragraphs 31, 91 and 92 of that document.[9]

These principles include: *the principle of legitimacy*, meaning that any verification system should correspond to the generally recognised principles and norms of the UN Charter and other fundamental sources of international law, and that there should be equality of rights and duties of all participants in the verification process; *the principle of effectiveness*, stipulating the need for prompt and genuine information about the state of affairs with the treaty compliance; *the proportionality principle*, meaning that the verification methods should correspond to the specificity of a treaty; *the principle of universality*, providing for the equal opportunity for every party to an agreement to verify the observance of an agreement directly or through the United Nations system, or by entrusting this task to a group of countries, possessing the necessary experience and technical means; *the principle of complementarity*, meaning a combination of various verification means and methods which are employed either simultaneously or stage-by-stage.

II

The modern Soviet approach to verification may be characterised by the following statement by M. Gorbachev: 'Now that major measures of real disarmament, touching upon the most sensitive sphere of national security, are on the agenda, the Soviet Union will demand the strictest system of verification and inspection, including international forms'.[10] One of the fundamental elements of the Soviet concept of comprehensive international security, based on the UN Charter principles and norms, is a 'strictly verified reduction of the states' military potential down to the limits of reasonable sufficiency'.[11] The Political Report of the Central Committee of the Communist Party of the Soviet Union to the 27th Party Congress (1986) underscored that 'all-embracing, rigorous verification is, perhaps, the critical element of the disarmament process. The crux of the problem, as we understand it, is that there can be no disarmament without verification, while verification without disarmament becomes senseless'.[12]

The verification matters have, for a long time, been a stumbling block in the way of disarmament, being used as the main pretext for not undertaking any substantial steps in that field. The basic argument has been the alleged 'closedness' of Soviet society, the reluctance of the USSR to accept 'all-out' verification, its inclination to non-compliance, in short, the presumption of bad faith on the part of the Soviet Union as a treaty partner. Such an approach impeded negotiations and produced detrimental effects on their results. Quite often the Western States, proceeding from a conviction of the inimical intent and treachery of the USSR, and at the same time conscious of the cataclysmic consequences of a nuclear war, were forced to start negotiating with the USSR. But having done so they would propose deliberately excessive and unacceptable verification requirements, thus undermining the negotiations.[13] Even if an agreement had been reached, the 'presumption of bad faith' caused public accusations against the USSR concerning its alleged non-compliance, even though such accusations have repeatedly been doubted by authoritative sources within the USA.[14] According to the paradoxical logic of such an approach even the lack of evidence of Soviet violations did not mean that no violations took place, but rather that they have been skilfully concealed.[15]

Even despite revolutionary solutions to verification problems, provided for by the Stockholm Conference Document and the INF Treaty, and notwithstanding the role the USSR played in their formulation and realisation, the notion that the Soviet Union has incentives to commit violations and is able to conceal them, that it is the USSR that should always be considered a potential 'defendant' in connection with non-compliance matters, is still a frequent starting point of analysis.[16] However, an opposite point of view has been spreading lately. For example, according to General R. Lajoie, Director of the US On-Site

Inspection Agency, neither he, nor those under his command, had any difficulties while verifying INF Treaty compliance on Soviet territory: 'The Soviets have been friendly, co-operative and flexible'.[17] The recommendations made by an American expert, A. Krass, concerning the fundamentals of trust in the relations with the USSR are worth mentioning:

> "First, we must assume that the Soviets have an objective interest in the success and preservation of agreements. Second, we must be willing to be reassured by evidence of Soviet compliance. Third, we must maintain confidence in our own intelligence capabilities and recognise that the more militarily significant a violation is, the less likely the Soviets can keep it hidden. Finally, we must treat ambiguities, technical violations, and misunderstandings in a calm, businesslike, and confidential manner on the assumption that the other side has an interest in clarifying and correcting any incidents of noncompliance.[18]

The lack of mutual trust, instigation of distrust in the USSR, as well as some domestic reasons, have led to what the Soviet Foreign Minister E. Shevardnadze described as a 'verification allergy'. Speaking at a press conference in Washington, D.C. on 23 September, 1988 he said: 'We do not try to conceal the fact that for quite a long time our attitude towards all kinds of verification, on-site inspections in the first place, has been reserved.'[19] The fundamental change in the Soviet attitude towards verification that happened in the mid-1980s, was an integral part of drastic reforms, taking place in the domestic and foreign policies of the Soviet Union.

It is axiomatic that the internal and external policies of a country are interrelated. Accordingly, an adequate perception of a state as a member of the international community by its other members is only possible when the latter understand the policies of the former.[20] Predictability and openness in the international behaviour of a state are a function of its domestic plans and intentions. In the interrelated and interdependent world of today the international community is entitled to a degree of predictability and openness in the domestic policies of a state.

The process of Perestroika now under way in the Soviet Union, and its policies of glasnost and openness, are a clear indication of where the USSR intends to channel its resources, of the goals it sets itself, its true intentions and future programmes as well as the allocation of its economic and intellectual capabilities. Now, more than ever, Soviet foreign policy is dictated by its internal policies and the interest it has in concentrating on creative activities to make its country a better place to live. That is the reason why it needs lasting peace, disarmament, predictability and constructiveness in international relations.

A change in the Soviet position on verification, which was brought in line with current standards, made for a breakthrough in that area. The philosophy of the new Soviet approach to the problem of real verification is based first and foremost on the fact that because at present there exists a deficit of mutual trust, verification measures should become an integral part of a comprehensive system of international security, and a guarantee for its effectiveness in the military area. As we move along the road of reducing and eliminating some classes of nuclear weapons and limiting military capabilities to levels of reasonable sufficiency, the importance of verification will continue to grow. Without verification there can be no sufficient confidence in the observance of agreements, and, consequently, trust in a partner, without which further breakthroughs in disarmament are inconceivable. At the same time, verification measures should not turn every party to the agreement into a suspect. Verification should become a positive factor; it should be not only a measure allowing the detection of possible violations, but also a confidence-building measure. It should not perpetuate confrontation and suspicion, rather it must be a guarantor of 'natural' observance of voluntarily assumed obligations.

The Soviet Union is aiming for a businesslike, factual and serious approach to numerous verification issues, be they political or military and technological in nature. These issues should be resolved in a spirit of co-operation, through joint efforts, taking into account mutual concerns and pursuing the main goal – to guarantee the strict observance of assumed obligations. To follow such an approach means to ensure the productive resolution of the most complicated and sensitive items on the disarmament agenda.

Effective and adequate verification measures are an integral element of the latest Soviet proposals on arms limitation and disarmament.[21] These proposals embrace the whole range of modern arms: strategic and tactical nuclear weapons, chemical weapons, and conventional forces. They provide for the nuclear test ban, the prevention of placing weapons in space, the consolidation of disarmament accords in force, and the ABM treaty first and foremost. According to these proposals, depending on their specifics, the verification problem should be solved by the optimum combination of different verification measures, using national technical means (NTM), as well as advanced co-operation measures, including on-site inspections (OSI).

But when the 'verification allergy' was cured it turned out that the negotiating partners of the USSR had gone so far with demands for verification that they were not ready to comply with them themselves. The final stage of the INF Treaty negotiations presents an obvious case. According to one authoritative opinion: 'when the likelihood of concluding an INF Treaty seemed remote, the administration indulged its penchant for intrusive and non-negotiable verification measures. As the possibility of, and eagerness for, a treaty increased, . . . the administration was forced to scale back its OSI rhetoric'.[22]

An inconsistent and sometimes negative US approach to verification is an obstacle in the way of new agreements, be that on START or a chemical weapons ban. 'It turns out that the Russian proverb, "Trust but verify", applies only to the Soviet Union, not to the USA',[23] said E. Shevardnadze. Now that the first real measures to eliminate nuclear weapons have been agreed upon and are being carried out, and there is a chance to reach further agreements, the verification problem should not be allowed to become again an obstacle in the way of disarmament.

III

By now some experience has been gained in developing, negotiating, codifying and implementing the verification provisions of agreements on disarmament.[24] That experience clearly demonstrates both the effectiveness of the existing methods of verification based primarily on the use of NTMs and their future potential as verification techniques. The reliability of NTMs has been enhanced by technological improvements as well as by the introduction of special provisions in agreements which prohibit both interference with their functioning and attempts at deliberate concealment measures which impede verification.[25] The unimpeded functioning of NTM is made possible by other measures such as: agreed rules of counting systems covered by agreements; exchange of quantitative data on armaments; notification of upcoming activities regulated by an agreement, for example, test launches of missiles or their elimination.

The Antarctic Treaty and the document of the Stockholm Conference demonstrate the feasibility of working out and implementing such measures as OSI. The measures agreed upon in these documents guarantee the effectiveness and reliability of verification, as well as its legitimacy, and prevent it from being used as an instrument of interference in the internal affairs of other parties to the agreement.

Finally there is the discharge of verification functions by an international body – the IAEA safeguards – provided to guarantee compliance with the Non-Proliferation Treaty.

But it is the INF Treaty that contains the most remarkable verification provisions, the implementation of which will provide practical experience central to future agreements.

IV

The INF Treaty is the second ratified agreement in force between the USSR and the USA in the area of arms limitation after the ABM Treaty; it is the first one that provides for the physical destruction of nuclear missiles. The treaty strengthens strategic stability; it is a step towards the reduction of strategic offensive armaments, and it has implications extending beyond the boundaries of the bilateral relationship and nuclear arms limitation. The Treaty demonstrates the following possibilities: of undertaking radical reductions, even to the point of elimination, of the most sophisticated armaments; of the conduct of asymmetrical reductions with the goal of eliminating not only quantitative, but also geostrategic imbalances; of working out modalities for the participation of third-party states in the implementation of the substantive propositions of the Treaty; of the application of varied verification measures in aggregate, including the different sorts of OSI.

These precedents, created by the INF Treaty, found a reflection in the developed system of verification, which provided for: verification of the full elimination of weapons systems, including ancillary equipment, combat and industrial infrastructure, including different elements of the weapons system at different stages of their life cycle; asymmetrical verification (equal in size but different in numbers of inspections), founded in the difference in the quantities of the eliminated systems; verification on the territories of third-party governments, for whom the Treaty, with their consent, creates corresponding obligations.

Carefully formulated articles of the Treaty dedicated to the problems of verification are pertinent not only to the Treaty itself. As the pilot application of very promising verification measures which have been tested, the Treaty will serve as a model of verification techniques for more profound arms limitation measures.

The NTM clause is spelled out in the INF Treaty with a greater degree of detail than in standard provisions: in Article XII of the ABM Treaty, or Article V of the provisional agreement SALT I, and Article XV of the SALT II Treaty. Article XII of the INF Treaty demands the implementation of active co-operative measures of verification which facilitate the use of NTM, and its paragraph 3 stipulates implementing such co-operative measures with respect to deployment bases for road-mobile ground-launched ballistic missiles with the range of over 5,500 km. This last point was derived from the similarities between these missiles and the inter-mediate range missiles being eliminated. At the same time, this underlines the interconnection between the elimination of the INF weapons and the reduction of strategic nuclear arms, as well as the continuity of the verification measures. Though not 'intrusive' in the literal sense, the regime of verification through NTM established in the Treaty proves to be decisively more penetrating than in other agreements.

The Treaty contains an unprecedented number of various forms of OSI which amounts to a broad and deeply echeloned system comprehending all stages of the implementation of the Treaty: verification of baseline data about deployed armaments; observation of the process of elimination of the armaments, and observation of the missiles which have still not been dismantled; verification that the production of missiles covered by the Treaty will not be resumed.

In this way, the verification measures stipulated by the INF Treaty are aimed towards the achievement of synergistic effect; the parallel conduct of two forms of verification (NTMs and the various kinds of on-site inspections) complicates to the highest degree the *infraction* of the Treaty's articles.[26] This synergistic effect is also attained by way of inspecting a weapons system at different stages in its cycle of production and deployment, of inspecting each of the system's elements, as well as the infrastructure. This substantially increases the reliability of verification.

In sum, the stipulated system of verification, even should it not be 100 per cent effective, makes the expense involved in deliberately breaking the Treaty and covering up the fact incommensurate with the desired results. Expenses wasted on the cover up of prohibited activity, the impossibility of conducting an entire R & D and testing cycle on a system in violation of the agreement, and the threat to the prestige of the state in the event of being caught at cheating – all these things add together to make it economically, militarily, and politically pointless to violate the terms of the Treaty. Therefore the verification measures stipulated by the Treaty not only serve the goal of the timely detection of violations of its provisions; in addition, they serve as an effective deterrent to Treaty violations.

At the same time, the INF Treaty stresses verification measures which confirm the positive efforts of the parties, i.e. the steps taken in fulfilment of Treaty obligations, rather than verification measures which are directed towards compiling data on Treaty violations. The task of the inspections called for by the Treaty is to reveal the completeness and timeliness of the inspection measures, which are conducted with the co-operation of both the inspecting and the inspected parties. In this way verification reinforces mutual trust, trust which is already reflected in the fact of entering into such a far-reaching agreement. The system of verification stipulated by the INF Treaty reflects the aspiration to secure the fullest observation of the Treaty by its participants, while at the same time not treating them as suspects.

It is obvious that verification of the implementation of the reduction of strategic offensive arms should be more comprehensive and intrusive than the verification of the elimination of INF missiles. This derives, first of all, from the fact that a future agreement will regulate the reduction, and not the complete elimination, of weapons systems; after the agreement, the two sides will retain significant quantities of strategic armaments. The retention of these armaments entails the continuation of their production within agreed limits; flight tests; transit to the site of deployment or storage; rotation and exchange of systems on the sites of deployment and storage. Any one of these actions would be a violation of the INF Treaty; they wouldn't necessarily be so under the terms of a treaty on the reduction of strategic nuclear weapons.

Secondly, this derives from the wide range of systems to be eliminated, encompassing a variety of means and locations of deployment, as well as a variety of particulars in design and military application. The INF treaty eliminates mobile and fixed land-based missiles of eight deployed and two non-deployed types; at the same time, the reduction of strategic nuclear arrangements would have to comprehend: land-based mobile and fixed missiles of no fewer than ten types; sea-based missiles launched from submarines and surface vessels and possessing various flight patterns; aviation systems, which include both the warplanes themselves, and the weapons which they deliver – gravity bombs and guided missiles. Aside from that, the envisaged measures must include the reduction to agreed levels of the number of nuclear warheads and nuclear charges.[27]

Building upon the verification provisions of the INF Treaty, expanding and perfecting them where necessary with full regard for higher demands that would be made on verification by a START treaty, the two sides have agreed upon guiding principles for the verification of the reduction of strategic offensive arms. These measures will include baseline data exchanges and inspections to verify the accuracy of these data; on-site observation of the elimination of arms; continuous on-site monitoring of the perimeters and portals of critical production facilities; short-notice OSI of declared locations of arms comprehended by the treaty and suspect site inspection; procedures that enable verification of the number of warheads on ballistic missiles, including OSI, as well as observation by NTMs enhanced by co-operative measures.[28]

The implementation of these measures will demand the following, in addition to the expansion of the rights and obligations of the two sides in connection with verification:

— The realisation of additional technical co-operative measures, including such possible measures as the registration of missiles during production, with the guarantee that a missile will retain this identifying registration during its entire life cycle; the rigging of systems under production and covered by the agreement so as to facilitate the distinction of each different system by functionally related observable differences or by externally observable differences; exchange of data describing characteristic features of systems to be reduced; simple demonstration of armaments to be reduced before the inspection provisions come into force; the facilitation of the determination of the presence or absence of weapons systems covered by the agreement on, for example, delivery systems of dual usage.

— The wider usage of the newest technical means of verification – for example, automatic data recorders and sensors rigged to prevent scrambling and distortion and providing information to both sides in equal quantity.

— Bolstering the qualifications of inspectors, especially with respect to their juridical preparation (knowledge of the foundations of international law, including the rules for the interpretation of treaties; knowledge of the treaty on the reduction of strategic offensive arms; knowledge of the articles concerning inspections; knowledge of the relevant norms of the national law of the country where the inspection is being conducted).

For these purposes it would be desirable to examine the possibility of implementing a number of joint projects, including the conduct of joint training for inspectors, and the creation of joint enterprises for the production of the technical means of verification. The initial experience of the Standing Verification Commission, established by the INF Treaty, shows that the search for co-ordinated and compatible means of verification is a complicated process. This experience proves that it will be worthwhile to create such a joint enterprise or laboratory in advance of the future treaty's entry into force.

Evidently, both the useful experience gained through the implementation of verification measures in accordance with the INF treaty, and the measures agreed upon in the course of working out an agreement on the reduction of strategic offensive arms, can find application in both bilateral and multilateral efforts aimed at the supervision and verification of arms limitation and disarmament, including the elaboration of multilateral regulatory mechanisms within and outside the context of the United Nations.

V

The verification of disarmament and other security-building measures is, by its nature and scale, a global problem requiring an international approach to its solution. Obviously the share of multilateral agreements in that field will increase. Hence the growing role of international organisations, the United Nations in the first place. M. Gorbachev, in his well-known article 'Realities and Guarantees of a Secure World', proposed the establishment, under the auspices of the United Nations, of a mechanism for wide-ranging international verification of compliance with agreements aimed at reducing international tension and limiting armaments, and for monitoring the military situation in regions of conflict. The mechanism would use different forms, methods and means of monitoring and verification for the purpose of gathering information and transmitting it promptly to the UN. It would provide an impartial picture of events, bringing to light, in good time, preparations for military action. It would make surprise attacks difficult and facilitate measures to prevent development, expansion or intensification of military conflicts.[29] Consideration might be given to the merits of eventually instituting an international verification agency (IVA) as one possible option in the establishment of an international verification mechanism.[30]

The Agency would co-ordinate and, as appropriate, verify compliance with agreements and treaties on specific aspects of the limitation, reduction and elimination of armaments, with the consent of states-parties of course. It could also be entrusted with the task of verifying compliance with agreements on the reduction of international tension. Some other functions could well be within its authority. The IVA might be established as an integral part of the UN Secretariat or as an independent agency associated with the UN and other international organisations through co-operation agreements. There could also be a multilateral centre under the UN Secretary General which would assist in verification and which could subsequently become part of the IVA or operate in close contact with the Agency.

Far from ruling out the establishment of bilateral and multilateral systems to verify compliance with individual military and political agreements, efforts to institute an IVA presuppose the establishment of such systems.

These ideas have much in common with the proposals of other states: Finland – to establish a UN data base on disarmament and verification problems; France – to establish an international satellite monitoring agency'; the 'Group of Six' – to establish a machinery for the international verification of nuclear tests; Canada – to establish a satellite verification system PAXSAT. Thus there is under way a specific and productive dialogue on verification matters, with the partners introducing constructive and complementary proposals. A final conception of an international verification mechanism should be the result of a joint creative effort reflecting the balance of interests of all states and of the international community as a whole.

There is no doubt that verification is a critical element of disarmament. Its capabilities are constantly improving, new intrusive and penetrating forms of verification are being introduced which make it possible to monitor reliably the compliance with treaties in force and to develop further measures of disarmament. At the same time the use of the latest advances in science and technology for military purposes makes feasible the creation of weapons that can hardly be monitored, thus undermining agreements in force and precluding new ones. Quite obviously it is more reasonable not to develop new weapons and to limit and reduce existing ones, rather than to spur on the arms race whilst paying lip service to more sophisticated methods and techniques of verification. The obligation to eliminate weapons and to ban their production is the easiest one to verify.

Notes

1 *USSR–US Summit, Washington, December 7–10, 1987. Documents and Materials,* Moscow, 1987, p. 13

2 See: *The Soviet Union working for Disarmament, 1946–1960,* ed. V. Zorin, Moscow, 1961, p. 71.

3 E. Shevardnadze, 'Report at the USSR Foreign Ministry Workshop', *Viestnik MID SSSR* (The USSR Foreign Ministry Bulletin), 1988, No. 15, p. 33.

4 With kind permission of A. Stanislavlev I used some preparatory materials from our joint article, A. Stanislavlev and B. Tuzmukhamedov, 'This Seemed Unattainable', *International Affairs,* 1988, No. 3, pp. 25–33. I also used portions of my report, 'Legal Questions Arising under Intrusive Verification Provisions of the INF Treaty

and Future Arms Reduction Treaties', presented at the Sixth Conference of Soviet and US Lawyers on legal issues of arms limitation, 1988.

5 See also definitions of verification: S. Batsanov, 'Verification Issues in the Disarmament Process', *Problems of International Security and Disarmament*, Moscow, 1984, p. 94; I. Kotliarov, *International Verification by Space-Based Means*, Moscow, 1981, p. 28; A. Krass, 'The Soviet View of Verification', in *Verification and Arms Control*, Los Angeles, 1985, p. 38; E. Morris, 'Comparison of United States and Soviet Approaches to Verification', in *A Proxy for Trust*, Ottawa, 1986, p. 16.

6 See various opinions on verification as a guarantee in: Kotliarov, op. cit., p. 9; R. Timerbayev, *Verification of Arms Limitation and Disarmament*, Moscow, 1983, p. 33; O. Bogdanov, *General and Complete Disarmament* (International Legal Issues), Moscow, 1964, p. 281.

7 Timerbayev singles out such 'generally recognised principles of disarmament verification as an organic link of verification and disarmament, conformity of nature and scope of verification to those of disarmament measures, non-interference of verification in the internal affairs of a state' (op. cit., p. 194). Bogdanov earlier proposed essentially the same principles (op. cit., pp. 283–5).

8 UN Doc. A/S–10/2.

9 See also the Special Report of the UN Commission on Disarmament to the Third Special Session on Disarmament. UN Doc. A/S–15/3, para. 12, 'Verification in all its Aspects'.

10 *Pravda*, 17 February 1987.

11 *Materials of the Twenty Seventh Congress of the OPSU*, Moscow, 1986, p. 74.

12 Ibid, p. 67.

13 J. Newhouse cited a senior American official involved in arms limitation talks saying that, by suggesting the proposals for verification, the USA on many an occasion 'sought to satisfy the rhetorical commitment to arms control while using verification as the means of assuring that nothing would happen'. (J. Newhouse, *Cold Dawn: The Story of SALT*, New York, 1973, p. 70).

14 See 'Analysis of the President's Report on Soviet Noncompliance with Arms Control Agreements', *Arms Control Today*, April 1987, pp. 14–12A; 'Administration Compliance Report Prematurely Charges New Soviet ABM Violations', The Arms Control Association Background Paper, December 1987.

15 The Heritage Foundation complained in one of its publications: 'We have never found anything that the Soviets have successfully hidden'. (A. Katz, *Verification and the SALT: The State of the Art and the Art of the State*, Washington, 1979, p. 81).

16 Though judging by recent publications this statement is a lip service to a notorious tradition rather than a proof of authors' firm belief. See, for example, *Verifying Arms Control Agreements: The Soviet View*, US Congress, House, Washington, 1987, pp. 1, 15, e.a.; S. Goldman, *Soviet Compliance with Arms Control Agreements*, CRS Issue Brief 84131, Washington, 1988; M. Krepon, 'START Can Be Verified Too', *Washington Post*, 23 March, 1988, p. A27.

17 *Arms Control Today*, November 1988, p. 10.

18 A. Krass, 'The Politics of Verification', *World Policy Journal, Fall*, 1985, p. 750.

19 *Viestnik*, 1988, No. 19, p. 25.

20 See A. Kozirev, 'Trust and Balance of Interest', *International Affairs*, 1988, No. 10, pp. 3–12.

21 For a more detailed review of Soviet proposals concerning verification see V. Abarenkov, B. Krasulin. *Disarmament Reference Book*, Moscow, 1988, pp. 272—80. For an interesting, although not indisputable account of the Soviet position on verification, see A. Sherr, *The Other Side of Arms Control*, Boston, 1988, pp. 242–76.

22 J. Mendelsohn, 'INF Verification: A Guide for the Perplexed', *Arms Control Today*, September, 1987, p. 29. The author further quotes an administration official, who said: 'We never faced up to the implications of our own proposals'. Ibid, p. 26.

23 *Viestnik*, 1988, No. 19, p. 25.

24 For a detailed analysis of verification provisions in various treaties see Timerbayev, op. cit., pp. 46–67, 71–7, 106–12, 152–4, 157–69.

25 In a broad sense the term NTM implies means of observation, located beyond boundaries of jurisdiction of a state whose activities are being verified. While the term embraces many methods and techniques, there seems to be general agreement that space satellite systems form the primary NTM system. According to some sources the most advanced space surveillance systems have a ground resolution in the order of 10 cm., making it possible to detect from space objects on the Earth's surface of a size slightly larger than a tennis ball (*PAXSAT Concept: The Application of Space-Based Remote Sensing for Arms Control Verification*, Ottawa, 1987, p. 13).

26 Synergistic effect as a feature of verification is discussed in: Krass, *The Politics of Verification*, pp. 739–40; B. Lall *et. al.*, *Verifying a Ban on Ballistic Missile Defense*, New York, 1987, p. 33; S. Graybeal and M. Krepon, 'On-Site Inspections', in *Verification and Compliance: A Problem-Solving Approach*, Southampton, 1988, pp. 99–101.

27 See *USSR-US Summit, Washington, December 7-10, 1987*, pp. 143-5.

28 Ibid., pp. 145-6. See also *USSR-USA Summit, Moscow, May 29-June 2, 1988. Documents and Materials*, Moscow, 1988, pp. 83-4.

29 *Pravda*, 17 September, 1988.

30 For more details concerning the IVA see UN Doc. A/S-15/AS.1/15 submitted by the delegations of Bulgaria, Czechoslovakia and the USSR at the Third Special Session on Disarmament, 1988.

Part II
Effective Implementation of International Law

Section A. The Protection of Human Rights

6.

The International Protection of Human Rights and the Domestic Jurisdiction of States.

REIN A. MÜLLERSON

The relations arising in connection with the protection of human rights and freedoms are mainly relations between the state and the individual, i.e., internal state relations. Of course, not all relations in the field of protection of human rights are internal. Thus, relations arising between an individual and an international agency (the Human Rights Committee, the European Commission and the European Court of Human Rights) surely are not internal state relations. However, despite this, relations in the field of protection of human rights and freedoms are basically internal state relations and these rights and freedoms are secured chiefly by the state with the help of regulations of national law and internal mechanisms and procedures.

So when it is a question of international protection of human rights and international co-operation in this field, we inevitably come across problems of the relationship between international and domestic law, international human rights standards and the domestic jurisdiction of states. It should be stressed that the character of these problems is rather dynamic and they cannot be solved once and for all. Changes in the world as a whole and the development of international law and international co-operation in the field of human rights constantly introduce new elements into the solution of these problems.

International law has traditionally been, and to a considerable extent continues to remain, an inter-state law. But the emergence of inter-state organisations and various state-like entities (free cities, the Vatican, West Berlin, national liberation movements) have impaired the 'purity' of the inter-state character of international law norms, although these new subjects have not in substance changed the inter-state character of international law.

However, there is an increasingly felt tendency towards a departure from the purely state-centrist, 'étatist' character of international law. More and more often the states begin to create norms which do not regulate relations between them but are addressed to other formations and persons: juridical persons, including transnational corporations, international non-governmental organisations (NGOs), officials of international organisations and individuals as such. Although the norms meant to establish the legal status of individuals and juridical persons are frequently applied not directly to them (their demands are realised through the norms of domestic law), nonetheless the individual more and more often begins to come into direct contact with international law. This he/she does not do only in his/her capacity as an official of an international organisation or as a subject of the norms of private international law.[1] In the field of human rights the individual also appears not only as a passive beneficiary of international law norms in accordance with which the state grants him/her *definite* rights and freedoms, but as an active participant in the process of ensuring international standards in the field of human rights.

The final document of the Vienna meeting of the states participating in the Conference on Security and Co-operation in Europe obliges the states

> to respect the right of their citizens, independently or jointly with others, to make an active contribution to the development and protection of human rights and fundamental freedoms ... [including] the right of persons to supervise the implementation of and contribute to the fulfilment of the provisions of the CSCE documents and to join others with this aim.

Soviet science did not recognise the possibility for an individual to be a subject of international law. Lately, the situation has begun to change. This non-recognition of the international legal personality of individuals was to a definite extent, I think, the result of an 'étatist' approach to international law and international relations. In our country there was an overemphasis on the role and significance of the state inside society and on the world scene. The new thinking, putting man in the focus of our concerns and calling for the humanisation of international relations, cannot but take a new approach also to the role of man in international relations and his relationship to international law.

Most international norms in the field of human rights are so-called non-self-executing norms. They cannot in themselves, without the support of domestic legislation, guarantee for the individual his rights and freedoms. For this reason many provisions of the International Covenant on Civil and Political Rights directly speak about the obligation of States to ensure definite rights for individuals, with the help of national legislation. Consequently, such norms themselves cannot directly regulate the legal status of the individual.

However, does this mean that individuals themselves have no relation to international standards in the field of human rights and obtain all their rights only from the state through the medium of the norms of international law? I think this is not so. Such alienation of the individual from the norms of international law and the treatment of human rights as something bestowed on the individual from above is, as I have already said, a reflection of the 'étatist' approach to social relations. In my view, the norms of international law in the field of human rights, which oblige the state to secure for the individual the rights provided by them, at the same time give the individual the right to demand that the state honours its international obligations. It can be said that, in agreeing with international norms on human rights, the state assumes the obligation not only before the other states which are party to a respective international document, but also before all persons under its jurisdiction, and, first and foremost, before its own citizens.

Of course, difficulties can and do arise here in practice. If the legal system of a state does not envisage the operation of international treaties themselves on its territory (as, for example, in the United Kingdom, Scandinavian countries, etc.), the courts and other law-enforcing organs most likely will not be guided by international standards on human rights in settling a concrete case. In the Soviet Union international treaties themselves can operate in many fields of legal regulation, directly generating rights and obligations for the individuals. This is the case owing to the presence in many acts of a norm referrable to international law. However, such a norm is so far absent unfortunately in the field of ensuring civil and political rights. And even in countries where, under the constitution, international treaties are effective inside a country and are a component part of the law in that country, the provisions of these treaties on human rights may be and are declared by courts to be non-self-executing and, consequently, are not applied in concrete cases under consideration.

So, while not denying the importance of the operation of international law norms on the territory of a state, we must say that the implementation of international standards on human rights is impossible without the help of the relevant national legislation.

However, even if an international norm itself cannot ensure the rights and freedoms recorded in it, it can, if declared effective inside a state, suspend the application of a regulation of internal legislation standing in contradiction to it. For example, if the legislation of a country does not ensure the right to hold peaceful meetings envisaged in Article 20 of the Covenant on Civil and Political Rights, the article itself may serve as a basis for demands for ensuring this right. Individuals may, separately or in association with others, demand of the state fulfilment of its obligations, including changes in domestic legislation. In this case international standards serve as a legal base for the demands of individuals.

To my mind, all this testifies to the constant increase in the international legal standing of the individual and his ever-closer direct ties with international law. Also this testifies to changes in the scope and extent of the domestic jurisdiction of states in the field of human rights.

The fact that intra-state relations, as a rule, are not the direct object of international legal regulation does not mean that all questions connected with their legal regulation refer to the domestic jurisdiction of states. It would be incorrect to say that regulation of internal state relations belongs to the domestic jurisdiction of states, while the decision of all international matters lies beyond their domestic jurisdiction.

The relationship between matters constituting the domestic jurisdiction of states and matters that lie beyond this jurisdiction is not a mirror-like reflection of the spheres regulated by national and international law respectively. The sphere of domestic jurisdiction and the sphere of operation of internal law is not one and the same thing. The fact that some relations are regulated only or mainly by internal law does not mean automatically that their legal regulation is the internal concern of a given state.

In contrast, many international questions belong to the domestic jurisdiction of a state. S. V. Chernichenko points out, for example, that 'external affairs coming by their substance under the domestic jurisdiction of a state are in fact affairs concerning the activity of a state on the world arena which it decides in principle on its own account.'[2] And, conversely, in regulating internal relations (even if their legal regulation is carried out directly with the help of norms of national law), a state must take account of its international obligations. In this case it enjoys only a relative freedom of discretion.

There can be no direct answer to the question as to whether issues of protection of human rights belong to the domestic jurisdiction of states or not. Most glaring and mass violations of human rights, such as apartheid, genocide, racial discrimination, denial of the right to self-determination for whole peoples, are international crimes and, naturally, cannot come within the domestic jurisdiction of states. And this is so regardless of whether a particular state is a party to a relevant international treaty or not. The majority of leading international law scholars take the justified view that at least the prohibition of such practices as slavery and the slave trade, genocide, apartheid, torture, mass murder, prolonged and arbitrary detention, is a customary norm of international law.[3]

Apart from such mass violations endangering international peace and security, the provision for and protection of human rights are among the cases subject in many respects to the domestic jurisdiction of states. To the extent to which the states are obliged by international treaties to provide a definite number of rights and freedoms for people under their jurisdiction, these rights and freedoms, in the numbers and within the limits established by the respective treaties, do not remain within the domestic jurisdiction of states.

Consequently, while the direct regulation of human rights and their protection and provision are, as a rule, effected through the norms of domestic legislation of states, the practical aspect of such regulation within definite limits may lie outside the domestic jurisdiction of a state, because it must co-ordinate its law-making activity in this field with its respective international obligations. 'The objects of such obligations,' N. A. Ushakov writes, 'cease to belong to the sphere of the exclusive domestic jurisdiction of a state for which the obligation arises to adopt a relevant internal state act.'[4]

While the object of international law and the object of its regulation are most often relations in the framework of international state relations, in certain cases an object of such legal relations may be also a question of legal regulation of intra-state relations, in particular in the field of the protection of human rights.

The domestic jurisdiction of states is a rather mobile category. In socio-political respects, changes in the framework of domestic jurisdiction are due to the internationalisation of various spheres of social life and the growing interdependence of the world. From a legal perspective the extent of domestic jurisdiction depends directly on the development of international law. L. Henkin writes: 'That which is governed by international law or agreement is *ipso facto* or by definition not a matter of domestic jurisdiction.[5] We must agree with this postulate, although with some reservations.

Firstly, if a certain area of social relations becomes an object of international legal regulation, this does not mean that all matters arising in this area are fully withdrawn from the domestic jurisdiction of a state. Thus, questions of human rights do not enter into domestic jurisdiction to the extent that they become the object of international treaties or customary norms of international law. Many aspects of human rights and freedoms continue to remain under the domestic jurisdiction of states and the mechanism for ensuring international human rights standards continues to remain chiefly an internal matter for a state, for international law does not, as a rule, establish how a state should fulfil the obligations it has assumed.

Secondly, international obligations of different states in the field of human rights are not the same. While generally recognised norms in the field of human rights are obligatory for all states, as we have already said, the matter is different with regard to concrete treaty obligations. They are binding only on states which are parties to a concrete treaty.

Even for parties to treaties, questions relating to rights and freedoms envisaged in the treaties do not fully lie outside their domestic jurisdiction. As a rule, states themselves take care of individual violations of these rights. However, this does not imply a hostility to international legal standards in the policy of a given state in the field of human rights. Such individual cases of violation of international standards by a state become the object of international juridical examination only when this state has recognised the binding character of the respective international juridical procedures and mechanisms relating to the right of individuals to make complaints against a state, as specified in the respective treaties, and only when all internal means of protection have been tried. This warrants the conclusion that actions against particular individuals, rather than mass or systematic violations of international standards, belong basically to the domestic jurisdiction of states.

Lastly, the following question arises. As is known, special procedures for the implementation of human rights have been established on the basis of many international treaties on human rights. Thus, the Committee on Human Rights has the mission of contributing to the implementation of the international Covenant on Civil and Political Rights. It considers reports of states and individual complaints against states which have acceded to the optional Protocol to the Covenant. The Committee can also consider statements of one state against another if both states participating in the Covenant have made the relevant statement on the basis of Article 41 of the Covenant.

However, the question arises whether the existence of such special procedures and mechanisms excludes other means accessible to states. For example, can a state participating in the Covenant lodge a protest about a violation of human rights envisaged in the articles of the Covenant by another participating state or can they, for instance, take the matter to the International Court of Justice, provided, of course, both states have recognised the jurisdiction of the Court?

O. Schachter believes that this is hardly possible, since 'the treaty drafters apparently meant to limit means of implementation to those agreed in the treaties'.[6] However, L. Henkin believes that if the treaty itself does not contain other indications, any special mechanism set up for implementing obligations in the field of human rights does not replace, but merely supplements, other customary means applied in cases when international agreements are violated.[7] For his part, M. Sassoli points out that 'no one has given any proofs that observance of treaties on human rights is ensured only by special mechanisms'.[8]

I think the last point of view is correct. After all, a special mechanism of implementation is set up not in order to get round other means of implementing international treaties. On the contrary, special mechanisms and procedures are designed to serve as additional guarantees of fulfilment of international obligations by states rather than to replace the traditional means – protests, court and arbitration procedures and, when necessary, collective means of compulsion. In normal conditions, and as a rule, the states rather must strive to use these special mechanisms and procedures in the first place. However, there is nothing to prevent them from resorting to other means. This is specified also in Article 44 of the Covenant on Civil and Political Rights which lays down that the provisions on the implementation of the Covenant do not prevent the states which are party to the Covenant from resorting to other procedures for settling disputes on the basis of general and special international agreements between them.

In the limits in which questions of protection of human rights do not constitute the domestic jurisdiction of states, the concern of international organisations or other states for their observance is not interference in their internal affairs. At the same time, to prevent this concern from turning into impermissible interference, it must be shown in forms corresponding to the requirements of international law. Thus, an international organisation or agency can deal with cases of violation of human rights in any particular state only within the competence of this organisation or agency.

Western literature on problems of non-interference in internal affairs most often considers as impermissible interference only so-called 'dictatorial interference',[9] i.e. interference connected with the use or threat of compulsory measures. We can hardly agree with this above all because this is not stated in any norms of international law and does not even follow from them by any logical deduction. For example, the resolution of the UN General Assembly on 21 December 1965, about the impermissibility of interference in the internal affairs of states and the protection of their independence and sovereignty, not only condemns armed interference, but also bans other forms of interference, such as threats directed against the international legal status of a state or against its political, economic and cultural elements.

If the principle of non-interference referred only to the prohibition of violent, dictatorial interference, the bans contained in it would actually coincide with bans of the principle of non-use of force or its threat. Hence, interference must imply any measures of economic, political or other character aimed at applying compulsion to other state in the exercise of its sovereign rights.

However, on the other hand we should not forget that questions of human rights are not today matters fully subject to the sovereign consideration of a state. Consequently, these questions can be considered by other states and respective international agencies within the competence of the latter. Moreover, they can take measures permitted by international law with the aim of ensuring that a given state fulfils its international obligations in the field of the protection of human rights and freedoms. Of course, under prohibition is any armed interference, including so-called 'humanitarian intervention' (I do not speak here about the possibility and even necessity of interference under the aegis of the UN or by its decision, for example, in the case of such gross violation of human rights as genocide). Under prohibition are any measures of economic or political pressure which aim, not to put an end to violations of international standards on human rights, but to change the social or political system of another state.

It is difficult, indeed practically impossible, to state in advance those criteria which would help to determine in each concrete case whether or not a particular action is a violation of the principle of non-interference.

Naturally, we cannot regard as interference in internal affairs any talk, even on the part of officials, about the state of human rights in another country, especially if this talk corresponds to the real state of things. (It should be said in general that this refers to cases when definite violations of international human rights standards do really take place. If any state accuses another state of violating human rights without any grounds, this is interference or an attempt to interfere in internal affairs.) We can hardly treat as interference, moreover, requests and appeals of the leaders of one state to the leaders of another state about the destinies of specific persons, especially if such requests are confidential and do not serve any propaganda purposes. Further, we cannot regard as interference in internal affairs the use of special mechanisms created on the basis of international treaties on human rights. Permissible are protests and statements really aimed at the protection of the rights and freedoms of an individual if there are systematic violations of specific rights and if individual cases are not accidental excesses but testify to a definite policy pursued by a state.

At present, violations of human rights in different states are subject to consideration in the framework of the UN Human Rights Commission, and if systematic violations of generally recognised international standards really do take place, such consideration is not interference in internal affairs. Within the framework of the Commission also operative is procedure 1503, in accordance with which consideration is given to complaints of private persons testifying to systematic mass violations of human rights. This, too, is not interference in internal affairs of a state.

However, it is a case of interference when propaganda campaigns are organised, leading to the worsening of inter-state relations and aimed at discrediting the policy of a particular state, if no systematic violations of human rights are observed in that state.

One of the indispensable conditions for authorising interference by other states or by relevant international agencies, when it is a question of ensuring human rights in some other state, is the existence of real and systematic violations of human rights.

As for separate, accidental violations of international human rights standards in a particular state, which do not testify to a definite anti-human-rights policy, such violations can, to my mind, become subject to international consideration only in cases directly specified by appropriate international procedures (e.g., in the Human Rights Committee, the European Human Rights Commission or other agencies). In general, we see an expansion of different forms of international protection of human rights and, as a consequence, a corresponding narrowing of the sphere of domestic jurisdiction of states in this field.

It must be admitted that the Soviet Union's reserved attitude to control mechanisms in the field of the protection of human rights and its painful reaction to the slightest criticism (seen, if not as an encroachment on our sovereignty, at least as interference in our internal affairs) did not merely derive from ideological dogmatism but also testified to the fact that we had something to conceal in the field of human rights. Words were not matched with deeds.

Democratisation and the consolidation of the rule of law in our country are generated by internal processes which have their own momentum. As for international co-operation in the field of human rights, the Soviet Union is participating in it not in order to 'lift up' other countries to the generally recognised standards, nor with any propaganda purposes. Our participation in international treaties on human rights and our recognition of the respective international mechanisms and procedures should be seen first of all as additional guarantees for the protection of the rights of Soviet citizens. It can be even said that they are an indispensable external element in the building of a state governed by the rule of law in the USSR.

Notes

1 For more information see R.A. Müllerson, 'Private and Public International Law' in *International Law and the International System*, ed. W. Butler, Dordrecht, Boston, Lancaster, 1987, pp. 77–84.

2 S.V. Chernichenko, 'Subjective Boundaries of International Law and the Domestic Jurisdiction of the State', *Soviet Yearbook of International Law*, Moscow, 1986 (in Russian).

3 See O. Schachter, 'International Law in Theory and Practice', Vol. 178 Rd. C., p. 336; A. D'Amato, *International Law: Process and Prospect*, New York, 1987, p. 145.

4 N. A. Ushakov, *Non-Interference in Internal Affairs of States*, Moscow, 1971, p. 62 (in Russian).

5 L. Henkin, 'Human Rights and "Domestic Jurisdiction" ', in *Human Rights, International Law and the Helsinki Accord*, ed. T. Buergenthal, New York, 1979, p. 22.

6 Schachter, op. cit., p. 334.

7 Henkin, op. cit., p. 25.

8 M. Sassoli, 'Mise en oeuvre du droit international humanitaire et le droit international de l'homme: une comparison, *Anuaire Suisse de droit international*, Vol. XLIII 1987, p. 39.

9 See H. Kelsen, *The Law of the United Nations*, London, 1950, 770; Henkin, op. cit., p. 25.

Editorial Note

Unlike the chapter which follows, this chapter does not study the application of international law by Soviet courts because until now this has not been a choice open to Soviet courts. The possibility of giving this power to Soviet courts is under consideration at the present time and indeed this is one of the reasons for the thrust of the next chapter.

7.

The Application of International Law in the English Legal System[1]

COLIN WARBRICK

(a) Matters relating to sovereignty and the limits of jurisdiction of the U.K. and of foreign countries are matters affecting the prerogative and are primarily for the executive to determine. (b) It is undesirable that the U.K. courts and Her Majesty's Government should take differing views on a question of this kind. Consequently, unless Her Majesty's Government's conclusions are manifestly unreasonable or *manifestly contrary to international law* the courts should accept the view taken by Her Majesty's Government.

per Silkin, Attorney-General in *Rio Tinto Zinc Corporation et al.* v. *Westinghouse Electric Corporation* [1978] A.C. 547, at 593–4.

The Attorney-General's concession in the *Rio Tinto* case that the courts have the ultimate word on matters of international law has taken on an increasing significance as recent English cases have clarified the constitutional relationship between international and internal law and have done so in ways that increase the opportunities when international law questions might come before a municipal court.[2] It is necessary to emphasise the constitutional nature of this relationship against both those who would contend that the matter is ultimately and always one of international law, the strict monist hypothesis,[3] and those who suggest some variant of Judge Fitzmaurice's position that there is no 'common field' of operation of international and domestic law.[4] Generally, the latter view is to be preferred, even if it is not absolutely true. In English law, while considerations of constitutional theory have influenced the approach of the courts, matters of international legal theory have scracely ever done. International law does not, as a rule, demand that a State adopt any particular device for ensuring that its municipal law and decisions taken thereunder are compatible with its international obligations.[5] The very variety of mechanisms resorted to in the national legal systems shows the absence of any customary rule regulating the manner in which concordance is to be achieved. The general nature of international obligation is merely one of result, that concordance is, in fact, achieved.[6] If the political organs of the State take no action, whether from a belief that none is required or because of deliberate intention to violate the State's international obligations, or if they do act with inadvertence to or in wilful breach of those duties, the capacity of the domestic courts to take any steps to repair the deficiency by filling gaps, correcting errors, enjoining conduct or providing other remedies depends upon their constitutional authority *vis-a-vis* the other organs of government. There is no rule of international law which precludes them from doing so[7] (nor, in some cases, is there if the breach of international law is by the government of another State),[8] nor is there anything in such questions which makes them non-justiciable in the sense that they are questions of law which a domestic court does not have the capacity to resolve.[9] Indeed, there is an arguable case that if a domestic court has the constitutional capacity to review or control these acts of its own government, then it should do so to avoid the international responsibility of the State which will be the consequence of its failure to act. It is true that, exceptionally, an international obligation may require expressly a specific domestic response, for example, harmonisation treaties[10] or treaties 'creating' crimes.[11] Even here though, the domestic effect will be governed by domestic law. If there be a dissonance between the State's international obligations and some aspect of its internal law, the general rule is that the State is under an international obligation to make reparation,[12] not that the domestic law or decree or decision is rendered invalid or a nullity[13] in the law of the errant State[14] or must be so regarded by the law of a third-State.[15]

Essentially, the constitutional questions for States operating under the rule of law is whether the requirement of legality of government action extends to demanding compliance with international law as well as domestic law. If the answer be that, in principle, this should be the case, the inquiry shifts to how that result should be achieved. In any particular State it is necessary to know which organs of the State 'do' international law and which organs of the State control the 'doing' of international law.[16] In the United Kingdom, the traditional answers to these questions are that international law generally falls within the foreign affairs powers of the State, powers which are exercised by the Government and which are subject to only limited Parliamentary control and not ordinarily subject to judicial supervision.[17] The Attorney-General's observations, quoted at the head of this article, show that the government recognises that some questions of international law may properly come before English courts and that the courts should be the ultimate determiners of such matters. Foreign affairs powers of government are not in like case with domestic powers because a measure of control upon their exercise results from the interests of other States and the mechanisms of control of the international legal system. However, the expanding field of international law has brought within its ambit issues directly between the State and individuals where the traditional measures for securing compliance may be inadequate because of the absence of sufficient interests in any other State.[18] In these circumstances, there is a case for greater judicial control of governmental action. The availability of international legal rules is important because they provide 'manageable standards'[19] for judicial supervision, they make matters governed by them 'justiciable' in this sense, although other discretionary considerations may exclude or limit judicial intervention, for instance, matters of standing, of the availability and sensitivity of evidence, of the possibility of an internal remedy and the availability of an alternative external remedy. For some little time, writers have urged that domestic courts abandon their reticence and adopt a more receptive attitude to arguments based on international law.[20] In particular, it is argued that the courts can thereby contribute to achieving compliance with international law by securing the obedience of their own executive departments. The development of international rules which not merely have an effect upon individuals but which purport to confer rights on them directly, rights which will usually be exercisable against their own governments, is said to emphasise this argument, because the international machinery for securing the enjoyment of such rights is rudimentary or non-existent.[21] But the old concerns remain and they are genuine if sometimes exaggerated. The task for legislators and courts is to fashion a role for the internal examination of international law which takes these old interests into account, while providing effective protection for the new values of the international legal system. One way of doing this is by more effective parliamentary scrutiny of executive policy in foreign affairs. Despite a good deal of resistance, some progress has been made in this direction.[22] However, the main thrust of Parliamentary control is likely to be at the general policy level rather than examining the individual case, and, in any event, it should not be restricted to matters covered by rules of international law. On the other hand, the mere fact that a question of international law is in issue does not make the matter inevitably suitable for domestic judicial determination.[23] All legal systems have some devices which limit the judicial review of executive actions on the grounds of the sensitivity of the issue or of the expediency of the governmental process. While there can be debate as to where the line should be drawn, only a minority of opinion suggests that the line should be erased altogether. Overall, then, while there are convincing reasons why there should be a readier recourse to international law by domestic courts, it is equally important that these authorities should refine the processes for elucidating accurately what it is exactly that international law requires. Nothing will be more destructive of developments in this area if the techniques of municipal tribunals are seen to be capricious and unscientific, bending the materials of international law to support this or that preferred judicial policy.

It is suggested that in English law there are four kinds of case in which the court may be faced with a question of international law:

1. where the court may have direct access to the rules of international

law (applicable only for rules of customary international law);

2. where the rule of international law has been subject to some national act transforming it into an internal rule, for example, a statute

(a) to implement an international treaty;

(b) to exercise a competence under international law, whether based on customary law or treaty;

(c) to provide a domestic statement of customary international law;

3. where there is no specific domestic transformation of an international legal rule but where a principle of domestic law of general application allows the court to take international law into consideration, for example,

(a) statutory interpretation: the principle that Parliament is presumed not to have legislated contrary to the State's international obligations;

(b) where it must be decided whether some matter is in accordance with public policy;

4. where there is domestic authority that the court has no power to consider the questions, issues of international law notwithstanding, for example,

(a) many prerogative acts, including domestic acts of state; and

(b) foreign acts of state.[24]

I shall argue that the role of the court is distinct in each of these cases, although they have certain features in common. The one which they share which is the most important is that in any case where the court must consider international law, its first duty is to discover exactly what the rule of international law is. Establishing this varies in difficulty, not merely from source to source (it will be generally easier to find what a treaty provision is than what is a rule of customary law)[25] but from rule to rule. This problem may be alleviated somewhat where there is a domestic transformation of the rule but, even here, there have been circumstances where the court has preferred the international rule to the domestic version of it.[26] The transforming act also confines the inquiry the court must make: it is the particular rule which must be considered. In case 3, the inquiry is open-ended, into *any* international obligation of the State which may be relevant. In case 1, since the court is applying the international rule, the content of the rule and the consequences of any violation of it will be decided by international law, as will questions of whom may claim rights under the rule and upon whom it imposes duties. In case 2, the court may look at international law for the purpose of giving meaning to the transformed rule but, in applying that rule, it is to domestic law that the court must look as to rights and remedies and so forth. In these aspects, the court's role in case 3 is the same but, while the inquiry is potentially wider, there are more restraints on how a court may react when it has elucidated a relevant international rule. Thus, the approach to statutory interpretation is merely a presumption, so that clear words in the statute will, or some other presumption may, take priority. 'Public policy' is to be closely confined. Those judicial decisions which have touched upon the European Convention of Human Rights might appear to have eroded the distinction between cases 2 and 3. However their impact must not be overstated. At most the Convention has been used to reinforce decisions rather than being the reason for them, and the special regard paid by certain judges to the Convention may be explained by the unusual certainty with which it can be determined what it is that the Convention requires.[27] While the language of the Convention is itself quite broad, its interpretation is assisted by the extensive and readily available jurisprudence of the Court and the practice of the Commission.

The idea of the *dedoublement fonctionnel*[28] of the State in the international legal system finds a reflection in the process of the domestic application of international law. The Government always has an interest that the point of international law be decided accurately by its courts. Failure by them to do so correctly can lead to political difficulties with other States[29] and may involve the international responsibility of the State.[30] The Government's knowledge of State practice and the experience of its lawyers make its participation in the determination of the rule of international law particularly valuable. On the other hand, the Government may have an interest in the outcome of litigation[31] which may supersede its concern about the rule of international law. The desirability of having the Government involved in proceedings as an 'expert' about the condition of international law in cases in which it is not directly involved has to be balanced against the reluctance of the executive appearing to take the side of one party to a private suit. The undesirability of the Government having any special status of expert in litigation in which it has an interest has to be balanced against the injustices in principle, and in practice of the possibility of the court coming to a wrong conclusion on the matter of international law. In either case, the court must find the right balance, steering between the scepticism of Lord Cross in *The Philippine Admiral*[32] and the deference of Lord Fraser in *Rio Tinto*.[33] If it be appreciated that internal judicial decisions about international law always have some international impact, either as evidence of the state of the law or contributing to the development of international law, or if they are wrong, occasioning the responsibility of the State, then the special character of these judgments is apparant.[34] Equally, though, they are decisions of law and there is nothing in their nature which makes them unsuitable or unamenable to judicial determination. Where the court does decide that it ought not to render a judgment where a question of international law is involved, it should do so in terms which indicate that there are other reasons for its reluctance than the alleged non-justiciability of international legal questions in internal courts. It is suggested that the formulation of the Attorney-General, quoted at the head of this article, is correct. While the courts should be cautious about departing from the considered view of the executive as to the position in international law, nonetheless they have the final responsibility to decide the matter. Circumspection in face of the Government's opinion (which in my view ought ordinarily to be before the court)[35] acknowledges one of the fundamentals of the international legal system that, in the absence of any procedures specifically accepted by it, a State may insist upon its own view of what its international obligations are. It is for each State to decide how far it should subject this relatively untrammelled discretion at the international level to domestic judicial review. The more clearly are the domestic courts invested with authority to decide upon questions of international law, the more boldly might they differ from the position taken by the executive.

Case 1: the direct reception of international law – customary international law
The standard English international law textbooks demonstrate a bewildering confusion of terms to describe the place customary international law has in English law,[36] which reveals how mysterious had become the meaning of Blackstone's famous sentence: 'The law of nations ... is here adopted in its full extent by the common law and is held to be a part of the law of the land.'[37] In large measure, the mystery may have been dispelled by the judgment of the Court of Appeal in *Trendtex*,[38] 'may' because the judgments are not above reproach[39] and because it is possible to adopt an interpretation of *Trendtex* which very much limits its effects.[40] Lord Denning dealt shortly[41] with criticism of the *Trendtex* decisions and its welcome in the House of Lords in *I Congreso*[42] suggests that he was probably on strong ground in doing so. What he said in *Trendtex* is that, 'the rules of international law [by which he meant customary international law] are incorporated into English law automatically and are considered part of English law unless they are in conflict with an Act of Parliament.'[43] As I understand it, this is a general proposition, not limited to the rules on sovereign immunity which were before the Court, that allows the English Court to give effect to rules of customary international law unless precluded from doing so by an inconsistent statutory provision. This authority is given by a rule of the common law, which rule *itself* is further glossed upon by Lord Denning in these terms: 'If this Court is satisfied that the rule of international law on a subject has changed from what it was 50 or 60 years ago, it can give effect to this change ...'[44] This does not appear to be intended to narrow the effect of the former statement on incorporation but only to state the *stare decisis* point, or as Shaw, LJ put it: 'What *is* immutable is the principle of English law that the law of nations (not what *was* the law of nations) must be applied in the Courts of England.'[45] What we have, then, is an interpretation of a single rule of the common law which authorises an English court to apply any rule of customary international law in its present condition. This would appear to

leave the question of what is the present condition of customary international law, that is, the matter of its proof, much more like a question of fact (say, like a question of foreign law)[46] than the question of law, which it is.[47]

At its widest, *Trendtex* undoes the limitation suggested by Lord Atkin in *Chung Chi Cheung*[48] that the rules of customary international law are incorporated only so far as they are not 'inconsistent with rules ... finally declared by superior tribunals' and would mean that a rule of customary international law would override established common law rules.[49] It is a conclusion which has been challenged[50] and there are proper concerns about allowing the courts to roam through the broad acres of the common law armed with a reforming scythe fashioned, say, from the ringing phrases of the Universal Declaration of Human Rights,[51] arguing that the content of the Declaration is part of customary international law:[52] it would be impossible to anticipate which stalks might fall. There are, however, protections against an arbitrary harvest; certainly, there has been none since the judgments in *Trendtex* were handed down.

The protections against excessive judicial reliance on customary international law are of two kinds, neither of which turned out to be of great consequence in the *Trendtex* case. A litigant must *prove* that that is a rule of customary international law (though the proof is by argument and not by material evidence) and he must prove that the *content* of the rule is mandatory rather than permissive and, if mandatory, that he is the person entitled to benefit from the rule and the defendant is the person bound to perform the obligation imposed by the rule.[53]

The more controversial the rule, the greater the need for proof.[54] Statutory incorporation of a rule of customary law operates like conclusive proof of the existence of the rule:[55] superior judicial authority as strong evidence.[56] Executive opinion as to what the rule is has sometimes been regarded as good evidence;[57] sometimes the courts have treated it with suspicion.[58] Evidence of executive practice ought to be important since it contributes itself to the purported rule[59] (and in some cases, it might, as a unilateral statement or by creating an estoppel, itself bind the State in international law). Ideally, the investigation a domestic court should make ought to be the same as the one an international tribunal would undertake but expedition, cost, access to information all conspire to confine the inquiry.[60] Experience would suggest that greater reliance is placed on textbooks than would be usual in an international court and that there is a marked tendency to rely on national evidence.

Many rules of customary international law do not place obligations on States but confer powers or competence upon them: whether States might draw straight baselines from which to measure their territorial seas;[61] whom they might designate as their nationals;[62] to where and to whom they might extend their legislative jurisdiction.[63] Beyond those minimum competences which States are required to exercise,[64] it is a matter for a

State's discretion as to how much of its potential authority it will claim. The great and confusing case of *Keyn*[65] can be explained in these terms. International customary law allowed but did not require a State to exercise some criminal jurisdiction over persons on board foreign flag ships in its territorial sea. Even if English law could have been read to extend to foreign ships in the territorial sea, as a matter of domestic law, no court had been provided with jurisdiction to try such cases,[66] a deficiency which the permissive rule of customary international law could not make good.[67]

Even where international law imposes a duty upon a State, it is still necessary for the litigant in domestic proceedings to show that the duty is owed to him, a burden which will be very difficult to discharge where he is an individual rather than an international person.[68] It is possible that an individual may be able to show that *he* has rights in international customary law where those rights are fundamental human rights. In relation to English law, where the individual would have a plausible case, for example, that he has a right not to be tortured, there is inevitably a domestic provision protecting him which would render reliance on international law unnecessary.[69]

This narrow reading of the impact of *Trendtex* accords with the general nature of customary international law which recognises the rights and duties belonging to States rather than individuals. It allows the State to take advantage of this position by renouncing or compromising its rights, generally and in advance, or in a particular case after a wrong has been committed,[70] when it deems it to be in the State's interests to do so. It will be said to the contrary that the imperfect mechanisms of the international legal system for securing compliance need supplementation and, in particular, the courts of a State ought to be able to call to account against the standards of international law their own Executive Departments. Even if this policy argument is accepted, it is not required by international law nor is it allowable in English law, given the terms of the *Trendtex* judgments.

Case 2: transformation of the international rule:
statutory implementation[71]
The treaty-making power is vested in the executive [72] and there is no power of judicial review as to how the power is exercised.[73] This goes beyond a matter of constitutional theory, that treaty-making being by virtue of the Prerogative, [74] it is generally immune from judicial supervision,[75] for it is not easy to see what standards the courts would find to assess the legitimacy of a particular exercise of the power. It is true that the development of the concept of *ius cogens*[76] has introduced into international law the idea of an unlawful treaty but even if the standard of *ius cogens* were clear in international law,[77] there would be substantial problems of standing to raise such an assertion in English proceedings. If, then, the executive's power to make treaties is free from judicial restraint,

it is as clear that the power to give internal effect to treaties rests with Parliament. Neither the British Government nor that of any foreign State can rely upon a treaty to which it is a party before the English court in the absence of a Statute giving the treaty the force of domestic law.[78] Nor can an individual assert any rights under an unimplemented treaty, however significant may be its effect upon his interests.[79]

Accordingly, the normal situation when an English court comes face to face with the terms of a treaty is where domestic effect is given to its terms by legislation, that is to say, there will necessarily be an act of transformation. Provided that the Court is satisfied that it is the intention of Parliament to implement the terms of an international agreement, 'cogent evidence' of which was called for by Diplock, LJ in *Estuary Radio*,[80] then recent decisions have seen an 'internationalising' of the courts' approach to interpretation.

The judgment of Lord Diplock in *The Eschersheim*[81] goes as far as possible, commensurate with the doctrine of parliamentary sovereignty, in authorising the courts to give the 'international' meaning to implementing legislation. He said: 'If there be any difference between the language of the statutory provision and that of the corresponding provision of the convention, the statutory language should be construed in the same sense as that of the convention if the words of the statute are reasonably capable of bearing that meaning.'[82] What this amounts to is a two-stage investigation. What the treaty means must be established according to an 'international' interpretation of its terms. Once that meaning has been elicited, it must, as it were, be laid against the Act and, if the statutory language will bear the same meaning, then that interpretation of it should be adopted. The justification for this approach depends, then, upon the court getting the international interpretation correct. In a series of decisions culminating in *Fothergill* v. *Monarch Airlines*,[83] the English courts have demonstrated their receptiveness, not only to arguments based upon a purposive reading of the treaty text, but also to the aids to interpretation in the form of the *travaux préparatoires*[84] and authoritative versions of the text in other languages.[85] Such problems as remain seem practical rather than of principle, although it would be desirable if the House of Lords were to make it clear that the practice of any international organ charged with interpreting a treaty text should be taken into account and, if that interpretation be authoritative, that it be followed by the domestic court.[86] The conclusion is that, increasingly, English courts have sought the *meaning* of 'transformed' international rules in a manner that an international tribunal would adopt but that the *effect* of such rules is to be determined according to domestic law. It is an important conclusion because, as cases 1 and 2 show, domestic courts are capable of deciding questions of international law, something which, in other contexts as we shall see, they deny.

Case 3: the indirect effect of international law
This case covers a variety of instances where a court may have recourse to

international law (usually treaty law) in circumstances when there is no specific incorporation of the international rule. The principal example is where the court relies on the general presumption of statutory interpretation that Parliament did not intend to legislate in violation of the international obligations of the State.[87] Another example is where the court relies on international law to fill out the content of public policy. Although there is some dispute about it, the better view is that the statutory presumption extends to treaty law as well as to customary international law.[88] The presumption can, of course, only extend to those obligations existing at the time the legislation was enacted, unless the legislation indicates to the contrary. It is a presumption which was not of much practical importance (except, perhaps, as to the territoriality of legislation)[89] until the United Kingdom's ratification of the European Convention of Human Rights. Neither the Convention nor any other general human rights treaty to which the UK is a party has been implemented by domestic statute. Yet from time to time English judges have suggested that they might take the Convention into account in interpreting rules of English law.[90] The presumption is much weaker than the one described in case 2. It yields, of course, to the express words of a statute and may give way to other statutory presumptions, many of which, in any case, touch on matters which concern human rights.[91]

The significance of the presumption is most likely to arise with respect to the exercise of ministerial powers conferred by Act of Parliament. Increasingly, the government is understood to weigh the substance of proposed legislation against the European Convention and to put forward proposals which are, as far as possible, compatible with it. However, discretionary powers necessarily can be exercised in unforeseen ways. Parliament shows no inclination to put a specific fetter on the powers that they should be now in compliance with the Convention. More disappointingly for many international and administrative lawyers, the courts have shown an equal lack of appetite for conditioning discretionary authority in this way.[92] The alternatives are:

1. that the Minister was bound to exercise his powers in accordance with the State's international obligations; but this runs into the constitutional obstacle that the treaty has not been implemented;[93] or

2. that a Minister was bound to take into account those international obligations in reaching his decision (and, if the obligations were ones of customary international law or implemented treaty provisions, to show that his understanding of international law was correct).[94]

The weight of authority is against either limitation on the exercise of a minister powers. Indeed, a recent case, *R. v. Secretary of State for Foreign and Commonwealth Affairs*,[95] goes even further in denying any justiciable obligation on the Minister even though the statute required him to satisfy himself that the exercise of his discretion was 'permitted by international law'.[96] More recently still, however, the Divisional Court was more receptive to these kinds of arguments in *R.* v. *Secretary of State for the Home Department ex p. Brind*[97] (although finding no merit in the applicant's claim that the Minister's decision was contrary to the Convention). Whatever the present position in English law, the outcome of a case presently awaiting judgement by the European Court of Human Rights, *Soering*,[98] raises the possibility that the absence of a domestic remedy to challenge an exercise of a discretion against the Convention will involve a breach of Article 13, even if the decision was in substance compatible with the Convention. If this indeed is the way that *Soering* comes out, it will be a substantial policy reason for the English courts to revise their approach on this matter.

Rather than the mandatory non-justiciability argued for by the Court in *R.* v. *Secretary of State for Foreign and Commonwealth Affairs*, the courts should rely on the discretionary rules which apply in administrative law cases before the English courts, whether international law is involved or not.

In the area of challenge to statutory powers, the right of an individual does not depend entirely on the demonstration that his legal right has been interfered with. The rules of standing, however unclear they are in English administrative law, are developing a wider basis than specific legal interest.[99] The more the courts are prepared to see the function of administrative law as restraining within legal limits the exercise of the powers of Government, the more readily will they be prepared to grant persons the right to argue that the Government is going beyond its powers in international law. Standing is, of course, only the beginning and not the end of the litigation. Even an extended notion of standing does not mean that a court should grant a hearing on the merits to every person who claims that governmental action is contrary to international law. Considerations of justiciability of the issue[100] limit the court's involvement.

One factor arguing for judicial abstention on international matters requires examination. It is the argument that the State must speak with one voice in international affairs[101] and that it would embarrass the executive if the court were to hear challenges to Government action with respect to other States. Even if this is true, there is no reason why the 'one voice' should be the executive's. In the ultimate case, Parliament can speak the last word but where a question of law arises it seems axiomatic that the court should have the final say (unless precluded by Parliament), whether that law be international or domestic. This is particularly the case where the impact of the Government's decisions falls directly on individuals. But it must be a question of law. The Court cannot interfere on questions of policy, not because it would thereby embarrass the executive but because it has no standards for measuring policy judgments.[102] In the case of the Anglo-Icelandic fishing dispute, the treaty which eventually brought it to a conclusion[103] was not unlawful in international law, being simply a renunciation of the customary law rights of the United Kingdom.Even if it were admitted that some challenges to prerogative powers should be admitted and even though the recourse to power in this case had substantial adverse consequences on individual fishermen in the deep-water ports, no court could engage in a review of the treaty-making power. How would it calculate, to consider just one factor, the advantages of the new extended grounds shortly to be claimed by the United Kingdom with those lost off Iceland? This is a clear case. Other examples are more difficult to deal with: what if the claim is that a particular use of force is contrary to the Charter[104] or that the denial of trade union rights at security centres is contrary to International Labour conventions?[105] Such issues are not non-justiciable in the sense that there are no standards for the court to apply, because international law supplies some. They can only be so regarded if some kind of political question doctrine refers them exclusively to the executive to determine, perhaps on the ground that considerations of national security are involved.[106]

Quite apart from the general question of principle as to whether the courts should have recourse to international legal rules to control the exercise of executive power, any further expansion of the most favourable *dicta* in *Ashby*[107] comes up against certain practical obstacles. The most formidable one would seem to be the need to demonstrate that the exercise of the discretion is contrary to the international obligation. This is particularly true where the executive claims to have acted for a legitimate reason and where any breach of the obligation turns upon the wrongfulness of its motive. This was the argument in *Soblen*,[108] where the applicant maintained that the deportation decision was in reality for extradition purposes, but done in this manner in order to achieve his return to the United States, which the domestic law would not allow, and which the extradition agreement did not require. While conceding that the Court had the power to review an abuse of the ministerial power, the Court of Appeal found that Soblen had not been able to show that he was being returned for purposes not proper to the deportation power.[109]

The consequence of accepting that persons charged with exercising statutory powers are under an obligation to take into account any relevant international obligations of the State when making decisions will not necessarily mean that any eventual decision will be in accordance with international law. The official may say that, having considered the international legal implications of his decision, he still deems it the right one to take. However, making him spell this out serves two purposes. First, the international law question may be considered by the court to see if the official has reached the proper answer to it. Even if he has done so but is still determined to act contrary to international law, then the political price must be paid. The responsible Minister must be prepared to answer to Parliament as to why he deemed it necessary to ignore international law. The political process will not guarantee a remedy, but examination of an issue within the political arena ought, if constitutional theory is to have any practical meaning, to be of some consequence on some occasions.

Conclusion

Recent developments in English law, dating from *Trendtex* for customary international law and from *Salomon* for statutes implementing treaties, have increased the accessibility of international law to the English courts and, what is more, have done so in terms which emphasise that the inquiry the courts must make is to the 'international' meaning and effect of the international legal rules. The same progress cannot be reported in relation to unimplemented treaties, where the courts have not taken opportunities to scrutinise national laws and decisions against the international obligations of the State. It is an omission which is of practical consequence mainly in relation to human rights treaties and it might reflect judicial deference to the fact the Parliament has chosen not to enact legislation giving effect to the general human rights treaties. It cannot be ruled out that, if the courts did seek to rely on, say, the European Convention, as if it were domestic law, that a future Government might find it expedient to limit or even cancel its participation in the international regime. It cannot be ignored that the United States, where ratification of human treaties would have direct internal legal consequences, has not ratified any of the major human rights instruments.

Notes

1 Although this paper is a general survey, it is written with international human rights particularly in mind.

2 This paper is concerned with *English* law only. Despite the opinions of Solicitor-General to the contrary, see U.K.M.I.L. (1982) 53 B.Yb.I.L. 344, it is not clear that English law and Scots law are at one on the relationship between domestic and international law: see *Mortenson* v. *Peters* (1906) 8 F.(J) 93; *Kaur* v. *Lord Advocate* 1981 S.L.T. 322 and for comment, Evans, Treaties and United Kingdom; the Scottish Dimension (1984) J.R. 41. For a recent article which discusses many of the English authorities, see Schaffer, the Inter-relationship between Public International Law and the Law of South Africa (1983) 32 I.C.L.Q. 277.

3 *Interpretation of the Memel Statute* P.C.I.J. Series A/B, No. 49, 336; H. Kelsen, *Principles of International Law* (2nd ed. 1966, edited by R. W. Tucker), pp. 566–8; J. G. Starke, Monism and Dualism in the Theory of International Law 14 B.Yb.I.L. 66 (1936).

4 Fitzmaurice, The General Principles of International Law considered from the standpoint of the Rule of Law, (1957 – II) R.C. 1, 68–74. Ferrari-Bravo, 'International Law and Municipal Law . . .', in R. St J. Macdonald and D. M. Johnston (eds), *The Structure and Process of International Law: Essays in Legal Philosophy Doctrine and Theory* (1983), p. 715. Generally, international wrongfulness of a domestic governmental act does not involve invalidity but gives rise to international responsibility. In some special cases, there may be an inter-

national obligation to provide domestic remedy for actions claimed to be in violation of a State's international obligations, for example, European Convention of Human Rights, Arts. 6(1), 13.

5 D. P. O'Connell, *International Law* (2nd ed. 1970) Vol. 1., pp. 50–51.

6 Yb.I.L.C. (1977–II, ii), pp. 11–30.

7 Far from it, decisions of Courts can engage the international responsibility of the State, 3rd Report on State Responsibility by Professor Ago (1971–II, i) Yb.I.L.C., pp. 246–8; *Phillippson* v. *Imperial Airways* (1939) A.C. 332; for further comment, see W. Bishop, *International Law, Cases and Materials* (3rd ed. 1970), pp. 142–3.

8 O'Connell, above n. 5, pp. 794–7.

9 But for non-justiciability of foreign acts of state, see *Buttes Gas* v. *Hammer* [1981] 3 All E.R. 616, Lord Wilberforce, at 632–3; Collier (1982) C.L.J. 18.

10 For example, Convention on the Contract for the International Carriage of Goods by Road 1956, (1964) Cmnd. 2260; Carriage of Goods by Road Act 1965.

11 For example, Hague Convention for the Suppression of Unlawful Seizure of Aircraft 1970, U.K.T.S. 39 (1972) Cmnd. 4956; Hijacking Act 1971 (now Aviation Security Act 1982, part I).

12 I. Brownlie, *Systems of the Law of Nations: State Responsibility*, Part i (1983), chs. III, XIII.

13 But see Mann, The Consequences of an International Wrong in International and Municipal law (1976–77) 47 B.Yb.I.L. 1, 14–39; also Article 6, part II, International Law Commission Draft Articles on State Responsibility, Yb.I.L.C. (1982–I) p. 199.

14 This article rather concentrates upon the judicial application of international law. It is important to remember that the political organs themselves will have various devices for examining relationship between their policies and the State's international obligations. These range from such well-established institutions as the Legal Adviser's Departments in Ministries of Foreign Affairs to relatively new approaches such as the scrutiny of proposed legislation by Parliament against international legal standards. It is to be expected that these processes will have some impact, each on the other. For instance, the receptiveness of the Courts to an 'international' approach to the interpretation of statutes implementing treaties might condition the manner in which such legislation is drafted.

15 For example, see *Bradley* v. *Commonwealth of Australia* (1973) 47 A.L.J.R. 504.

16 This article is not concerned with the question whether there are internal limitations upon what internationsl obligations a State can undertake, eg. the proposed 'Bricker Amendment' in the United States, see Bishop, above n.7, pp. 110–112 and, for an example of the problem resulting from the limits of federalism, Byrnes and Charlesworth, Federalism and the International Legal Order: Recent Developments in Australia, 79 A.J.I.L. 622 (1985). It is not an issue which is likely to arise in the United Kingdom: *Blackburn* v. *Attorney-General* [1971] 2 All E.R. 1380.

17 F. A. Mann, *Foreign Affairs in English Courts* (1986), ch. 1.

18 In addition to human rights, there is, for example, the harmonisation

of commercial and family law, and aspects of economic and environmental law.

19 *Baker* v. *Carr* 369 U.S. 186. 217 (1962).

20 Falk, *The Role of Domestic Courts in the International Legal Order* (1964), chs. 1 and 3; Fisher, *Improving Compliance with International Law* (1981), ch. IX; Jenks, *The Prospects for International Adjudication* (1964), ch. 13.

21 *Filartiga* v. *Pena-Irala* 630 F.2d 876 (1980). The decision was widely welcomed but, for a note of caution, see Hassan, A Conflict of Philosophies: the *Filartiga* Jurisprudence (1983) 32 I.C.L.Q. 250.

22 See A. Cassese, *Parliamentary Control over Foreign Policy* (1980). In the United Kingdom, the most important development has been the establishment of the Select Committee of the House of Commons on Foreign Affairs.

23 *R.* v. *Secretary of State for Transport, ex p. Iberia Lineas Aereas de Espana*, unreported, see Current Legal Developments, 35 I.C.L.Q. 425, 426-7 (1986).

24 It is not proposed to examine this category in this article, see F. A. Mann, above n. 17, chs. 9 and 10.

25 The fact that it was faced with a complex question of customary law rather than with a treaty provision was one reason the Supreme Court would not investigate the international legality of the Cuban nationalisation decrees in *Banco Nacional De Cuba* v. *Sabbatino* 376 U.S. 398, 428. It might be thought that it should be the complexity of the rule rather than its formal source which, if anything, should be relevant but this is apparently not the case: see *Ethiopian Spice Extraction Share Co.* v. *Kalamazoo Spice Extraction Co.* 543 F.Supp.1224. For the State Department suggestion, see (1983) 77 A.J.I.L. 141. For the settlement of the claims, (1986) 80 A.J.I.L. 344. For a recent United Kingdom example see *Maclaine Watson & Co. Ltd.* v. *Department of Trade and Industry etc.* [1988] 3 All E.R. 257, 301-307 (the *ITC cases*).

26 The clearest example is *Corocraft* v. *Pan American Airways* [1969] 1 Q.B. 616. Given the interpretation of the statutory language by the Court of Appeal, see [1984] 1 All E.R. 1, the decision of the House of Lords in *Alcom* v. *Republic of Columbia* [1984] 2 All E.R. 6, is arguably another; see Ghandi (1984) M.L.R. 597.

27 Duffy, English Law and the European Convention of Human Rights (1980) 29 I.C.L.Q. 585. I am much indebted to this article.

28 Scelle, 'Le Phénomenè juridique de dédoublement fonctionnel', in *Rechtsfragen der Internationalen Organisation: Festschrift für Hans Weberg*, p. 324; also McDougal, 'The Impact of International Law upon National Law: a Policy-oriented Perspective', in McDougal and Reisman, *International Law Essays, a Supplement to International Law in Comparative Perspective* (1981), pp. 445-8.

29 See *Alcom*, above n. 26.

30 *Philippson*, above n. 7.

31 Note the allegations that the Government was interested in the outcome of the *British Airways* v. *Laker* case because of the possible consequences of the American case for the privatisation of British Airways: see *The Times*, 13 September 1984, p. 1.

32 [1976] 1 All E.R. 78, 91.

33 *Rio Tinto Zinc* v. *Westinghouse Electric Corporation* [1978] 1 All E.R.
    434, 475; '... I can hardly conceive that if any British court, or your
    Lordships' House sitting in its judicial capacity, was informed by Her
    Majesty's Government that they considered the sovereignty of the
    United Kingdom would be prejudiced by execution of a letter of
    request in a particular case *it would not be its duty* to act on the
    government's view and to refuse to give effect to the letter.'
    [Emphasis added].

34 H. Lauterpacht, Decisions of Municipal Courts as a Source of Inter-
    national Law (1929) 10 B.Yb.I.L. 65.

35 After the Court of Appeal decisions in *Alcom*, above n. 26, the Govern-
    ment was represented by an *amicus curiae* in the hearing before the
    House of Lords. In *Intepro Properties* v. *Sauvel and the Republic of
    France* [1983] 2 All E.R. 495, neither the French Government (the
    effective defendant) nor the British Government were represented on
    what was quite a difficult point of diplomatic and state immunity.
    Hunter, Proving Foreign and International Law in the Courts of
    England and Wales, (1977-78) 18 Va.J.I.L. 665, 691 notes that there is
    no obligation to indicate on the pleadings that a point of international
    law will be raised.

36 I. Brownlie, *Principles of Public International Law* (3rd ed., 1979),
    while expressing doubts about the value of the terminology (pp. 44,
    59), uses 'incorporation' and 'transformation' to describe the compet-
    ing explanations for the recourse to customary international law by
    the English Courts, pp. 45-9; D. W. Greig, *International Law* (2nd ed.,
    1976) takes 'adoption' and 'incorporation', pp. 55-7; O'Connell,
    above n. 5, uses 'adoption' and 'transformation'.

37 Commentaries on the Laws of England (1857) Vol. IV, C.V. p. 66.

38 [1977] 1 All E.R. 881.

39 See the doubts of Stephenson L.J., [1977] 1 All E.R. 881, 904 suggest-
    ing that the Court of Appeal was bound by its decision in *Thai-Europe
    Tapioca Service* v. *Government of Pakistan* [1975] 3 All E.R. 961 that
    the doctrine of absolute immunity had been incorporated into English
    law. This opinion seems to have convinced Donaldson J. in *Uganda
    (Holdings)* v. *Government of Uganda* [1979] 1 W.L.R. 481. For
    academic endorsement, see F. A. Mann, above n. 17, pp. 120-23.

40 Duffy, above n. 17.

41 *Hispano Americana Mercantil* v. *Central Bank of Nigeria* [1979] 2
    Ll.L.R. 277, 279; 'All I would say about that is that *Trendtex* was not
    decided *per incuriam*'.

42 [1981] 2 All E.R. 1064, 1070 per Lord Wilberforce; *Alcom* v. *Republic
    of Colombia* [1984] 2 All E.R. 6, 8-9 per Lord Diplock.

43 [1977] 1 All E.R. 881, 888.

44 Ibid., 890.

45 Ibid., 910 (emphasis in original). For academic approval, Butler, Inter-
    national Law and Municipal Law: some reflections in British Prac-
    tice, 24 Coexistence 67, 74-76 (1987).

46 Morris, *Conflict of Laws* (3rd ed. (1984)), ch. 3.

47 See generally, Hunter, above n. 35. For example, *Trendtex*, above n. 38
    although in *I Congreso* [1977] 1 Ll.L.R. 536, 554, Robert Goff J. did
    allow in some written evidence.

48 [1939] A.C. 160, 169.

49 What it amounts to is that previous English decisions on the point of international law will not be binding on subsequent courts but will be evidence of what the state of international law was at the time they were given. The contemporaneity of a judgment rather than its hierarchical authority will be more important.

50 See Duffy, above n. 27 at p. 601. This is supported by *Kaffaria Property* v. *Government of Zambia* 1980 2 S.A. 709.

51 G.A. Res. 217A (iii).

52 A view which commands a wide measure of support, Humphrey, 'The Universal Declaration of Human Rights: its History, Impact and Juridical Character', in Ramcharan, ed., *Human Rights: Thirty years after the Universal Declaration* (1979), pp. 21, 28-37. *Hostages Case* (1980) I.C.J. Rep. 1, 43.

53 One reason why so many of the judgments in this area concern sovereign immunity is that the person claiming the immunity in internal law, a foreign State, was the identical person to the one entitled to immunity in international law.

54 Brownlie, above, n. 36, pp. 47-9. See the remarks of Lord Wilberforce in *I Congreso* [1981] 2 All E.R. 1064, 1069, 1072.

55 For example, State Immunity Act 1978.

56 *Chung Chi Cheung*, above n. 48, subject to the observations in that case that judgments of superior tribunals are *binding* as to the state of customary international law.

57 *The Fargernes* [1927] p. 211, though here it was the application of the international rule rather than the rule itself about which the Executive spoke.

58 *R.* v. *Secretary of State for the Home Department ex p. Thakrar* [1974] 2 All E.R. 261.

59 See Akehurst (1975) 38 M.L.R. 71.

60 Though the inquiry may be very extensive, for example, *In re piracy iure gentium* [1934] A.C. 586; *ITC cases,* above n. 25. In the Federal Republic of Germany, such questions are hived off to the Constitutional Court allowing a more intensive investigation of the question of international law, see Rupp, International Law as part of the Law of the Land: some aspects of the operation of Article 25 of the Basic Law of the Federal Republic of Germany (1976) 11 Tex. I.L.J. 541, 546. The recent English cases involving state immunity have involved elaborate inquiries into the practice of other States but, since that practice consists largely of judicial decisions, they cannot be regarded as typical of the Courts' approach to customary international law.

61 *Anglo-Norwegian Fisheries cases* (1951) I.C.J. Rep. 116.

62 *Nottebohm case* (1955) I.C.J. Rep. 4.

63 *The Lotus case* (1927) P.C.I.J. Rep. Series A, No. 10.

64 *Corfu Channel case* (1949) I.C.JU. Rep. 4.

65 *R.* v. *Keyn* (1876) 2 Ex. D. 63 C.C.R. 65.

66 The deficiency was put right by the Territorial Waters Jurisdiction Act 1878.

67 Marston, *The Marginal Seabed* (1981) p. 136-7 suggests a rather narrow ratio for *Keyn* but not one which undermines this example.

68 Were it not for the fact that the relevant rules are made part of domestic law by the Immigration Rules, the claim of a refugee to be entitled to

non-refoulment as a matter of customary international law seems the most likely example, cf. *R.* v. *Secretary of State for the Home Department ex p. Bugdaycay et al.* [1987] 1 All E.R. 940.

69 *Ireland* v. *United Kingdom* Eur. Ct. H.R.s Series A, vol, 25; *Donnelly* v. *United Kingdom* App. No. 5577/72, 4 D.R. 64.

70 For example, United Kingdom – Iceland Treaty surrendering previously claimed high seas fishing rights of the United Kingdom, U.K.T.S. (1976) No. 73, Cmnd. 6545; United Kingdom – United States Exchange of Notes on Co-operation in the Suppression of Unlawful Narcotic Drugs into the United States, U.K.T.S. (1982) No. 8, Cmnd. 8470 which allows United States officials to stop and search British vessels on the high seas; see Siddle, Anglo-American Co-operation in the Suppression of Drug Smuggling (1982) 31 I.C.L.Q. 726. A State may choose not to press its rights in a particular case. Most importantly, there is no right of an individual in international or domestic law to diplomatic protection: *China Navigation Co.* v. *Attorney General* [1932] 2 K.B. 197; *R.* v. *Secretary of State for Foreign and Commonwealth Affairs, ex p. Pirbhai,* unreported, see Current Legal Developments (1988) 37 I.C.L.Q. 1008–1010.

71 Brownlie, above n. 36, p. 59 refers to the 'pointlessness' of transformation except in the purely formal sense of deciding whether formalities of domestic law necessary to allow a municipal court to take cognisance of the international rule have been complied with. There are, however, as has been indicated, substantive issues which arise. The act of transformation may change the nature, but not the content, of the rule, as statutory transformation of treaty law does in English law. It should be noted that the tradition of statutory transformation in English law is to make the minimum provision necessary to give effect to the international obligation, e.g. United Nations Act 1946; compare the Australian Charter of the United Nations Act 1945 (Cth) referred to in *Bradley* v. *Commonwealth of Australia* (1973) 47 A.L.J.R., 504.

72 *Attorney-General for Canada* v. *Attorney-General of Ontario* [1937] A.C. 326.

73 *Blackburn* v. *Attorney General* [1971] 1 W.L.R. 1037.

74 *The Parlement Belge* (1878–79) 4 P.D. 129; Wade, *Administrative Law* (5th ed. 1982) p. 215 casts doubts upon this proposition because treaties have no effect in domestic law. Treaties are not without consequence for internal litigation, see *ITC cases,* n. 25, per Kerr L.J. at 291–3. Compare also the argument of Elkind and Shaw, below n. 93.

75 Although *Council of Civil Service Unions* v. *Minister for the Civil Service* [1985] A.C. 374 has changed fundamentally the courts' view of their powers with respect to the Prerogative, the position does not seem to have changed in relation to treaty-making, see Lord Roskill at p. 418 (the *G.C.H.Q. case*).

76 Vienna Convention on the Law of Treaties 1969, (1980) U.K.T.S. No. 58 Cmnd. 9764, Art. 53.

77 Sinclair, *The Vienna Convention on the Law of Treaties* (2nd ed. 1984), pp. 215–18.

78 *The Parlement Belge* (1880) S.P.D. 197.

79 *Malone* v. *Metropolitan Police Commissioner* [1980] Q.B. 49. *I.R.C.* v.

Collco Dealings [1962] A.C. 1, 22 per Lord Reid, 'Although the infringement of a treaty may cause loss to individuals, the only person properly entitled to complain of such infringement is the other party to the treaty.'

80 *Post Office* v. *Estuary Radio* [1968] 2 Q.B. 740.

81 [1976] 1 All E.R. 920.

82 Ibid. at 924.

83 [1981] A.C. 251. Note the observations of Lord Fraser at p. 289 on the propriety of relying on Arts. 31-3 of the Vienna Convention on the Law of Treaties to interpret a treaty text, the Vienna Convention not having any implementing legislation. The possibility of relying on a customary law basis for the content of Arts. 31-3 is perhaps an indication of the more formal approach taken by Scots to reliance on treaties by domestic courts, above, n. 2. For other cases advancing the 'international' approach to treaty language, see *Stag Line* v. *Foscolo Mango* [1932] A.C. 328; *Buchanan (James) & Co. Ltd.* v. *Babco Forwarding and Shipping (U.K.) Ltd.* [1977] 3 All E.R. 1048. For a general review, see Higgins, 'The United Kingdom', in F. G. Jacobs and S. Roberts (eds.), *The Effect of Treaties in Domestic Law* (1987), pp. 123-40.

84 Urged most strongly by Lord Diplock in *Fothergill*, above n. 92, at 283.

85 Ibid., per Lord Wilberforce at 273-4.

86 Warbrick, The European Convention of Human Rights and English Law (1980) 130 N.L.J. 852. This is not to say that international decisions can be directly implemented, see *Attorney-General* v. *BBC* [1981] A.C. 303, especially Lord Scarman at p. 354; and more generally, Drzemczewski, European Convention in Domestic Law (1983) pp. 314-22.

87 *The Le Louis* (1817) 2 Dods. 210; *R.* v. *Jameson* [1896] Q.B. 425; Maxwell, *The Interpretation of Statutes* (12th ed. 1969), pp. 183-6.

88 That the presumption is so restricted, see Evans, above n. 2, Cross, *Statutory Interpretation* (1976), pp. 142-4 makes the distinction between presumptions of general application (in which category *The Eschersheim* belongs) and presumptions for use only in doubtful cases (which would include Case 3).

89 Craies, *On Statute Law* (7th ed. 1971), pp. 469-70; *Air India* v. *Wiggins* [1980] 2 All E.R. 593. Here, the rule may be stated too emphatically because international law does allow extra-territorial criminal legislation in some circumstances. For example of English law being so interpreted, see *R.* v. *Kelly* [1982] A.C. 665.

90 *Kaur*, above n. 2, suggests that the English cases are wrong, a view endorsed by some judges who have heard cases where a Convention point has been argued, e.g. Roskill, L.J. in *R.* v. *Chief Immigration Office ex parte Bibi* [1976] 3 All E.R. 843, 848-9. After the flurry of individual judgments in the 1970s, the general approach to the Convention has become increasingly cautious, e.g. *R.* v. *Home Secretary ex p. Chundawara* [1987] Imm. A.R. 277.

91 For example, *R.* v. *Governor of Pentonville Prison ex p. Azam* [1974] A.C. 18.

92 This is a matter of English administrative law, the details of which it is not possible to explore here. See *Fernandes* v. *Secretary of State for the Home Department* [1981] Imm.A.R.1; *Ibid.* v. *Kirkwood* [1983] 2 All

E.R. 390 *Ibid, ex p. Brind* (1989) N.L.J. 1751. Mann, above n. 13 at p. 17: '... there does not appear to be any evidence at all in support of the suggestion that a British legislative, executive or judicial act, valid under British law, could ever be null and void on the ground of being contrary to customary international law.' This was written contemporaneously with *Trendtex* and the accompany footnote (95) reveals a reservation that that decision might affect the general proposition. See also *Guilfoyle* v. *Home Office* [1981] Q.B. 309 and the comment of Crawford 52 B. Yb.I.L. 308, 309, (1981). For a survey of recent decisions, see Current Developments 38 I.C.L.Q. 965–977 (1989). Note that the Government preserved its position in international law by making an Article 15 declaration after the European Court had found a provision of the Prevention of Terrorism (Temporary Provisions) Act 1984 incompatible with the Convention in *Brogan et al.* v. *United Kingdom* E. Ct. H.R. Series A, vol. 145B.

93 See Elkind and Shaw, The Municipal Enforcement of the Prohibition against Racial Discrimination (1984) 55 B. Yb.I.L. 169, discussing *Ashby* v. *Minister of Immigration* [1981] 1 N.Z.L.R. 222. The authors make a strong argument for the limiting effect of treaties on ministerial powers, arguing that there is no constitutionally prohibited interference with private rights in such cases, pp. 233–44.

94 This would be an application of the 'unreasonableness' principle. See *Associated Provincial Picture Houses* v. *Wednesbury Corporation* [1948] 1 K.B. 223; *Secretary of State for Education* v. *Tameside M.B.C.* [1977] A.C. 1014. Wade, *Administrative Law* (5th ed. 1982) pp. 347–88; Craig, *Administrative Law* (1983) pp. 353–71. See Jowell and Lester, Beyond *Wednesbury:* Substantive Principles of Administrative Law (1987) P.L. 368, 371–381. It cannot be said that ignoring the State's international obligations will always be unreasonable, though the Attorney-General's concession seems close to admitting that to act in a manner 'manifestly' (whatever that means) contrary to international law is a kind of manifestly unreasonable conduct. Note Lord Diplock in *British Airways Board* v. *Laker Airways Ltd.* [1984] 3 All E.R. 39, 54; 'Where a decision is one which concerns the relations between the United Kingdom and a foreign state, a very strong case needs to be made out to justify a court of law in holding a decision to be *ultra vires* under the *Wednesbury* principle'.

95 Lexis, CO/342/88, 29 July 1988 per Henry J.

96 Diplomatic and Consular Premises Act 1989, Ss. 1(4), 2(2).

97 *Times Law Report*, 30 May 1989, but see now the Court of Appeal in *Brind*, above n. 92.

98 *Soering* L Eur. Ct. H. Rs. Series A, vol. 161.

99 Cane, The Function of Standing Rules in Administrative Law (1980) P.L. 303, 326–8. Also Fisher, above n. 13 on the need to expand standing qualifications for the better domestic enforcement of rules of international law.

100 Cane, above n. 99, suggests that most of the difficulties presently dealt with by standing rules would be better met by considerations of the justiciability of the issues. One of his criteria pointing in the direction of non-justiciability is the possibility of alternative remedies: see *Iberia Lineas Aereas de Espana* above n. 23. Although an alternative remedy at the diplomatic level will often be available theoretically where a question of international law arises, the possibility will more

often be practically remote and, for the individual, something not within his initiative to pursue.

101 *The Arantzazu Mendi* [1939] per Lord Atkin at p. 264. The Executive does not appear to be bound to follow the Court if it has spoken first or has interpreted the Executive's position in a way unacceptable to the Government. The Courts sometimes have difficulty in understanding what the Government's position is, e.g. *Gur Corporation* v. *Trust Bank of Africa Ltd* [1986] 3 W.L.R. 583, per Nourse L.J. at p. 604. Wilmshurst, Executive Certificates in Foreign Affairs: The United Kingdom (1986) 35 I.C.L.Q. 157 and Warbrick, Executive Certificates in Foreign Affairs: Prospects for Review and Control, ibid., 138.

102 Note now the interesting case of *Bulk Oil (Zug)* v. *Sun International Ltd.* [1984] 1 All E.R. 386 where the Government's policy not to allow the export of oil to Israel was being challenged as being contrary to European Community Law; for the outcome, *Bulk Oil (Zug)* v. *Sun International (No. 2)* [1986] 2 All E.R. 744.

103 Above n. 70.

104 There is a substantial obstacle for an individual challenging the exercise of military force on the ground that it is contrary to international law. His participation in the enterprise, even if it amounts to aggression, is not unlawful in international law, see *Hostages case (U.S.* v. *List)* 8 War. C.Tr.34.

105 See Corby, Limitations on Freedom of Association of Civil Servants and the ILO's Response (1985) 15 I.L.J. 161.

106 Even here, the bar would seem not to be absolute, *G.C.H.Q. case* above n. 82; *R.* v. *Secretary of State for the Home Department ex p. Ruddock* [1987] 2 All E.R. 518.

107 Above, n. 93.

108 *R.* v. *Governor of Brixton Prison, ex parte Soblen* [1963] 2 Q.B. 243.

109 Ibid., p. 302. So long as the courts are reluctant to order discovery of documents bearing on foreign affairs decisions, litigants will face well-nigh impossible burdens of proving their claims in such cases; see also *Air Canada* v. *Secretary of State for Trade (No. 2)* [1983] 1 All E.R. 910. The matter will hardly be improved by the proposed Official Secrets Act 1989.

8.

Democracy, Human Rights and Conflict in Northern Ireland.

ALPHA CONNELLY

The Court, being aware of the danger such a law poses of undermining or even destroying democracy on the ground of defending it, affirms that ... States may not, in the name of the struggle against ... terrorism, adopt whatever measures they deem appropriate.

The Court must be satisfied that ... there exist adequate and effective guarantees against abuse. (European Court of Human Rights)[1]

Democracy and human rights

Democracy and human rights go hand in hand. All international catalogues of human rights afford some recognition to this fact. Recognition may be implicit, as in the choice of rights to be protected, or explicit, as when the limits of individual freedom of action are drawn by reference to the requirements of a democratic society. For example, the International Covenant on Civil and Political Rights includes in its list of individual protected rights those commonly associated with the democractic process: the right to vote, the right to take part in the conduct of public affairs, the right of peaceful assembly, the right to freedom of association, and the right to freedom of expression.[2] The exercise of the right of peaceful assembly and of the right to freedom of association may be curtailed to the extent that is 'necessary in a democratic society' in order to protect a number of specified public interests such as the maintenance of public order or morality. No explicit reference to the standard of a democratic society is made in the provision for restriction on freedom of expression; but entitlement to a fair and public hearing is subject to the exception that the press and the public may be excluded from all or part of a trial for reasons, *inter alia*, of 'national security in a democratic soceity'.[3]

Some regional instruments for the protection of human rights draw a more direct link between democracy and respect for human rights. One such regional instrument is the European Convention on Human Rights. In the Preamble to this Convention, the Governments signatory thereto 'reaffirm their profound belief in those Fundamental Freedoms which ... are best maintained on the one hand by an effective political democracy and on the other by a common understanding and observance of the Human Rights upon which they depend.'[4] As in the case of the International Covenant on Civil and Political Rights, the rights protected by the Convention include many of the traditional democratic rights. The right to freedom of expression and the right to freedom of peaceful assembly and to freedom of association are guaranteed in the Convention itself,[5] while, under a supplementary Protocol, States Parties 'undertake to hold free elections at reasonable intervals by secret ballot, under conditions which will ensure the free expression of the opinion of the people in the choice of the legislature'.[6] Again, as in the case of the International Covenant, necessity in a democratic society provides a yardstick by which to measure the legitimacy of curtailment in the public interest of the exercise of a right but, unlike the Covenent, this yardstick is used not solely in relation to the right of peaceful assembly and the right to freedom of association but has been extended, under the Convention and its Protocols, to restrictions on the exercise of a number of other rights such as freedom of expression, freedom of movement and the right to privacy.[7] As with the Covenant, entitlement to a fair and public hearing is subject to the qualification that the press and public may be excluded from all or part of a trial in the interest, *inter alia,* of national security in a democratic society.[8]

Evidence of the link between democracy and respect for human rights is to be found not only in the international texts themselves but also in the application and interpretation of these texts by international bodies, especially those bodies which have been established under treaty to review and to ensure compliance by States with their international human rights obligations. As might be expected from the wording of the texts and their respective geo-political scope, regional bodies have been more assertive than their global counterparts in overtly having recourse to democratic principles and ideas as an aid to the interpretation of protected rights.

In particular, the European Commission and European Court of Human Rights have frequently had recourse to 'the common heritage of political traditions, ideals, freedom and the rule of law'[9] shared by the Contracting Parties in choosing between different interpretations of a State's obligations under the European Human Rights Convention. Moreover, this approach has not been limited to the interpretation of those rights formulated by reference to democracy in the text itself, but has been employed generally in relation to all the rights guaranteed by the Convention and supplementary Protocols. For example, the Court has interpreted the right to a fair trial to include access to a court, and has said in support of this interpretation that 'in civil matters one can scarcely conceive of the rule of law without there being a possibility of having access to the courts'; that were the right to a fair trial 'to be understood as concerning exclusively the conduct of an action which had already been initiated before a court, a ... State could ... do away with its courts, or take away their jurisdiction to determine certain classes of civil actions and entrust it to organs dependent on the Government'. Such a narrow interpretation of the right to a fair trial had therefore to be rejected since it imported 'a danger of arbitrary power'.[10] Also, it has interpreted the term 'law' not merely by reference to the existence of a norm in domestic legal systems, but has required that a norm, to qualify as law, be 'formulated with sufficient precision to enable the citizen to regulate his conduct'[11] and not confer such wide discretion on a public authority as to permit the arbitrary exercise of power by the authority. In relation to the right of personal liberty, it has stated that, 'in a democratic society subscribing to the rule of law ..., no detention that is arbitrary can ever be regarded as "lawful" ';[12] and, in relation to interference with correspondence, that, to the extent that the domestic law did not 'indicate with reasonable clarity the scope and manner of exercise of the relevant discretion conferred on the public authorities', it did not afford 'the minimum degree of legal protection to which citizens are entitled under the rule of law in a democratic society'.[13] Furthermore, there is now substantial case law on how the Commission and the Court assess the necessity in a democratic society of a restriction on individual liberty. While attaching some weight to the view of the national authorities as to the necessity of the impugned measure, they insist on the existence of a 'pressing social need' for the restriction and require proportionality between the effect of the restriction on the individual and the public interest which it serves.[14]

It is no accident that massive violations of human rights frequently occur where power is heavily concentrated in the hands of one person or of a group of persons not subject to democratic control. This does not mean that the existence of democratic institutions will of itself ensure respect for human rights. Even in a democracy, vigilance is required if human rights are not to be infringed. There is always a danger that the rule of the majority may become the tyranny of the majority, or that a democratically-elected Government may abuse the democratic process in order to perpetuate its power. One situation in which vigilance is required is when democratic institutions are under serious attack. Here the threat to human rights may emanate not only from those who would overthrow the system but, more subtly, also from the institutions themselves. In response to the attack, the Government may resort to measures which infringe human rights and thereby ultimately erode its own democratic base.[15]

International instruments allow for the dilution of respect for human rights where there is a serious threat to the stability of the State. In time of public emergency threatening the life of the nation, Governments may take measures which, but for the existence of the emergency, would be violative of their human rights obligations.[16] Typically, such measures are legitimate provided they are not inconsistent with the State's other obligations under international law and go no further than is 'strictly required by the exigencies of the situation'. In deciding whether or not the conditions for derogation by a State from its international human rights obligations have been satisfied, international bodies take into account such considerations as whether safeguards exist for the individual and whether less severe measures would have sufficed in the circumstances.[17]

Northern Ireland

In the late 1960s, a deep sense of grievance stemming from discrimination in areas such as employment, housing and local government led to the emergence of a civil rights movement in Northern Ireland. Civil rights groups took to the streets in marches and demonstrations, and were on occasion met with harsh opposition on the part of the authorities. Those discriminated against were Catholics, and many Catholics, for religious and historical reasons, identified more with the population of the Republic of Ireland than with their Protestant neighbours in Northern Ireland. The environment was ripe for a resurgence of violent Irish nationalism.

The initial response of the British authorities to the violence was to use the army to back up the civil power and then, some three years later, to suspend the regional Government and legislature in Northern Ireland and to assume direct central control from Westminster in London.[18] Special powers of arrest and detention were brought into operation, at first under existing legislation, and later under legislation specifically passed to deal with the situation.[19] As time passed, other restrictive measures were introduced. Foreigners suspected of involvement in terrorism could be excluded from the United Kingdom by executive order.[20] Within the United Kingdom itself, a form of internal exile was implemented. Persons could be barred from Northern Ireland or from Great Britain.[21] Paramilitary organisations were proscribed.[22] And, more recently, the voice of violent dissent has been excluded from the airwaves.[23]

It is intended to examine some of the measures taken by the British authorities in response to the resurgence of violence in Northern Ireland for their compatibility with respect for two areas of individual liberty, namely, personal liberty and freedom of expression. The measures will be evaluated by reference to those democratic principles and values which the United Kingdom has undertaken internationally to uphold.

The United Kingdom is a democratic State, party to many international human rights treaties, including the International Covenant on Civil and Political Rights and the European Human Rights Convention. In that the European Convention draws a strong link between democracy and respect for human rights, and the European Commission and European Court of Human Rights apply democratic principles in interpreting the rights guaranteed by the Convention, it is primarily by reference to the standards enunciated by these organs that the action of the British authorities will be assessed. They are essentially the standards of Western liberal democracy, and not being universally approved, feature much less in catalogues of human rights, such as the International Covenant on Civil and Political Rights, which aspire to universality. However, in so far as the Covenant provides broader guarantees of a democratic kind than its European counterpart, these will also be taken into account.

(i) Personal liberty

The typical response of governmental authority when faced with a serious threat to public peace is resort to special powers of arrest and detention, and such was the response of the British authorities to the resurgence of political violence in Northern Ireland. These powers are commonly associated with military dictatorships and other forms of autocratic government where they serve as instruments of popular oppression. In a democracy, they are special in that they signify a deviation from the norm and are justified by reference to extraordinary circumstances. If they are not to replace the norm and thereby erode the democratic foundation of the State, they must be limited in their stringency and duration by the seriousness of the threat to the democratic order. It is necessary that the implementation of the measures, and the need for them, be kept constantly under review, and that safeguards exist for the individual against their abuse.

The special powers of arrest and detention enjoyed by the authorities in Northern Ireland have been reviewed and revised on a number of occasions over the last twenty years.[24] In general they have been restricted, and safeguards have been progressively introduced, but the powers still deviate significantly from the norm in a democratic society, and several, if they are to comply with the United Kingdom's international obligations, depend for their justification on the existence of an emergency situation in Northern Ireland of sufficient magnitude to require such measures. The legal position is complicated by the fact that, since 1973, the powers have been conferred and regulated by two sets of legislation, one set, the Northern Ireland (Emergency Provisions) Acts, applying only in Northern Ireland, and the other, the Prevention of Terrorism (Temporary Provisions) Acts, applying both to Northern Ireland and to Great Britain.[25]

Originally, the powers were very broad. It was not necessary that a person be suspected of having committed an offence. An individual could be detained on suspicion of 'acting, having acted or being about to act in a manner prejudicial to the preservation of the peace or maintenance of order'.[26] A wider power allowed detention simply 'for the preservation of the peace and maintenance of order',[27] and was at times used to detain persons who were not themselves regarded as posing a threat to public peace or order but from whom it was thought information about the activities of others might be gleaned. Such 'trawling' provisions, with their adverse effect on the liberty of persons who pose no threat to public order and who are not suspected of any offence, are unacceptable in a democracy under normal conditions and are justified, if at all, only by a very serious threat to the democratic institutions of the State. Indeed, when the powers were scrutinised by the European Court of Human Rights, they were found to be incompatible with the right to personal liberty under the European Human Rights Convention, but were held to be justified in view of the existence of a public emergency in Northern Ireland from 1971 to 1975, an emergency brought about by 'a massive wave of violence and intimidation' creating 'a particularly far-reaching and acute danger for the territorial integrity of the United Kingdom, the institutions of the six counties and the lives of the province's inhabitants'.[28]

In 1973–74, some narrowing of the grounds for detention was introduced by reference to the concept of terrorism. Terrorism was defined as 'the use of violence for political ends [including] any use of violence for the purpose of putting the public or any section of the public in fear',[29] and a person could be detained on suspicion 'of having been concerned in the commission or attempted commission of any act of terrorism or the organisation of persons for the purpose of terrorism'.[30] Although the power of arrest in relation to terrorism has not been retained under the most recent Northern Ireland legislation, the Northern Ireland (Emergency Provisions) Act of 1987, it is still available under the Prevention of Terrorism legislation. Under the latter, a constable may arrest without warrant a person who is suspected of being or having been 'concerned in the commission, preparation or instigation of acts of terrorism'.[31]

Terrorism is not itself an offence. It is a description for a range of activities which themselves are branded as criminal. From a human rights perspective, detention on suspicion of involvement in terrorism is an advance on arrest in the interests of the preservation of peace or maintenance of order, but falls short of the specificity usually required in a democratic society for deprivation of liberty in connection with suspected criminal activity.

The European Human Rights Convention requires suspicion of an offence,[32] and although the European Court has taken the view that the commission or attempted commission of an act of terrorism or the organisation of persons for the purpose of terrorism are 'well in keeping with the idea of an offence',[33] in the author's view it would not be compatible with the Convention standards for a person to be arrested on suspicion of terrorism without being told the facts as well as the legal authority on which the arrest was based.[34] A person is entitled to know for what suspected terrorist activity or involvement he or she is being held. In other words, although arrest in connection with terrorism will not of itself fall foul of the international standards for lack of specificity, it will offend against them if the detainee is not promptly informed of the actual or alleged behaviour which has given rise to the arrest.

One of the marked differences between the Northern Ireland Acts and the Prevention of Terrorism legislation, as regards arrest and detention, concerns the powers conferred by the former on the army in Northern Ireland. The Prevention of Terrorism legislation does not confer any special powers on members of the army but, since 1973, under the Northern Ireland Acts, a member of Her Majesty's forces on duty in Northern Ireland has enjoyed a power of arrest on suspicion of *any* offence.[35] The safeguards are that the detainee may only be held by the army for a short period (up to four hours) and that suspicion of some offence is required. However, the fact that many persons arrested by the army have not been subsequently transferred into police custody, as would be expected if a serious offence was suspected, must give rise to concern.[36]

In cases of detention for suspected criminal activity, the European Human Rights Convention requires that the suspicion be objectively based, i.e. reasonable.[37] This requirement is a typical safeguard in a democratic society against arbitrary detention. The Prevention of Terrorism legislation has always incorporated the safeguard that the suspicion be reasonable or based on reasonable grounds.[38] In contrast, throughout the 1970s and most of the 1980s, Northern Ireland emergency legislation allowed arrest, whether in connection with terrorism or a specific offence, purely on suspicion.[39] Only in 1987 was a requirement that the suspicion be based on reasonable grounds introduced and applied both to arrest by a police officer and the army.[40]

Whatever the reason for detention, it is important that there be some limit to its duration, and that continued detention be subject to review and authorisation by an authority other than the arresting officer. Deprivation of liberty entails serious consequences for the individual. Not only are freedom of movement, social contact and privacy drastically curtailed, employment may be jeopardised and family life disrupted. Respect for the inherent dignity and worth of the human being requires that these consequences be minimised and that detention be continued only where an overriding public interest is served. The international texts all contain safeguards in this respect, and frequently require independent control by the judiciary after a period of detention.[41]

The original special powers in Northern Ireland allowed for indefinite detention. Although no time limit was placed by law on detention, some of the powers were exercised in a way which limited the period of detention in practice.[42] Internment without trial was, however, used from 1971 until

1975 when a change in policy led to its discontinuance. During these years, many persons were detained for long periods without being charged with an offence or brought to court. Such detention clearly conflicts with the international guarantees relating to personal liberty, but was found by the European Court of Human Rights to be justified in Northern Ireland at the time because of the existence of a public emergency threatening the life of the nation.[43] Internment without trial has not been used since 1975, and it is doubtful whether the conditions which might justify the use of such a measure, i.e. a public emergency threatening the life of the nation, have existed at any time in Northern Ireland since then. Violence has continued, but neither its scale nor its frequency suggest an emergency of this kind.

Perhaps surprisingly, it is the Prevention of Terrorism legislation which allows for longer periods of detention without charge than the Northern Ireland Acts. Under the former, a person may be detained initially for forty-eight hours, and, after that, for a further period not exceeding five days provided such an extension is granted by the Secretary of State. Detention for seven days without judicial review of the detention offends against international human rights standards. In particular, it offends against the guarantee that a person being held on suspicion of a criminal offence should either 'be brought promptly before a judge or other officer authorised by law to exercise judicial power' or promptly released.[44] Indeed, the European Court of Human Rights held in November 1988 that a period of detention of four days and six hours without being brought to court violated this guarantee.[45] The response of the British Government to this decision of the Court was to enter a notice of derogation on 22 December 1988, i.e. to rely on the existence of a public emergency in Northern Ireland to justify such powers. However, since the condition precedent for derogation – the existence of a public emergency – seems to be lacking, the purported derogation would appear to be of no effect, and the legislation, on the face of it, in allowing for the detention of a person for a period of seven days without being brought to court, appears to be contrary to the United Kingdom's obligations under the Convention.[46]

Under the Northern Ireland (Emergency Provisions) Acts of 1973 and 1978, persons detained in connection with terrorism could be held for up to seventy-two hours on police authority alone.[47] This power overlapped with special police powers under the Prevention of Terrorism legislation and has not been retained under the 1987 Act. It is the Prevention of Terrorism Act which now applied to such situations, i.e. a person may be detained for up to forty-eight hours on police authority alone and, after that, for a further period not exceeding five days on the authority of the Secretary of State. The Northern Ireland legislation still allows detention by the army for up to four hours (on suspicion of any offence).[48]

Other safeguards have been introduced into the legislation over the years. Recent safeguards in Northern Ireland include the introduction of a right of access to a solicitor and a right to have someone, such as a relative or friend, informed of the detention. A committee established by the British Government in 1978 to inquire into police interrogation procedures in Northern Ireland discovered that in practice persons detained under emergency legislation were not allowed to consult with a solicitor before they were charged.[49] The committee recommended that such detainees should have an absolute right of access to a solicitor after detention for forty-eight hours,[50] and this recommendation was implemented by legislation some eight years later, in 1987.[51] The same legislation provides that a detainee 'shall be entitled, if he so requests, to have one friend or relative or other person who is known to him or is likely to take an interest in his welfare told that he is being detained [under emergency legislation] and where he is being held in police custody'.[52] As with access to a solicitor, compliance with the request may be delayed in certain circumstances, but the right is absolute after detention for forty-eight hours. These rights were conferred on detainees in England and Wales under ordinary criminal legislation some three years earlier;[53] and given that the European Commission of Human Rights had found in 1981 that the refusal to allow two men detained under emergency legislation to contact their wives and let them know of their arrest was in breach of the men's right to respect for family life,[54] the delay in introducing these safeguards is regrettable.

(ii) Freedom of expression

Freedom of expression has been described by the European Court of Human Rights as 'one of the essential foundations of a democratic society, indeed one of the basic conditions for its progress and for the self-fulfilment of the individual'.[55]

There is no prior censorship by law of the written word in the United Kingdom. Organisations and persons who support the use of violence for political ends may have their views printed in books, journals and newspapers and distributed, subject to the constraints of the ordinary criminal law. One such constraint is that a person who solicits or invites support, including financial support, for a proscribed organisation is guilty of an offence.[56] Likewise, a person who seeks contributions, financial or otherwise, in connection with acts of terrorism is guilty of an offence.[57] In so far as these offences constitute restrictions on freedom of expression, they are probably compatible with international human rights standards and with 'the essential foundations of a democratic society'. Not only can they be justified on a ground of public interest such as the protection of public safety or national security or the prevention of crime, but they are not overly restrictive in that what is penalised is support for paramilitary organisations and contributions to acts of terrorism. The political views of these organisations, their members and supporters are not as such denied expression. The target of the law is assistance to the violent expression of these views.

Of dubious compatibility with the international human rights standards, however, is the recent introduction of restrictions on the spoken word in the broadcasting media.[58] Not only is the voice of political violence to be denied direct transmission, but so also is the voice of organisations associated with political violence in Northern Ireland, whether or not the words spoken are supportive of the use of violence. In October 1988, the British Home Secretary, in the exercise of his legal powers, directed both the British Broadcasting Corporation and the Independent Broadcasting Authority

> to refrain from broadcasting any matter which consists of or includes any words spoken ... by a person who appears or is heard on the programme in which the matter is broadcast where (a) the person speaking the words represents or purports to represent a specified organisation, or (b) the words support or solicit or invite support for such an organisation.

The specified organisations include not only organisations such as the Irish Republican Army which are proscribed by law, but also Sinn Fein, Republican Sinn Fein and the Ulster Defence Association, all lawful organisations.

Doubt as to the compatibility with international human rights standards of these instructions lies not so much in the public interest served by them, as in their scope. They are currently being challenged by the National Union of Journalists, and if no domestic remedy is forthcoming, the challenge will almost certainly be carried to Europe in the form of a complaint to the European Commission of Human Rights. Here the crucial issue is likely to be the necessity for such censorship in a democratic society. While some aspects of the directives, such as the ban on words which are supportive of a proscribed organisation may, as noted above in relation to the written word, be justified as necessary in the interests of national security, public safety or the prevention of crime, their application to all words spoken by a representative of one of the specified lawful organisations appears to be overly broad and to offend against the criterion of proportionaly applied by the European Commission and European Court of Human Rights.[59] This is particularly so with respect to Sinn Fein, an organisation which fields candidates in local and Parliamentary elections and whose candidates have on occasion been duly elected as representatives for their constituencies. The directives make some concession to this fact in that they exempt from the ban words spoken in the course of proceedings in Parliament, or by or in support of a candidate at a Parliamentary, European Parliamentary or local election pending that election, but this concession, welcome as it is, probably doesn't go far enough. Sinn Fein representatives speak out on a range of social issues such as poverty, housing and unemployment, and not only at election time. Their political activity is not limited to support for the armalite. It must be doubted whether there is in the United Kingdom a 'pressing social need' to exclude everything said by Sinn Fein representatives from being broadcast on radio or television except during an election. Such exclusion, by reason of its breadth, appears to be excessive.

In this connection, it may be relevant that it is the words actually spoken which are censored. A report of the words spoken is not. Hence the views of a Sinn Fein representative on, for example, unemployment, may be reported but not directly broadcast. In this way, it may be argued, democratic values are preserved. This, in practice, however, leads to the somewhat ridiculous situation whereby an interview with a representative of Sinn Fein may be televised in which the words actually spoken by the Sinn Fein member may not be broadcast but a voice-over paraphrasing the actual words spoken is permissible. Do the words spoken present a greater threat to public safety than a report of the words? Indeed, what is the danger to public safety of broadcasting the actual words spoken? Is there not rather a danger to democracy presented by the banning of the direct expression of views on important social issues merely by reason of the source of those views?

Another recent measure also strikes at the heart of the democratic process and raises some of the same issues as the broadcasting ban. This measure does not cut off publicity for the spoken word, but rather requires that a statement be made. The requirement is that a candidate at a local election in Northern Ireland or at an election to the Northern Ireland Assembly (presently suspended) make a declaration that, if elected, that person will not by word or deed express support for or approval of a proscribed organisation or acts of terrorism connected with Northern Ireland.[60] Breach of such a declaration is not a criminal offence. The remedy lies with electors and members of the relevant elected authority, any one or more of whom may apply to the High Court for a determination that a person has acted in breach of the terms of a declaration. Should the High Court so determine, the person will be disqualified for membership of the relevant body for a period of five years.

These legislative provisions are aimed principally at Sinn Fein candidates. They have been criticised as counterproductive in that they provide 'the elected extremist with the opportunity at a time of his own choosing, probably when party fortunes are at a low ebb, to boost electoral support by claiming that the declaration is a symbol of oppression which must be cast aside'.[61] From an international human rights perspective, the requirement that such a declaration be made impinges upon freedom of expression in that it seeks to fetter the expression of support for political violence. It may be said to serve a number of legitimate public interests such as the protection of public safety or national security or the prevention of crime, but its necessity in a democratic society for the attainment of these goals is questionable. Similarly, disqualification as a result of the breach of a declaration by verbal support for a proscribed organisation or acts of terrorism may be said to constitute an interference with freedom of expression which requires to be justified by sufficient public interest. Whether a particular interference can be regarded as necessary in a democratic society or not will depend, in a contested case, on such matters as the actual words spoken, the context in which they were spoken, and the political situation in Northern Ireland at the time.

The requirement that a declaration be made, and disqualification for breach of a declaration, also raise issues pertaining to the electoral process and to participation in public life. While the European Convention on Human Rights is surprisingly weak on the electoral guarantees it affords,[62] the International Covenant on Civil and Political Rights specifically acknowledges the right of every citizen to take part in public affairs and the right to stand for election under conditions which will guarantee the free expression of the will of the electors, without distinction of any kind including political opinion and without unreasonable restrictions.[63] The requirement that a declaration be made may be challenged as a fetter on the free expression of the will of the electorate, as importing a distinction based on political opinion, and as an unreasonable restriction on the freedom to stand for election and to take part in the conduct of public affairs. Disqualification may likewise be challenged as politically discriminatory and as an unreasonable restriction on the right to take part in the conduct of public affairs.

The United Kingdom is not party to the Optional Protocol to the International Covenant on Civil and Political Rights whereby an individual may complain to the Human Rights Committee of an alleged violation of the Covenant. Since this avenue of individual redress is closed, it is to be hoped that, in their consideration of the next report of the United Kingdom on the implementation of its obligations under the Covenant,[64] members of the Committee will closely scrutinise both the requirement that election candidates make a 'declaration against terrorism',[65] and the broadcasting ban, for compatibility with the Covenant.

Such measures entail a direct tinkering by the Government with the democratic process, and there is a real danger not only that the process will be undermined, but also that, in seeking to protect the public from acts of violence, the Government will play into the hands of anti-democratic forces. A significant minority of the population of Northern Ireland have little faith in the democratic process. They have seen and suffered discrimination over the years, and are impatient with the slow pace of reform. They perceive the democratic process as controlled by an oppressive majority and as having little to offer them. To silence or reduce what voice they have in that process may be expected to encourage non-participation and increase sympathy for violence as the only means of achieving real improvement in their condition.

Conclusion

Several factors contribute to a social order in which human rights are respected. Democracy is one of them. Where democracy is threatened, so is respect for human rights. One peculiar threat arises when the institutions of a democratic State react to attack by adopting measures which may themselves undermine the democratic foundation of the State. It has been argued that, whether or not there exists 'a public emergency threatening the life of the nation', the legitimacy of the measures taken in response to such attack should be judged by reference to the democratic underpinning of the State.[66]

Since this chapter has been concerned with the limits in a democracy of legitimate State responses to destabilising violence, particular attention has been paid to measures which are arguably incompatible with democratic values. Special measures to deal with political violence are acceptable in a democracy. A Government is entitled, indeed is expected, to protect the lives and property of citizens, to maintain public order and to defend the democratic institutions of the State. Special times may require special measures. The point is that, in a democracy, not every measure in pursuit of these goals is acceptable. Only such measures as are necessary to achieve them and are consistent with basic democratic values are to be regarded as legitimate.

For the last twenty years there has existed in Northern Ireland a serious threat to the established order. In response, the British authorities have resorted to a series of extraordinary measures in order to protect public safety and national security. The question arises whether some of these measures, in curtailing civil and political liberty, may in fact endanger the very democracy they seek to preserve.

The United Kingdom is a democratic State, party to a number of international human rights treaties in which the link between democracy and respect for human rights is recognised. The form of democracy espoused by the United Kingdom is traditional, Western liberal democracy, and it is therefore primarily by reference to the liberal democratic values of the European Human Rights Convention that the action of the British authorities in Northern Ireland has been assessed. Where the International Covenant on Civil and Political Rights affords more extensive protection than the European Convention, reference has also been made to the standards set forth in this text. Since the United Kingdom is party to these international treaties, the action of the authorities in Northern Ireland has been examined by applying to it not some hypothetical ideal or the author's own preferences, but criteria which the United Kingdom itself accepts.

Two areas of individual liberty were chosen for examination, personal liberty and freedom of expression. Only a general survey was attempted, since a thorough study of either area is beyond the scope of this chapter. The survey reveals that, in both areas, the compatibility of some of the measures taken by the State with its democratic foundation is open to doubt. In that additional safeguards have progressively been introduced in relation to arrest and detention, these are to be welcomed, but there is still cause for concern, e.g. as regards the length of time a person may be detained without being charged or brought to court and the fact that a person may be detained without being informed at the time of the arrest or shortly thereafter of the behaviour (or alleged behaviour) which has led to the arrest. Whereas the position with respect to personal liberty has improved somewhat, in contrast, freedom of expression has been reduced by measures which strike directly at the democratic process. The broadcasting restrictions, particularly the banning from the airwaves of words spoken by a representative of Sinn Fein irrespective of content, and the requirement that candidates at local and Northern Ireland Assembly elections make a declaration against terrorism, seem to overshoot the mark and not to be necessary in order to achieve the intended purpose. These measures run a real risk not only of being counterproductive in terms of protecting public safety but also, more fundamentally, of further eroding confidence in the democratic process as a means of achieving political change.

The yardstick suggested in this paper for testing the legitimacy in a democracy of State response to political violence is applicable to measures restrictive of individual liberty in general, not merely to measures curtailing personal liberty and freedom of expression. For example, in relation to Northern Ireland, the impact of exclusion orders on freedom of movement and the intrusion upon privacy occasioned by house searches should similarly be scrutinised for compatibility with democratic standards.

As regards the United Kingdom, it has been observed that the democratic values underpinning the State are most clearly articulated in the case law of the European Commission and European Court of Human Rights. In that the United Kingdom is party to the European Human Rights Convention and subscribes to the international review procedures established under the Convention, there is a degree of international scrutiny. It is submitted that the same criteria should be used by national review bodies and watchdogs. While some reference has been made by national bodies to the international standards, especially to the provisions of the European Human Rights Convention,[67] a more direct and explicit reference to democratic principles is recommended. The employment of these criteria by national bodies will not only enhance safeguards at the national level but will afford additional protection where the avenue of international scrutiny is not available. For example, there can be only limited international scrutiny of the need for exclusion orders, since the United Kingdom is not party to the Fourth Protocol to the European Convention on Human Rights under which the right to liberty of movement is guaranteed.[68]

This chapter has been concerned solely with State response to political violence and the danger such response at times presents to respect for human rights and democracy in the name of defending these very values. Moreover, it has been concerned only with the effect of certain measures on two areas of civil and political liberty. No attempt has been made to deal with the human rights grievances which fuelled the resurgence of violence in Northern Ireland in the late 1960s. Although the legitimacy of these grievances has been recognised, and although much has been done to tackle them, much remains to be done. Housing ghettos, discrimination in employment, and separate education all contribute to a social environment in which human potential is frustrated and human dignity diminished. It is only by determined State action in these and other fields to heal wounds and to reduce divisions that 'the inherent dignity and the equal and inalienable rights of all members'[69] of the population of Northern Ireland may be realised. It is a formidable task. Meanwhile, vigilance is required to ensure that the State does not itself add to the problem by 'undermining ... democracy on the ground of defending it'.[70]

Notes

1 *Klass and others,* Judgment of 6 September 1978, Series A, No. 28, paras. 49–50, 2 E.H.R.R. 214 at 232. See also *Malone,* Judgment of 2 August 1984, Series A, No. 82, 7 E.H.R.R. 14 at 45; and *Leander,* Judgment of 26 March 1987, Series A, No. 116, para. 60, 9 E.H.R.R. 433 at 453.

2 Arts. 19, 21, 22 & 25.

3 Art. 14 (1). Moreover, Art. 1 of the Covenant guarantees to all peoples the right of self-determination. Self-determination is a democratic concept. It signifies the right of a people to control its own affairs and to reject control or rule by others. On the essence of the concept see, e.g., D. Ronen, *The Quest for Self-Determination,* Yale University Press, 1979, ch. 3.

4 See also the Preamble to the American Convention on Human Rights wherein the signatory States reaffirm their intention to consolidate a system of personal liberty and social justice based on respect for the essential rights of man 'within the framework of democratic institutions'.

5 Arts. 10 & 11.

6 First Protocol, Art. 3.

7 Art. 8, 10, 11 and fourth Protocol, Art. 2.

8 Arts. 6 (1).

9 See the Preamble to the Convention.

10 *Golder,* Judgment of 21 February 1975, Series A, No. 18, paras. 34–5, 1 E.H.R.R. 524 at 535–6.

11 *Sunday Times,* Judgment of 26 April 1979, Series A, No. 30, para. 49, 2 E.H.R.R. 245 at 271. See also, e.g. *Silver and others,* Judgment of 25 March 1983, Series A, No. 61, para. 88, 5 E.H.R.R. 347 at 372; and *Muller and others,* Judgment of 24 May 1988, Series A, No. 133, para. 29.

12 *Winterwerp,* Judgment of 24 October 1979, Series A, No. 33, para. 39, 2 E.H.R.R. 387 at 403.

13 *Malone,* Judgment of 2 August 1984, Series A, No. 82, para. 79, 7 E.H.R.R. 14 at 45.

14 For a recent summary of the principles applied by the court, see *Gillow,* Judgment of 24 November 1986, Series A, No. 109, para. 55.

15 Cf. the view of C. Walker that '... the rule of law has more often been injured by overweening governments than by terrorist bombs', *The Prevention of Terrorism in British Law,* Manchester University Press, 1986, p. 216.

16 See, e.g., Art. 4 of the International Covenant on Civil and Political Rights, and Art. 15 of the European Convention on Human Rights. It should be noted that Parties may not, even in time of war or other public emergency, derogate from their obligations to ensure certain rights, e.g. the right to freedom from torture.

17 See, e.g., *Lawless,* Judgment of the European Court of Human Rights of 1 July 1961, Series A, No. 3, 'The Law', paras. 31–8, 1 E.H.R.R. 15 at 32–4; and *Ireland* v. *The United Kingdom,* Judgment of the European Court of Human Rights of 18 January 1978, Series A, No. 25, para. 218, 2 E.H.R.R. 25 at 96.

18 Direct rule was introduced on 30 March 1972.

19 Civil Authorities (Special Powers) Act (Northern Ireland) 1922; Northern Ireland (Emergency Provisions) Acts 1973, 1978 & 1987; and Northern Ireland (Emergency Provisions) (Amendment) Act 1975; Prevention of Terrorism (Temporary Provisions) Acts 1974, 1976, 1984 & 1989.

20 Prevention of Terrorism (Temporary Provisions) Act 1974, s. 6; 1976 Act, s. 6; 1984 Act, s. 6; 1989 Act. s. 7.

21 Prevention of Terrorism (Temporary Provisions) Act 1974, s. 3; 1976 Act, ss. 4 & 5; 1984 Act, ss. 4 & 5; 1989 Act, ss. 5 & 6.

22 Northern Ireland (Emergency Provisions) Act 1973, s. 19 & Sch. 2; 1978 Act, s. 25 & Sch. 2; and s. 1 & Sch. 1 of the Prevention of Terrorism (Temporary Provisions) Acts 1974, 1976, 1984 & 1989.

23 On 19 October 1988, by the Home Secretary, acting under s. 29 (3) of the Broadcasting Act 1981 and clause 13 (4) of the Licence and Agreement made between Her Majesty's Secretary of State for the Home Department and the British Broadcasting Corporation on 2 April 1981.

24 See, e.g., Report of the Commission to consider legal procedures to deal with terrorist activities in Northern Ireland, Cmnd. 5185, 1972; Report of the Committee to consider in the context of civil liberties and human rights measures to deal with terrorism in Northern Ireland, Cmnd. 5847, 1975; Review of the Operation of the Prevention of Terrorism (Temporary Provisions) Acts 1974 and 1976, Cmnd. 7324, 1978; Report of the Committee of Inquiry into Police Interrogation Procedures in Northern Ireland, Cmnd. 7947, 1979; Review of the Operation of the Prevention of Terrorism (Temporary Provisions) Act 1976, Cmnd. 8803, 1983; Review of the Operation of the Northern Ireland (Emergency Provisions) Act 1978, Cmnd. 9222, 1984.

25 Part 1 of the Prevention of Terrorism Act does not apply to Northern Ireland: see, e.g., s. 28 (2) of the 1989 Act.

26 Regulation 11 (1) made in 1956 under the Civil Authorities (Special Powers) Act (Northern Ireland) 1022.

27 Regulation 10 made in 1957 under the Civil Authorities (Special Powers) Act (Northern Ireland) 1922.

28 *Ireland* v. *the United Kingdom,* Judgment of 18 January 1978, Series A, No. 25, para. 212, 2 E.H.R.R. 25 at 93.

29 Northern Ireland (Emergency Provisions) Act 1973, s. 28, and the Prevention of Terrorism (Temporary Provisions) Act 1974, s. 9 (1). See also the Northern Ireland (Emergency Provisions) Act 1978, s. 31 (1); and the Prevention of Terrorism (Temporary Provisions) Act 1976, s. 14 (1); 1984 Act, s. 14 (1); 1989 Act, s. 20 (1).

30 Art. 4 of the Terrorists Order made under the Northern Ireland (Temporary Provisions) Act 1972.

31 S. 14 (1).

32 Art. 5 (1) (c).

33 *Ireland* v. *the United Kingdom,* Judgment of 18 January 1978, Series A, No. 25, para. 196, 2 E.H.R.R. 25 at 88. See also *Brogan and others,* Judgment of 29 November 1988, para. 51.

34 See *X.* v. *the United Kingdom,* Judgment of the European Court of Human Rights of 5 November 1981, Series A, No. 46, para. 66, 4 E.H.R.R. 188 at 212. See also Art. 9 (2) of the International Covenant on Civil and Political Rights.

35 Northern Ireland (Emergency Provisions) Act 1973, s. 12 (1); 1978 Act, s. 14 (1); 1987 Act, s. 14.

36 See D. P. J. Walsh, *The Use and Abuse of Emergency Legislation in Northern Ireland,* The Cobden Trust, 1983, p. 39.

37 Art. 5 (1) (c).

38 Prevention of Terrorism (Temporary Provisions) Act 1974, s. 7 (1); 1976 Act, s. 12 (1); 1984 Act, s. 12 (1); 1989 Act, s. 14 (1).

39 As to the sufficiency and relevancy of the suspicion in relation to the arrest of a suspected terrorist, see *McKee* v. *Chief Constable for Northern Ireland* [1984] 1 W.L.R. 1358.

40 Northern Ireland (Emergency Provisions) Act 1987, ss. 13 (1) & 14 (1).

41 See Art. 5 (3) of the European Covention on Human Rights, and Art. 9 (3) of the International Covenant on Civil and Political Rights.

42 See *Ireland* v. *the United Kingdom,* Judgment of the European Court of Human Rights of 18 January 1978, Series A, No. 25, para. 82, 2 E.H.R.R. 25 at 52.

43 Ibid., paras. 188–224, 2 E.H.R.R. 25 at 85–97.

44 Art. 5 (3) of the European Convention on Human Rights; Art. 9 (3) of the International Covenant on Civil and Political Rights.

45 *Brogan and others,* Judgment of 29 November 1988, paras. 55–62.

46 Only in an inter-State case may the legislation by challenged *in abstracto* as contrary to the United Kingdom's obligations under the Convention. As regards individual applications, since Art. 25 of the Convention requires that an individual applicant claim 'to be the victim of a violation ... of the rights set forth' in the Convention, only a person who has been detained under the legislation may complain to the European Commission of Human Rights about the legislation, and moreover only about its application in his or her case. See *Ireland* v. *the United Kingdom,* Judgment of the European Court of Human Rights of 18 January 1978, Series A, No. 25, para. 240, 2 E.H.R.R. 25 at 103–4.

47 1973 Act, s. 10 (1); 1978 Act, s. 11 (3).

48 Northern Ireland (Emergency Provisions) Act 1978, s. 14 (1).

49 Report of the Committee of Inquiry into Police Interrogation Procedures in Northern Ireland, Cmnd. 7497, para. 123.

50 Ibid., para. 277.

51 Northern Ireland (Emergency Procedures) Act 1987, s. 15.

52 Ibid., s. 14.

53 Police and Criminal Evidence Act 1984, s. 56 & 58; cf. Criminal Law Act 1977, s. 62.

54 *McVeigh, O'Neill and Evans* v. *the United Kingdom,* Report of 18 March 1981, paras. 235–40, 5 E.H.R.R. 71 at 106–7 and 25 *Decisions and Reports of the Commission* 15 at 52–3.

55 *Müller and others,* Judgment of 24 May 1988, Series A, no. 133, para. 33.

56 Prevention of Terrorism (Temporary Provisions) Act 1989, ss. 2 (1) and 10 (1).

57 Ibid., s. 9 (1).

58 See note 22 above.

59 See above p. 5.

60 Elected Authorities (Northern Ireland) Act 1989, ss. 3–9.

61 Note by Standing Advisory Commission on Human Rights on Government's Recent Announcements Affecting Northern Ireland Dealing with Terrorism and Terrorist Related Activities, 19 January 1989, p. 13.

62 See First Protocol, Art. 3.

63 Art. 25.

64 See Art. 40.

65 This is the phrase used in the legislation. See Elected Authorities (Northern Ireland) Act 1989, Sch. 2.

66 Cf. the 'limiting principles' advocated by C. Walker, op. cit., p. 8.

67 See, e.g., Review of the Operation of the Northern Ireland (Emergency Provisions) Act 1978, Cmnd. 9222, 1984, pp. 8, 55, 59, 66, 68, 100 & 119.

68 Art. 2. A limited degree of international scrutiny is available under the Convention itself, e.g. the compatibility of an order with respect for family life, guaranteed by Art. 8, may be raised in an appropriate case.

69 See the Preamble to the Universal Declaration of Human Rights 1948, the Preamble to the International Covenant on Civil and Political Rights 1966, and the Preamble to the International Covenant on Economic, Social and Cultural Rights 1966.

70 See introductory quotation.

Section B. The Settlement of Disputes by Arbitral and Judicial Means.

9.

International Arbitration in the External Policy of the Soviet Union.

GALINA G. SHINKARETSKAYA

The position of the Soviet Union towards international arbitration did not stay one and the same throughout its history. The position has changed as the situation inside the country has changed. In the first years of the Soviet state its external policy was formed by V. I. Lenin, who understood the necessity to live and develop together with other 'bourgeois' states. A socialist state was not going to 'fly to the moon', he wrote in an article 'On the slogan of the United States of Europe' as early as 1915.[1] Concrete external policy decisions were still being taken immediately after the Revolution by people who were still within the tradition of the Russian political science of the nineteenth and early twentieth century.

The interest in peaceful means of dispute settlement and in arbitration in Russian political science began to appear at the beginning of the nineteenth century in the works of V. Ph. Malinovsky, and became especially vivid at its end, when internationalisation of the economy and the development of economic relations in the whole world demanded that effective means of dispute settlement be introduced into international relations, means which could be used immediately, without any special diplomatic preparations.

During the second half of the nineteenth century many brilliant scholars appeared in Russia: Katchenovsky, Nezabitovsky, Stoyanov, Korkunov, Ulianitsky. A very special place among them belongs to Kamarovsky, who initiated a systematic survey of the problems of peaceful settlement of international disputes. His principal work devoted to this problem, 'On the International Court of Justice' was published in 1881. Kamarovsky was of the opinion that an injury to a state's interests committed by another state underlies every international conflict. To remedy such a situation a definite method is required, and only that method can be supposed just and equitable which corresponds to the gravity of the injury. Kamarovsky put forward two methods – arbitration, and a permanent court of justice. Kamarovsky's work has not lost its importance even now and helps those in our socialist state who look for ways to establish the rule of law. Of course Ph. Ph. Martens was world famous. Basing himself on the works of his predecessors, Martens was not only able to write a classical fundamental work, 'Modern international law of civilised nations', but also to take part in the preparation of the materials for the Hague Conference of 1899. Many books by Russian scholars were translated into foreign languages and became part of world legal culture. Kamarovsky's ideas on the permanent court set forth in his draft statute were realised in the Permanent Court of Arbitration; their echo we find even in the Statute of the International Court of Justice.

After the Great October Revolution when the Government, headed by Lenin, was revising treaties concluded by Tsarist Russia, it did not reject Russia's obligations in the field of peaceful settlement. The Hague Convention was kept in force, and Russia's membership in the Permanent Court of Arbitration retained. Readiness to use arbitration was expressed in some acts of the Soviet Government. As an example, let us take the Moscow Conference on the reduction of weapons, which took place in December 1922. At this time the Soviet state thought it vitally important to build a world without weapons or wars, and so was ready to submit its disputes to arbitration. In the amendments to the draft treaty on non-aggression and arbitration submitted by Poland, the Soviet delegation suggested a new art. VI: if a difference arises between the parties, except questions which have already been decided in peace treaties, this difference should be settled by an arbitration procedure. This broad formulation is a clear reflection of the ideas of those who drafted the 1899 and 1907 Hague Conventions. If a treaty on non-aggression and arbitration were adopted, it would have occupied a very special place in the politics of the USSR and its allies.

At the Moscow Conference our country put forward a proposal which was not to appear again in the practice of the USSR: an undertaking to submit territorial disputes to arbitration. This proposal can be fully appreciated only when one recollects that for Soviet Russia at that time a large part of her borders were disputed by other states. Later on all Soviet Governments firmly rejected any proposal to submit territorial disputes to arbitration. It was quite recently, in 1982, that the USSR, when accepting obligations in the Law of the Sea Convention to use arbitration, declared that she did not accept arbitration with respect, *inter alia*, to disputes concerning sea boundaries and delimitations or disputes involving historic bays. Peaceful settlement of disputes was seen by the Soviet Government, like many others at the time, as an integral part of the norms prohibiting the use of war as a means of national policy. Adoption of the General Act of 1928 was a step forward after the adoption and enforcement of the Kellog–Briand Peace Pact of 1928.

Another interesting phenomenon which emerged in the first years of the new Soviet state was a mixture of two classical forms of arbitration, that is commercial or civil arbitration and international or public arbitration. The reason for this was that private property was abolished and state ownership of the means of production was proclaimed. Thus the state became involved in civil relations. So the state could appear as a party in a civil dispute even with a foreign company. With the introduction of the new – more market oriented – economic policy in Soviet Russia in the 1920s, one aspect of this policy was the granting of concessions to foreign companies, on the basis of agreements between the state and such companies. In his speech before the 8th All-Russia Congress of People's Deputies, Lenin suggested the inclusion of arbitration clauses in such agreements. This idea was adopted, and the clause became typical for concession agreements. Foreign companies showed a great interest in concessions and the Soviet Government received several thousand applications. All in all about one hundred concessions were granted. The concessions continued until about the mid-1930s, diminishing gradually as the administrative system became ever more predominant. Until then the concessions did play some role in the development of the Soviet economy.

Commercial arbitration was also used in the practice of inter-state relations. In 1934 negotiations were held between the USSR and Japan on the sale of Chinese Eastern Railways. This is the southern branch of the railway built by Russia in 1897–1903 through the territory of China to the Pacific Ocean. Since 1924 it was under joint USSR – China management. The sums due for the railway were planned to be paid with goods. The Soviet Government proposed to include in the purchase agreement a provision that possible differences with respect to the goods should be solved by arbitration; an impartial president of the arbitration court might be appointed by some foreign commerce chamber with a solid international reputation, e.g. commerce chambers of England and the USA were mentioned. However the proposal did not materialise, because Japan insisted upon the appointment of a representative of the Japanese foreign ministry.

Another interesting aspect of Soviet policy in the early period was the readiness to submit to arbitration matters which have traditionally been supposed to be non-justiciable, matters which were once considered as 'concerning the honour and dignity of a state'. In 1923–24 the Soviet Government was accused of intending to bring about a coercive change in the social structure of capitalist states. In December 1923 the US Secretary of State said that an instruction of Comintern allegedly existed on how to make a revolution in the USA. The people's comissar for foreign affairs proposed that the USSR and the USA submit the matter to an arbitral court. The USA declined the proposal. A similar situation arose with respect to an alleged 'Comintern letter' which was used in Britain in 1924 as a means to rupture Anglo-Soviet relations. The Soviet Government again suggested going to arbitration to clear up the question. Again the suggestion was declined.

From the mid-1930s when lawlessness began to prevail in internal

Soviet affairs, the Soviet attitude towards legal means of dispute settlement and arbitration changed. Hardly a single scholarly article on the subject was published at this time. There was no official approval of any dispute settlement technique except negotiations. Nonetheless, a proposal was put forward in 1938 inviting Japan to turn to arbitration to settle the dispute on the re-demarcation of the border near the Hasan Lake.

After the Second World War a Cold War atmosphere prevailed. Although the war was ended, force still seemed to be a natural way of life to the leaders of both the USSR and the USA. This was no climate for 'good neighbour' relations. The lofty ideas of the UN Charter were far from being put into practice. The Soviet Union did not object to Article 33 of the UN Charter, where international arbitration is provided on the same basis as other means of dispute settlement, both voluntary and compulsory forms. However the Cold War years were unhappy ones for the International Court of Justice, which is most dependent on the international situation. Many governments (not only the Soviet) did not at that time believe in legal methods for the conduct of foreign policy. The number of treaties providing for arbitral settlement was very limited. The Soviet leaders spoke very disapprovingly of the United Nations Organisation and showed disbelief in its organs and its place in international relations. Thus I. V. Stalin said in one of his interviews to *Pravda* that the UN was turning essentially from a universal organisation to an organisation dominated by the Americans, acting in the interests of American aggressors.[2] In 1946 A. Vyshinsky, a close associate of Stalin, expressed his agreement with those who anticipated that if a dispute was referred to a court, even the International Court of Justice, that would not be a suitable forum to resolve it.[3]

As a consequence, scientific research in the field of international law was of no interest for the state, and was actually stopped. This was possible because all research was directed by the state itself or by its institutions. Scholarly views on international arbitration at that time are very difficult to follow, because there were hardly any publications on the problem. The literature on the International Court of Justice was almost as sparse. Those who did write on these questions, for ideological reasons, criticised severely 'imperialist' tactics in international politics. This was obligatory for every author. Being specialists, they could not but speak of arbitration and judicial procedure. So they used two languages: a calm and business like one when saying something about the problem and a harsh, even rude, one when making a general assessment. One can easily see this in the works by the then member of the ICJ, S. B. Krylov who published from time to time articles about what was going on at the ICJ. This 'compulsory hypocrisy' is also clearly seen in the title of a doctoral thesis published in 1952: 'The struggle of the Soviet Union against American – English Imperialists': efforts to use arbitration for aggressive purposes'.

Nonetheless the USSR did become a party to a treaty providing for arbitral settlement in 1948. This was the Convention on Navigation on the Danube. Formally the body to settle any dispute concerning the interpretation or application of the Convention was called a 'conciliation commission', but it bore many features which are usually considered to belong to compulsory arbitration: this body could be created by the request of only one party to the dispute. The neutral member of the body would be appointed by the President of the Danube Commission itself. Its function was not only to establish facts, but to decide the merits of the case. The decision was to be final and binding.

This general approach (of hostility) to international arbitration did not change with the 20th Congress of the Communist Party of the Soviet Union in 1956. Very few new treaties containing an arbitration clause were adopted by the USSR. It was the permanent practice of Soviet delegations at international conferences to declare reservations to such clauses. The Soviet example was, of course, followed by socialist countries. Very few of them undertook to arbitrate. Of course in commercial matters arbitration could not be completely avoided. That is why socialist countries, and the USSR among them, did join international conventions on commercial arbitrations (e.g. the New York Convention of 1958, the European Convention of 1961, the Moscow Convention of 1972). They also amended their domestic legislation accordingly.

The Soviet position towards international arbitration as well as that of the socialist countries was confirmed once again with the Helsinki Meeting on security and co-operation in Europe in 1975. Having signed the Helsinki Act they all declared (just like the other participants at the Meeting) their adherence to the principle of peaceful settlement of international disputes and their obligation to use peaceful means fixed in the Charter. Their special attitude became clear at the Montreux 1978 meeting of experts. The experts present there were to fulfil the task set by the Helsinki Act, namely, to analyse whether the existing system of dispute settlement could be completed with some special method for relations between the European countries. In the centre of the discussion in Montreux was the draft submitted by the Swiss delegation, which was prepared in 1973, even before the Helsinki meeting, and which received a special mention in the Final Act. The heart of it was compulsory arbitration for all disputes between the countries participants in the Helsinki process, where there was not settlement by voluntary means.

Socialist states did not support the Swiss draft and submitted their own document in which the idea of obligatory consultations was put forward. The reasoning of the socialist states for rejection of arbitration in this case seems quite convincing. What was under discussion was an all-Europe means of peaceful settlement of all disputes, independently of their essence and character, and the obligation provided in the Swiss draft was so broad and indeterminate that it would hardly be realistic to believe it would be effective. Too broad obligations of this kind seem to have long been proved useless. The diminishing practice of the Permanent Court of Arbitration shows that even those states which have paid lip-service to compulsory arbitration have not frequently used the Court. General and declaratory obligations are not at all popular nowadays.

Treaty practice of states provides good examples for this. We can see that the arbitration clause depends directly on the scope of substantial obligations. One finds the clause mostly in treaties with limited numbers of participants, and with limited spheres of application both geographically and functionally: for instance, constitutional conventions creating international organisations or agreements regulating diseases in animals. In cases such as these, the position of the USSR and other socialist states does not differ substantially from that of all other states.

Soon after the Montreux meeting a change came in the position of the Soviet Union. In 1982, when signing the Law of the Sea Convention, the Soviet delegation opted for arbitration and for special arbitration to be used for the settlement of disputes concerning the interpretation or application of the Convention. The scope of the obligation is rather limited, since the Soviet delegation declared all reservations allowed in the Convention. So the jurisdiction of the arbitration or of a special arbitration does not cover delimitation disputes, disputes concerning military activities and disputes which are under discussion in the Security Council. If one recollects that a state party to the Convention may not agree to submit to a judicial procedure for many disputes stemming from the exercise of its sovereign rights or jurisdiction, one can understand that very few disputes where the Soviet Union is a party will be in fact submitted to adjudication. The acceptance of arbitration in the Law of the Sea Convention was not a wholly voluntary step on the part of the USSR:[4] provisions on the obligatory procedures constitute an integral part of the 'package deal'. So in accepting the Convention as a whole every state party has to accept these provisions as well.

Nevertheless this recognition of the two purely legal means for the settlement of disputes is remarkable. Firstly, notwithstanding many exclusions, the principle is there that the Soviet Union accepted compulsory jurisdiction over all disputes connected with the Convention. The significance of this broad obligation prevails over the importance of the reservations. Maybe in future my country will revise its reservations. There are two possible ways to achieve this: to give an *ad hoc* consent for a particular case to be submitted to an arbitral court; or the so-called forum prorogatum. Secondly, it has to be said that the Soviet Union was one of the first states signatories to the Convention to declare for arbitration, which does demonstrate a measure of good faith. Third, it was for the first time in its history that the USSR showed a readiness to let her actions (indeed, a good many of them, the USSR being a great maritime power) be tested by an independent, impartial body with a compulsory character.

I personally am not at all sure that the choice of arbitration was a happy one. As I understand it, the USSR delegation opted for arbitration as the lesser of two evils, the alternative being judicial settlement. I think the Soviet delegation was looking for a means to ensure as much autonomy as possible for the parties. In some respects the arbitration procedures provided for in the Convention are no less rigid than the procedure of the International Law of the Sea Tribunal. In any case the arbitration procedure is not loose enough to guarantee the desired autonomy of the disputing state. Let us take the central point of the arbitration procedure - the choice of arbiters. The respondent state has not many possibilities to determine choice: it has either to accept the person suggested by the claimant state from the very beginning or to suggest, in its turn, a person agreeable to the claimant. Otherwise the choice will be made by the UN Secretary General or President of the Law of the Sea Tribunal.[5] My opinion is that the people who opted for arbitration had the image of *ad hoc* arbitration in their minds. However, the option is not a decision for ever.

A real change in the position of the Soviet Union towards arbitration has come only with the beginning of Perestroika in 1985. Then international law specialists acquired influence through their writings concerning what should be done in this field.

There are interesting developments concerning arbitration among socialist countries. During the forty-year history of the Council of Mutual Economic Assistance, all international disputes between socialist states in the field of economic and scientific - technical co-operation have been settled by negotiations or through bilateral joint commissions. Because these means did not prove sufficient, the idea of arbitral settlement of international disputes has gradually come to be discussed by scholars and other specialists interested in the problems of CMEA.

The first step in this direction was made during the preparations of the text of the Convention on responsibility for damage caused by a radiation emergency case during international transportation of waste nuclear fuel from nuclear power stations. A protocol was added to the Convention which provided for *ad hoc* arbitration of the damage caused by the radiation emergency case. Special arbitration rules were included in the Protocol. One can feel the influence of the notion of commercial arbitration in the Protocol: the disputes lying within the jurisdiction of the arbitration concerned essentially economic matters and the procedure was to be used *ad hoc*. Nevertheless, this was a most significant development.

The Protocol paved the way for future steps in this direction. At the third special meeting of the Session of CMEA, several countries (Bulgaria, Hungary, the GDR, Cuba, Poland, the USSR and Czechoslovakia) expressed their interest in studying, within the CMA permanent commission, the question of dispute settlement by arbitration concerning international agreements on economic and scientific - technical co-operation. As the result of several meetings of experts from the interested states, two drafts were worked out: a draft article on the undertaking to arbitrate to settle disputes and draft rules of the arbitration. The drafts were discussed at the meeting of the Permanent Legal Commission of CMEA in December 1988 and finally approved by the Executive Committee of CMEA in May 1989. The results of the several years of work seem rather limited: the arbitration clause (the so-called 'standard article') is to be included in treaties on economic and scientific – technical co-operation between CMEA countries only if they have reached agreement on this.

On the other hand, the clause signifies for the first time a possibility of using international arbitration. According to the standard article, if there is a dispute between the parties to a treaty concerning its interpretation or implementation, which the parties are unable to settle by way of negotiations or other mutually agreed means, one of the parties may, after a reasonable time, turn to arbitration. The parties can agree on the rules of procedure. If they do not, there are standard rules. According to the rules, every party to the treaty can appoint four of its citizens to the list of arbiters, who possess 'respective qualifications in the field of international law and knowledge of the questions of international economic and scientific – technical co-operation'. The arbitration itself, when deciding a case, applies international treaties, the agreement in which the arbitration clause is included, special treaties concluded by the CMEA countries, and – what is very important – principles and other generally accepted norms of international law, as well as international customs recognised by the parties as international legal norms. Non-appearance of one of the parties does not prevent the tribunal from conducting the proceedings and reaching a decision.

One may not expect that from tomorrow all CMEA countries will begin to use arbitration. The clause will probably be a rare element in treaties. Nevertheless the wall of silence around legal means of dispute settlement has been broken. If good conditions for the rule of law in international relations continue to exist, the clause will appear more often.

Arbitration cannot be considered in isolation. It is only one of the techniques used by any state in its foreign policy. Whether a state undertakes to arbitrate depends mainly on the place given by the state to the idea of the rule of law. From this point of view we can expect that the use of arbitration by the Soviet Union will expand in relations with socialist, capitalist and developing countries. There are already indications of this: speeches by M. S. Gorbachev and E. A. Shevardnadze in the General Assembly, and preparations to conclude a treaty on application to the ICJ for settlement of specific categories of disputes between permanent members of the Security Council. These show the growing readiness of the USSR to subject her actions to international judicial control. And since arbitration has for a long time been more popular in the Soviet Union than the ICJ, it is very likely that it will be more used in the future.

Notes

1 V.I. Lenin, 'On the Slogan of the United States of Europe', *Full Collection of Lenin's Works,* Moscow, vol. 26, p. 354, in Russian.
2 I.V. Stalin, *Talk to a Pravda Correspondent, Moscow 1951,* 11–12, Moscow, in Russian.
3 *The USSR, Ukrainian SSR and the Belorussian SSR Delegations at the Second Session of the UN General Assembly,* Moscow, 1948, p. 556 (in Russian).
4 The Soviet Representative at the Third UN Conference on the Law of the Sea stressed that the most important thing was to prevent disputes by elaborating substantial rules in such a way that they would be mutually acceptable and effective e.g. UN Doc. A/Conf. 62/SR.68, 5 April 1976.
5 See United Nations Convention on the Law of the Sea, Annex VII, art. 3 (e); Annex VIII, art. 3 (e).

10.

The Principle of Peaceful Settlement of Disputes: A New Soviet Approach

ELENA E. VILEGJANINA

Given the improvement in the international environment, and increasing awareness of the international community of states of the need to build a world free of violence, the international legal principle of peaceful settlement of disputes is gaining more importance. In 1982 The Manila Declaration on the Peaceful Settlement of International Disputes was adopted; in 1987 the Declaration on the Enhancement of the Effectiveness of the Principle of Refraining from the Threat or Use of Force in International Relations was taken up (a number of provisions of this Declaration, and provisions of Section III in particular, deal with the peaceful settlement of disputes); the 43rd session of the United Nations General Assembly approved the Declaration on the Prevention and Removal of Disputes and Situations which may Threaten International Peace and Security and the Role of the United Nations in this Field. All these documents were adopted by consensus as a result of the collective efforts of the UN member states, including the USSR. They reflect both the contemporary state of development of international law and the modern level of international legal consciousness.

The universal mechanism of the United Nations is not the only forum where both the principle and the means of peaceful settlement of disputes are being developed. On the agenda of the Conference of Security and Co-operation in Europe, for example, there is the question of the elaboration of acceptable methods for the peaceful settlement of disputes which would complement existing methods. Two meetings of experts of the states participants have already been held to discuss this problem: in 1987 in Montreux and in 1984 in Athens. The third one will take place, according to the Vienna document of 1989, in Valetta in 1991.

The existing means of peaceful settlement under international law are well known. They are enumerated in Article 33 of the UN Charter, the most important source of modern international law. According to the Charter the parties to a dispute shall seek a solution by negotiation, inquiry, mediation, conciliation, arbitration, judicial settlement, resort to regional agencies or arrangements. Almost the same list of means is incorporated in other principal international instruments such as the Helsinki Final Act, the Manila Declaration and others.

Naturally, this catalogue is not exhaustive and cannot be by its nature. Interstate relationships constantly give rise to new methods which meet the new needs and circumstances of a given case. In this connection we can mention, for example, consultations, institutionalised in international law in recent years as a method of peaceful settlement of disputes. The USSR actively favoured the development of consultations and suggested in 1978 that this very method could be used as a European method of peaceful settlement. Consultations are embodied in a number of universal conventions such as the Vienna Convention on the Representation of States in Their Relations with International Organisations of a Universal Character, and the Vienna Convention on Succession of States in Respect of Treaties and in some other cases.

States also turn to the so-called 'combined' methods which combine traits of some already existing means, say conciliation and arbitration. We can mention in this context the Commission on Claims, provided for by the Convention on International Liability for Damage caused by Space Objects. The mechanism of this Commission was elaborated with the active participation of the Soviet Union. Acting as a conciliatory body it can be, with the consent of the parties to a dispute, transformed into an arbitration body and give a binding decision.

There is no doubt that methods of peaceful settlement, which combine some features of conciliation and arbitration, had been familiar to international law much earlier. The Convention on Navigation on the Danube, 1948, provides for the creation of a conciliatory commission with a binding decision-making power. We can refer to numerous commissions created after World War II under the agreements on settlement of property claims. The possibility of transforming these conciliatory bodies into arbitration tribunals is a characteristic of these organs which is of particular interest in the context of this article. These commissions were created as conciliatiary on an equal basis, but if the parties failed to find a solution, an additional member was elected to the commission and it acted as an arbiter formulating a binding award.[1] This experience of combining conciliation and arbitration was utilised by succeeding international legal practice. To some extent it was absorbed by the convention on space damage, but on another level – in a universal legal instrument for the regulation of quite different relations.

Progress in respect of the International Court of Justice has been difficult until now. As a member of the United Nations the USSR is *ipso facto* party to the Statute of the International Court of Justice since the foundation of this body. But the general Soviet attitude towards the Court has been for a long period cautious and reserved. Naturally this political approach considerably influenced the development of Soviet legal doctrine. Soviet international lawyers did not analyse the ICJ and its practice thoroughly. There have been only three studies which concentrated fully on the problems of international adjudication. The last one, 'The International Court of Justice' by F. I. Kozhevnikov and J. V. Sharmazanashvily, was published in 1971. Later publications on different aspects of the peaceful settlement of disputes touch upon the activity of the International Court very briefly in the context of other issues, and contain no profound study of the Court's precedents. In the juridical literature the general opinion prevailed that international adjudication could play only a very modest part in the peaceful settlement process. This view was based on a series of arguments of a procedural and conceptual nature. In the view of some authors, adjudication is a very complex and formal procedure and thus cannot be as adequate and effective as, for instance, negotiations. As to compulsory jurisdiction, it was considered contrary to the principle of the free choice of means of peaceful settlement.[2] This thesis was supported by the argument that only limited numbers of states made declarations on the acceptance of the compulsory jurisdiction of the Court. Even fewer states made these declarations without any reservations. Some lawyers shared the view that the main reason for the ineffectiveness of the Court was rooted in its composition, where judges representing Western legal systems formed a constant majority.[3] Another reason which predetermined the general trend of the Court's activity was the nature of disputes.[4] When juridicial aspects prevail over political ones in disputes and requests for advisory opinions, the Court gave, as a rule, just judgments and acceptable advisory opinions. Yet once the political aspects of a dispute or of a request for an advisory opinion played a large role, the Court gave often ill-based decisions and advisory opinions.[4]

This tendency to seek connections between the ineffectiveness of the Court and the categories of disputes put under its consideration – political or legal, justiciable or non-justiciable – can also be found in Western international legal doctrine.[5] Western scholars proposed different approaches for the categorisation of intergovernmental disputes but finally all discussions concerning this issue – among both Western and Soviet scientists – came to the conclusion that it is impossible to draw in advance any boundary between categories of disputes or to determine on this basis whether a given dispute can be solved by the International Court of Justice.[6]

In the Court's practice there were several cases when parties to a dispute interpreted the nature of their controversies from different angles. Nonetheless this did not affect the Court's decision on its jurisdiction over the dispute nor the 'justice' of the final judgment. For example, in the case of the American diplomatic and consular staff in Tehran the questions submitted to the Court were of a purely juridical nature and did not go beyond the framework of the diplomatic law. However, Iran considered this case political and refused to participate in the proceedings before the Court.

Another example is the case concerning military and paramilitary activities in and against Nicaragua. It was directly connected with political events in the Caribbean region. The US objected against consideration of this case by the Court 'because of the express allocation of such matters as the subject of Nicaragua's claims to the political organs under the United Nations Charter'.[7] The Court found itself competent to consider the case, since the consideration of the whole situation by the Security Council did not preclude the Court from consideration of the legal aspects of the case. These examples demonstrate that the nature of the dispute and its admissibility by the Court are not predetermined objectively, but rather depend on the approach which is chosen for the settlement of the dispute.

So the thesis about the correlation between the character of decisions and the composition of the Court seems doubtful. In the 'Nicaragua v. USA' case, in the advisory opinion on the United Nations Headquarters Agreement (Palestine Liberation Movement), and some others which met the requirements of contemporary international law, the majority of the judges represented Western systems of law.

Notwithstanding the above considerations, the effectiveness of the Court, the quality of its judgments and their acceptability for parties, depend in the long run upon the part which international law is allowed to play in international relations. International law cannot have any serious weight in an atmosphere of constant interstate tension: 'inter arma silent leges'. Law and international institutions, including adjudication, can be effective only in the context of stability and coexistence between members of the world community. At present the political climate favours an increasing role for international law. The growing concern of the community of states to enforce the legal basis of international relations, to make more efficient the institutions and mechanisms set up for providing stability and legal order among states, provide an urgent context for the more effective use of the International Court of Justice. It has a new significance in the view of the growing realisation of its status as the principal judicial organ of the United Nations responsible for the maintenance of international peace and security. This new attitude to the ICJ has been making an impact in recent Soviet doctrine.[8]

A real estimation of the present role of the ICJ and its weight in the peaceful settlment process requires an analysis of its practice, including the consequences of its judgments for the settlement of disputes; an understanding of the dynamics of acceptance by states of its compulsory jurisdiction; and an analysis of the structure of these obligations and a lot of other issues. As they cannot be dealt with within the scope of a chapter, attention will be concentrated on one aspect, the most indicative one from the point of view of the contemporary role and prestige of the Court in international relations. I will focus on its activity in recent years.

Throughout the history of the Court states have referred their controversies for its consideration about fifty times. Not all these disputes were solved by the Court: sometimes the ICJ found the issue outside its competence, sometimes parties to a dispute found another way to a solution. Hence, by relying on simple arithmetic calculations, we can conclude that the Court deals each year with an average of one dispute. However, this primitive approach does not give an adequate picture of the real role of the ICJ. First of all it is necessary to take into consideration that there were different periods in the activity of the Court: more energetic and more passive ones. Its functioning decreased at the end of the 1970s but nowadays the popularity of the Court is constantly growing.

The cases which have been considered by the Court or which are under consideration by the Court now, are very varied in their political significance, in the questions raised, and in the procedural issues. Some of these cases have the importance of precedents, and their study is of practical and scientific interest. One of the trends of the comtemporary activity of the Court has been the predominance of cases on delimitation issues, in particular maritime delimitation. For the first twenty years of the Court's history it dealt with questions of maritime law in only two cases.[9] Subsequently, quite a number of cases have been solved by the court: two cases on the continental shelf boundary in the North Sea (*Federal Republic of Germany (FRG)* v. *Denmark* and *FRG* v. *Netherlands*, in 1967-9); two Fisheries Jurisdiction Cases (*Great Britain* v. *Iceland* and *FRG* v. *Iceland*, in 1972-4); four Maritime Boundary Cases (*Greece* v. *Turkey*) in the Aegean Sea in 1976-8, *Tunisia* v. *Libya* in the Mediterranean Sea in 1978-82, *United States* v. *Canada* in the Gulf of Maine in 1981-4, *Libya* v. *Malta* in the Mediterranean Sea in 1982-5); and one case on the review and interpretation of the Court's decision of 24 February 1982 on the continental shelf dispute between Tunisia and Libya (1984-5).[10] Two cases on maritime delimitation are under the consideration of the Court at the time of writing (May 1989). These concern the land and maritime frontier dispute between El Salvador and Honduras, and the maritime boundary between Greenland and Jan Mayen, between Denmark and Norway.[11]

Let us consider the evolution of the nature of the questions put before the Court and its respective decisions. Great Britain initiated in 1972 proceedings before the Court in a case against Iceland. The application was caused by the claim of the government of Iceland to a fisheries jurisdiction zone up to fifty nautical miles. Great Britain asked the Court to decide that this claim of Iceland was without basis in international law and that the fisheries regime in that area should be determined by agreement of the parties. The Court indicated in its decision that the parties were obliged to negotiate with the purpose of elaborating an equitable solution, which was to take into account, on the one hand, the preferential fishing rights of Iceland, taking into account the dependence of the population of Iceland on fisheries and, on the other hand, the Great Britain's historical fishing rights in the area. A decision with a similar context was taken by the Court in another case, raised by the Federal Republic of Germany against Iceland on the basis of similar circumstances.

The substance of the dispute between Greece and Turkey on the delimitation of the continental shelf was not considered by the Court. It is interesting, however, how the questions were scrutinised by Greece in its application to the Court. Greece asked the Court to decide that, in accordance with the principles and norms of international law, the Greek islands, as part of the territory of Greece, had their own continental shelf, and that therefore Greece had sovereign and exclusive rights to explore and utilise the shelf resources. The application contained also a request to indicate the shelf delimitation line between Greece and Turkey in accordance with the norms of international law applicable in this case. Unlike the previous case, the dispute between Greece and Turkey put before the Court the maritime law concept of the legal status of the shelf of the islands. In the case between Tunisia and Libya the parties requested the Court to indicate the principles and rules of international law which may be applied for the delimitation of the area, taking account of equitable principles and relevant circumstances, as well as the recent trends admitted at the Third Conference on the Law of the Sea. The parties also asked the Court to specify the practical ways in which the aforesaid principles and rules applied in their particular situation. In its decision the Court gave an elaborate scheme for the settlement of the dispute. It indicated that delimitation was to be effected in accordance with equitable principles and taking account of all relevant circumstances. It considered that no criterion for the delimitation of the shelf area could be derived from the principle of natural prolongation as such. At the same time the Court identified the factors and circumstances that should be taken into account for delimitation. Finally the Court indicated the geographical points of the line of delimitation. In their case, the United States and Canada submitted to the Court their dispute on the delimitation of the continental shelf and fishing zones in the Gulf of Maine. It should be mentioned that this was the first case joining these two issues in the practice of the ICJ. The Court gave in its judgment the geographical points of the single maritime frontier line.

In these cases which have been referred to the ICJ, complex issues of delimitation in frontier areas are regulated by specific sets of rules of international law. In this chapter I do not attempt to analyse the contents of all these cases (they are already examined in the juridical literature). I cite them only in order to illustrate and to support the view that controversies relating to frontiers, and to the sea in particular, are one of the major aspects of the Court's activities. Its judgments on these questions have the importance of judicial precedents and to a great extent determine the contents of international legal rules.

The importance of this process was emphasised by C. Wilfred Jenks at a very early stage of the Court's activity. In his view:

> while the Statute of the International Court provides that its decisions are binding only in the case before the Court and as

between the parties thereto, this provision merely precludes the application to the Court of the doctrine of the binding force of precedent and does not in any way impair the immense, persuasive authority of the decisions of the Court. As the body of international judicial precedent grows, a new element in a universal system may gradually assume decisive importance.[12]

In this field the significance of the ICJ grows. The tendency is obvious, not only from the point of view of the quantity of cases referred to the Court (though in number terms it may look modest), but also in the general trend of formulating more specific questions to put before the Court. If earlier parties addressing the Court brought to it questions formulated in relatively general terms – asking about the applicable legal norms – later the Court has been asked to be much more specific in deciding boundary questions.

There is no doubt that the dispute in the recent practice of the Court which has greatly raised its prestige in the opinion of the world community and which, at the same time, has confirmed the universal value of international law, is the case concerning military and paramilitary activites of the USA in and against Nicaragua. The major importance of this case lies in the way which the Court has approached the question of applicable law. The United States made a reservation to the declaration of acceptance of the jurisdiction under Article 36, Paragraph 2 of the Statute which withheld from the Court's jurisdiction 'disputes arising, under multilateral treaty, unless (1) all the parties to the treaty affected by the decision are also parties to the case before the Court, or (2) the United States of America specially agrees to jurisdiction'.[13] The notion of 'multilateral treaties' also includes the UN Charter which incorporates fundamental principles of international law such as non-use of force and sovereign equality. Nonetheless the Court did not hold the opinion that obligations deriving from these principles have only a conventional character. The ICJ confirmed in its judgment the obligatory character of these principles for states, regardless of their participation in a treaty. The Court pointed to the customary content of international law principles, such as non-intervention in the affairs of another state, non-use of force, state sovereignty and peaceful maritime commerce. In support of this view the Court emphasised the importance to be attached to such international instruments as declarations adopted by consensus. The Court referred to a declaration on 'Principles of International Law Concerning Friendly Relations and Co-operation among States in Accordance with the Charter of the United Nations'; to the Definition of Aggression; to certain other UN Declarations, and to the Helsinki Final Act, where the principles regulating interstate relations were formulated. This ICJ judgment can be considered as expressing contemporary qualification of international law and its basic principles as a value of the whole community of states, a *sine qua non* of its development in peace.

Taking into account all these factors, we come to the conclusion that under present conditions the ICJ is able to become an effective and prestigious principal judicial organ responsible for security and peace in the world. The Court is needed today to transform the modern international community into a legal community of states, accepting the primacy of international law.

Some concrete proposals aimed at radically changing the role of the International Court of Justice were advanced in the article by M. Gorbachev, 'Realities and Guarantees of a Secure World', a new approach to the idea of compulsory jurisdiction which may be one possible way to make the International Court more active. In this context I propose to consider the existing system of acceptance of the compulsory jurisdiction of the ICJ. It takes its origins from the Permanent Court of International Justice dating from the epoch of the League of Nations – which had many fewer members than the present United Nations. The concept of compulsory jurisdiction, in conformity with Article 36, paragraph 2 of the Statute of the Court, provided for every state to determine the limits of its acceptance according to its own interests. This is a procedure which may to a minimum extent promote the submission of disputes to judicial settlement in an international community with more than 160 participants.

We cannot see any significant increase in the number of states accepting the compulsory jurisdiction of the ICJ. The number of participating states changes but on the whole it remains the same as it was in the fifties and sixties – about fifty states. Since the seventies a number of states withdrew their declarations: they included Bolivia, Brazil, Guatemala, Iran, France and the USA. At the same time declarations on the acceptance of ICJ jurisdiction as compulsory were made by Barbados – in 1980, Nauru – in 1987 and Surinam – in 1987. A series of states chose to amend their previous declarations, for example, Malta. In 1983 Malta amended its declaration made in 1966 adding to the list of disputes withheld from the jurisdiction of the Court cases concerning territory, the continental shelf and other areas and their resources under the jurisdiction of Malta; questions of delimitation; measures against or preventing pollution or contamination of the marine environment in the zones adjacent to the coasts of Malta.[14] The disadvantages of such a system of acceptance of compulsory jurisdiction emerged in a number of cases submitted to the Court, when a state refused to participate in proceedings by invoking its reservations. These were the cases of Nuclear Tests, and of Military and Paramilitary Activities, already mentioned above.

In my view, one of the ways to make the Court and the law itself more efficient in international relations is to elaborate a different approach to compulsory jurisdiction. There could be an arrangement between states to submit to the Court disputes which have arisen in certain specific mutually-agreed spheres of relations. At the first stage it could be quite a narrow specific area. This could be widened step by step through agreements between the interested states. Such an approach would develop an interconnected system of mutual obligations towards the International Court of Justice which would become thereby a serious factor in promoting stability in the world.

It is only logical that the first step in the direction of widening obligations relating to the jurisdiction of the ICJ would be made by the permanent members of the UN Security Council, who are 'primarily responsible for the maintenance of international peace and security'. The Soviet Union has launched this idea of the acceptance of the compulsory jurisdiction of the ICJ on a mutually agreed basis. It has taken up the intitiative of consultations with other permanent members of the Security Council. This initiative has received a positive reaction. The Soviet–American contacts on this issue have progressed actively, and after several rounds of consultations the parties managed to elaborate basic elements of the notion of mutually agreed conditions for the acceptance of ICJ compulsory jurisdiction.

This step by two permanent members of the Security Council could orient other states in determining their position towards the International Court of Justice. If such an approach were to be adopted by other states, mutually agreed compulsory jurisdiction would become a considerable factor for the consolidation of trust, stability and democratisation in international life.

The Soviet Union, for its part, has begun reviewing its reservations made to multilateral conventions concerning the ICJ jurisdiction. In accordance with an act adopted on 10 February 1989 by the Presidium of the Supreme Soviet, the USSR withdrew its earlier reservations and accepted the jurisdiction of the Court as compulsory over disputes connected with the interpretation and application of a number of fundamental human rights conventions. These are the Convention on the Prevention and Punishment of the Crime of Genocide, 1948; the Convention for the Suppression of the Traffic in Persons and of the Exploitation of Prostitution, 1949; the Convention on the Political Rights of Women, 1952; the International Convention on the Elimination of all forms of Racial Discrimination, 1965; the Convention on the Elimination of all forms of Discrimination against Women, 1979, and the Convention against Torture and Other Cruel, Inhuman or Degrading Treatment or Punishment, 1984.

Taking this decision the Soviet Union was seeking to enhance the international legal order and to promote the primacy of international law both internationally and domestically.

Notes

1 Report of International Arbitral Awards. UN, Vol. XIV.
2 D. B. Levin *The Principle of Peaceful Settlement of International Disputes*, Moscow, 1977, p. 99 (in Russian).
3 D. B. Levin, ibid., p. 99.
4 F. I. Kozhevnikov and G. V. Sharmazanashvili, *The UN International Court of Justice*, Moscow, 1971, pp. 3–4. V. D. Kudryavtsev, *The Competence of the UN International Court of Justice*, Moscow, 1970, p. 14 (in Russian).
5 M. Vaucher, Le problème de la justiciabilité en droit international de différends dits 'politiques' et 'non-juridiques' et les notions de competence exclusive et de competence nationale. Article 15(8) du Pacte de la Société de Nations et article 2(7) de la Charte de l'O.N.U. Étude de droit sociologique: Paris, 1951; C. Rousseau, *Droit international public*, Paris, 1958; J. Charpentier, *Institutions internationales*, Paris, 1975, pp. 49–50.
6 Brierly, *The Basis of Obligation in International Law and Other Papers*, Oxford, 1958, pp. 96, 97, 100, 102, 106; George Schwarzenberger, *A Manual of International Law*, London, 1960, vol. I, p. 234; A. Kaplan and de B. Katzenbach, *Law in the International Community*, New York, 1962, pp. 100–101; G. Scelle, *Cours de droit international public*, Paris, 1948, pp. 695, 696; J. L. Simpson and H. Fox, *International Arbitration*, London, 1959, p. 44; *The Emergence and Development of the Soviet Sciences of International Law*, Moscow, 1975, p. 190 (in Russian).
7 *International Court of Justice Reports*, p. 27.
8 E. Evgenyeve and F. Kozhevnikov, 'The Role of the UN International Court of Justice in the Peaceful Settlement of Disputes', *Soviet State and Law*, 1986, No. 10; R. A. Müllerson, Review of the Book 'World Ocean and International Law' (Moscow 1986), *Soviet State and Law*, 1986, No. 6, p. 148 (in Russian).
9 Corfu Channel Case (*Great Britain* v. *Albania*), 1947–1949; Fisheries Case (*Great Britain* v. *Norway*), 1949–1951.
10 *ICJ Yearbook 1987–1988*, The Hague, 1988.
11 ICJ Application instituting proceedings – Maritime Boundary in the Area between Greenland and Jan Mayen, *Denmark* v. *Norway*.
12 C. Wilfred Jenks, *The Common Law of Mankind*, London, 1958, pp. 105–6.
13 *ICJ Yearbook 1984–1985*, The Hague, 1985.
14 *ICJ Yearbook 1987–1988*, The Hague, 1988.

11.

The UK, the Compulsory Jurisdiction of the ICJ and the Peaceful Settlement of Disputes

ANTHONY CARTY

Introduction

The UK remains the only permanent member of the Security Council which is a party to the optional clause jurisdiction of the International Court of Justice (the ICJ). The United States and France have abandoned the clause at a time when they were engaged in litigation which was to bring into question their military and security strategies, in the Nicaragua Case[1] and the Nuclear Tests Case [2] respectively. These incidents appear to suggest that the supposedly defunct doctrine of a 'vital interests' limitation of international adjudication of inter-state disputes is in fact still very much alive. What is one to make of the continued adherence of the UK to the optional clause? Does it signify simply that the UK has never been tempted? So, for instance, it has not been the subject of ICJ litigation since the Fisheries Jurisdiction Cases of 1974.[3] How far is there a danger that major disputes between the UK and others come before the ICJ against its wishes? The UK acceptance of the optional clause includes the reservation that it may refuse to submit to a case brought within twelve months of the acceptance of jurisdiction by a state for the purpose of pursuing a dispute with the UK.[4]

There is apparently firm UK support for adjudication by the ICJ precisely to resolve serious international conflict. So, in the context of the Nicaragua conflict, the UK representative in the UN Security Council said that all UN members should accept the compulsory jurisdiction of the World Court. The UK insisted upon the primary importance of upholding the rule of law in international relations: 'We invariably accept judgments of the ICJ in cases to which we are parties.'[5] So the official UK position is that the ICJ remains a central part of the structure of the UN as a peacekeeping organisation. There is no place for a doctrine of vital national interests, or a so-called political question doctrine, when it is a matter of deciding what is suitable for submission to the ICJ.

Later it will be seen that such categorical thinking underlay the original UK acceptance of the optional protocol in 1929, as it underlies the recent

UK *prise de position* over the Falklands dispute.[6] However, there is a very basic assumption behind the UK approach to its international legal relations which is extremely difficult to represent fairly, but which, in my view, renders the UK commitment to adjudication highly problematic. How to introduce it, i.e. within what legal categories or institutions, is not straightforward. It is no use to try to add to the British literature on the optional clause since 1945. Waldock sets the tone in examining whether and how far other countries have been willing to match the UK commitment. The danger of subjective reservations, and of the indefinite or revocable nature of the time commitments, etc, have led to a very refined analytical treatment of the nature of the optional clause.[7] Nonetheless the only really relevant observations that have been made in this context have been Jenning's remarks about the one national security reservation which the UK made to its optional clause in 1957, and for a very short time. Besides excluding hostilities, it gave to the UK the power to exclude any question which, in its opinion, affected the national security of the UK.[8] This reservation was the occasion for some especially involved comment.

Jennings began by saying that he thought the reservation reasonable as national security is a matter of which the government is the sole trustee; it is a matter on which an international court can have no useful opinion, nor is it entitled to have one. Yet this is precisely why it seems that the reservation will be unlikely to be able to stand alongside the Court's statute. This is for a double reason. The category of national security is potentially comprehensive and it is a category not capable of any kind of juridical assessment. If the reservation is void, the whole acceptance is void.[9] In my view it is possible to interpret this difficult passage as meaning that, while a national security reservation is incompatible with the juridical character of the engagement to accept the compulsory jurisdiction of the ICJ, as the tribunal exclusively competent to handle matters of a legal character, nonetheless questions of national security are not, in any case, juridical and, consequently, they are not justiciable.

This chapter will consider the possibility that the UK does not in fact, the optional clause acceptance notwithstanding, regard questions of its national security as subject to the rule of law. The basic material used to present this argument will be the UK practice of informal agreements, the implications of the official secrets debate, and, in particular, the recent legislation on that subject. The significance for international law will be considered in a case study of the House of Commons debate on the US bombing of Libya from bases within the UK. The question involved the international law relating to self defence and yet the entire extent of the relations between the US and the UK involved the 'play' of informal and therefore secret agreements and strategies for action for which the essential factual justifications were also kept secret.

The conclusion of the argument is not intended to be dogmatic. The primary point to suggest is that there are contradictions within official UK positions. How these would be resolved either in a crisis or simply when the question might be put, e.g. in arms control negotiations, is not clear. This chapter will make suggestions. At the same time a detailed consideration of the original UK acceptance of the optional clause will show that it is based on a problematic view of the nature of international law and of how far it can be taken to have developed. This in turn suggests that an effective programme for the development of the compulsory jurisdiction of the ICJ has to accept also the need to tighten up the legal foundations upon which it would resolve disputes. However, it will also be firmly indicated that, underlying the approach of the UK to questions of defence and security, there is a deeply entrenched view that these matters depend by their very nature upon the maintenance of imponderables, in particular the uncertainty which has to be inherent in the notion of nuclear deterrence. So there is a real danger that in the event of a conflict similar to those which France and the US have faced, the UK would respond in like manner. Nonetheless, this is not to doubt the sincerity of the state which began the Cold War period by invoking the jurisdiction of the ICJ in the Corfu Channel Case – the most important judgment of the court on the use of force before the Nicaragua Case.[10]

The Place of 'Informal' Agreements in the UK's Defence Policy

The interest of the theory of informal agreements is that it raises the question of whether a matter is thought juridical and so suitable for judicial review. In a recent analysis of the matter, provided by a member of the Foreign Office Legal Department, Aust points out that[11] a state in the exercise of its sovereignty is free to deny itself the advantages of concluding a legally binding treaty in order to benefit from the advantages of informal instruments. Aust discusses a large range of such agreements. Matters relating to security and defence are only one. It appears that in the latter case the simple advantage is the flexibility which comes from secrecy. So, for instance, the UK/US Memorandum of Understanding on UK participation in the Strategic Defence Initiative research programme is treated as confidential and will not be made available even to Parliament.[12]

A short review of the UK's military nuclear relations with the US will show that this particular instance is consistent with an overall pattern. Aust also refers to material which is supplementary to a treaty such as the 1963 UK/US Agreement on Polaris Missiles.[13] Article 2/2 provides for each party's representative to enter into '... such technical arrangements, consistent with the Agreement, as may be necessary'. This type of understanding goes back as far as the Mutual Defence Assistance Agreement of 27 January 1950.[14] It provides that the US will furnish such equipment, information, etc. as may be mutually agreed to assist in the production, overhaul, etc. of materials for common defence. To carry out programmes the respective governments will enter into supplementary arrangements covering specific projects, which will set out the nature and amount of the contributions to be made by each government, the description and purpose of the facilities to be established, appropriate security and proprietary rights and other details.

It is useful to give a full account of the overall shape of the military/ security agreements which have been concluded between the UK and the USA, culminating in the arrangements for the Trident system. There is an exchange of notes on the Setting up of a Missile Defence Alarm System in the UK.[15] This is intended to have the effect of an agreement within the context of NATO. At the same time there is an Exchange of Notes on the Setting Up of a Ballistic Missile Early Warning System in the UK.[16] The scheme is to be operated by the RAF in accordance with a joint plan which will be developed and agreed between the RAF and the USAF. There is also an Agreement between the two governments for co-operation on the uses of atomic energy for mutual defence purposes. This is mainly about the exchange of classified information, etc., and maintaining mutual standards of classified and secret documents.[17]

Of crucial importance for defence relations – and indeed for a definition of what is meant by the UK's independence as a nuclear power – is the agreement with respect to the Supply of Ballistic Missiles by the US to the UK.[18] The US shall supply to the UK an agreed number of intermediate range ballistic missiles and training to facilitate the deployment by the Government of the UK of the said missiles, only in the UK at such sites and under such conditions as agreed between the two governments. Ownership of the equipment passes to the UK as soon as it is in a position to man and operate the missiles. They will be manned and operated by UK personnel. The decision (esp. par. 7) to launch these missiles will be a matter for joint decision by the two governments. Any such joint decision will be made in the light of the circumstances at the time and having regard to the undertakings of the two governments assumed in article 5 of the NATO Treaty. Par. 8 of the Treaty specifies that the term missile does not mean warhead. The nuclear warheads provided remain in full US ownership, custody and control in accordance with US law. Par. 9 provides that the arrangements recorded here are consonant with the NATO Agreement and the Mutual Defence Agreement of 1950.

There is a further exchange of notes concerning the Trident System. In July 1980 the UK Prime Minister asked the US President if he would supply Trident I on a basis generally similar to that followed in the case of Polaris, with sufficient missiles and re-entry vehicles, less only the warheads themselves, enough to maintain four submarines (or five if the UK so prefers), with a close co-operation of the two governments to ensure compatibility of equipment. The successor to Polaris should be assigned to NATO, like Polaris. The Prime Minister continued: '... and except where the UK may decide that supreme national interests are at stake, the successor force will be used for the purposes of international defence of the

Western alliance in all circumstances'. The US response has been that the Polaris Sales Agreement shall be deemed to apply as well to Trident I weapons systems and all references to Polaris will be taken as references to Trident.[19]

How far do these actual treaties imply informal agreements? Clearly the two states have to agree a plan, or having agreed a plan, to observe a plan with respect to the operation of the missile warning system; they have to resolve upon or then to observe agreed procedures on joint decisions with respect to the launching of the missiles; or, perhaps most fundamentally of all, the question arises whether the nuclear military equipment provided by the US could legitimately be used for purposes quite unconnected with NATO, because a UK national interest required it? There is a definite third-party interest in how the terms of these agreements may be implemented. They provide the framework for mutual defence in the face of the threats that NATO is supposed to counter. NATO itself is supposed to complement and be compatible with the UN Charter.

This survey assumes that one may begin from the firm ground of a publicly concluded treaty. However, it is well known that one crucial dimension of UK – USA military and security relations concerns the terms under which the US enjoys the use of military bases within the territory of the UK. It is equally well known that these terms remain the subject of secret informal agreements, or perhaps merely understandings or exchanges. This issue will be the nub of the controversy in the case-study of the US bombing of Libya from UK territory. It would pre-empt this study to speculate about all the international legal issues to which this 'situation' might give rise. However, the general issue can be seen to be whether and how far the UK accepts and exercises responsibility for how its territory is used. As such the matter can be illustrated by reference to the wartime agreement on the lease of bases to the USA in the Caribbean. The agreement provides, *inter-alia*, that in emergency or war, the USA may exercise in the territories, or surrounding waters, airspace etc., all such rights, power and authority as is necessary to conduct military operations which are deemed desirable by the USA. At the same time it must show, in the terms of par. 4 of the Preamble to the Treaty, regard to the principles of good neighbourliness and friendly co-operation[20]

The Legal Basis for UK State Practice and the Official Secrets Act, 1989[21]

In the case study of the bombing of Libya another essential issue was the reliability of the evidence that Libya had been responsible for terrorist bombing in Berlin, and, as well, that it intended further bombing. Without knowing this evidence, and without knowing precisely on what understanding of international law the UK was acting, one cannot determine conclusively whether its conduct has been contrary to international law. This is not to say that the UK can successfully appeal to its own national standards of conduct to justify non-observance of international standards. However, a review of the UK understanding of the relationship of the rule of law as such to the issue of national security is bound to afford some indication of how it might behave in a crisis where international litigation was pending. At the same time it affects decisively the capacity of independent opinion to assess legally the implications of an incident such as the Libyan bombing.

So it is important to consider how the new Official Secrets Act regards official information about foreign affairs. There is an overriding prohibition of the disclosure of information from within the government service where, to take the terms of section 2 of the Act, the effect of disclosure is to damage the interests of the UK abroad or seriously to obstruct the promotion or the protection by the UK of those interests abroad. The legislation goes further and prohibits any disclosure which is likely to have any such effects. Section 3 extends the prohibition in similar terms to international relations in general. Where information relates to security or intelligence as such, the officers concerned are absolutely forbidden to disclose anything (section 1 of the Act).

It clearly remains open to the courts to review whether a disclosure is in fact likely to injure the security, defence or international relations interests of the UK. However the legislation is regarded as restrictive for reasons given by the White Paper with respect to the decision to exclude a public interest defence.[22] This demonstrates what can be meant by the view that a matter should be regarded as a prerogative of one branch of the state, the executive, rather than of the other two, and particularly, of the judiciary. Its relevance to international affairs is stressed even more by the fact that the duty of non-disclosure, with respect to international relations, extends to information provided in confidence to crown servants, from other states or international organisations (sect. 3.1.b).[23] So the Government regards it as too unclear a legal test to invite the court to ask whether a disclosure, 'likely to be damaging' in the above explained senses, is nonetheless thought by the accused to be in the public interest, e.g. to bring a certain malpractice within the Government to the attention of the public. This defence is excluded if the prosecution can show that the disclosure itself is likely to be damaging in the specific senses enumerated already. Such a weighting of public interest in favour of the executive away from Parliament – which is not a special category to which disclosures can be made – is consistent with the view that international arrangements, particularly as they affect security, are not properly to be framed in purely juridical terms.

A crucial common ground between the notion of informal agreement, which has been discussed already, and the Official Secrets Act, is the element of secrecy. Clearly, an informal agreement is a document. The White Paper[24] makes clear that documents and information, as such, are not formally put under a security classification. The prosecution has to satisfy the court that damage is done to elements of security, defence and international relations. The test is, as has been noted already, stricter for security than it is for the other two headings and this applies to 'documents' as well. So sect. 1.4.b refers to information or a document which falls within a class or description of information, disclosure of which would be likely to have a damaging effect on the work of, or of any part of, the security and intelligence service. As already noted, even this does not have to be proved if the defendant is a member of these services. The test in the other two cases is more mild. It refers to information or a document the disclosure of which would be likely to have a damaging effect (sects. 3.2.b and 2.2.c). However, it has to be stressed how broadly defined is the concept of harm and that there is no general public interest defence. So it would be criminal to be responsible for the disclosure of any document which would be likely to prejudice the capability of, or of any part of, the armed forces of the crown to carry out their tasks, etc., or quite literally, would be likely to damage the interests of the UK abroad, or would obstruct the promotion or protection by the UK of those interests, or would be likely to endanger the safety of British citizens abroad (sect. 2.2.c; 3.2.b).

The White Paper says[25] that it is possible to argue a public interest element, but it must be within the above tests. It excludes the possibility that an independent element be considered, for example that secrecy is being used to conceal misconduct or malpractice within the government, or in any other conceivable sense.[26] It would not now be possible to argue that observance of international standards or the protection of, e.g. rule of law standards within the UK, were relevant to the criminality of conduct, if it would be argued that the conduct was still likely to prejudice the factors or elements already outlined.

The US Bombing of Libya from the UK.

The terms under which the UK Foreign Secretary said the US might use the UK to bomb Libya take, once again, the shape of an informal agreement.[27] In the course of concluding the emergency debate on the subject in the House of Commons on 16 April 1986, he declared (col. 955, Hansard) that specific conditions had been imposed on the US action, with very strict rules of engagement, with very specific Libyan targets demonstrably involved in terrorist activity. However, when these remarks gave rise to the optimistic response that there was clearly in existence a published agreement, the Foreign Secretary replied that (col. 957) it was not a question of a publishable agreement but a series of exchanges between the UK Prime Minister and the President of the USA.

Throughout this debate the Government came back to a basic point that disclosure of precise information would jeopardise the security services. So the Prime Minister said that to demonstrate that Libya was involved in attacks on the US would mean referring to secret intelligence and would thereby jeopardise sources (cols. 876–7). This reasoning is very similar to that part of the White Paper which prohibits security disclosures in absolute terms. The reasoning for the absolute prohibition on disclosure is that to have to demonstrate in court that disclosures do or are even likely to damage the security services exposes these services.[28] The element of secrecy also extended to the vital question of the legal advice tendered to the Government in respect of the action taken. The Prime Minister stated that the action was within the terms of article 51 of the UN Charter and, in particular, that her legal advice was that the selection of targets was within article 51 (cols. 731–2). These were parts of her response to the claim of Dr Owen that, under the Charter, the government had an obligation to prove that the terms of article 51 had been fully observed and to produce the relevant evidence before the Security Council (col. 725).

St John Stevas stated with confidence that if the Prime Minister had been advised by those who know more about legality than he did, that there would be a clear breach of international law, then she would never have given her support for the action (col. 901). Yet the most penetrating legal objection was made by Dr Owen, to the effect that article 51 could only be satisfied if we could produce concrete evidence that without an air strike there would be planned raids in the future, putting our citizens, and those of the US or others, at risk. He did not believe we could show there had been a taking out of a camp containing terrorists who were due to leave Libya on terrorist activities. Yet only this would justify the claim for the use of article 51. The Prime Minister, he argued, had not given the technical grounds for her decision (col. 943). The concluding response of the Foreign Secretary is not without interest and may give some indication of the legal advice which the Government had received.

The right of self-defence is not defined in article 51. The article recognises the right as inherent and it does not have to be seen as a passive right. The right of self-defence includes the right to destroy or weaken one's assailants, to reduce his resources and to weaken his will so as to discourage and prevent further violence (col. 954). This is a remarkable definition of self-defence and, not to overstate the case against the UK policy of secrecy, it might be suggested that it does cover every action which the US took in Libya and thereby provides a standard of conduct which might be challenged in an international tribunal against the actual hard facts concerning what the US did in the event.

Nonetheless there is still complete uncertainty about the exact terms under which the US took its military action, i.e., not merely what it might have been allowed by the UK to do, but whether UK permission was even required. Once again, this does not affect the UK's international legal responsibility towards a country such as Libya. However, it does give a strong indication of how far the UK is willing to allow such an incident to be brought under the rule of law and under independent judicial or other critical review.

It is common ground that there is an agreement on military bases between the UK and the US and that it is secret. In the House of Commons debate the question was whether the agreement provided for joint UK – USA agreement on the use of the bases. The former Prime Minister Heath (the assumption being that only Prime Ministers know the terms of the agreement) affirmed that the UK Premier had a right of veto (col. 893). Former Premier Callaghan agreed. However, Benn insisted on putting the question, 'Why are we not allowed to know the conditions under which this country could be taken into war by a Prime Minister using the Crown prerogative?' If a Prime Minister had refused consent, he enquired, is there provision that when there is an overriding American national interest, British agreement is not required? (col. 905).

In the *Guardian* newspaper of 19 April 1986 there was a note on the intervention of Heath in the debate of the 16 April. It was stated that there was a special secret annex to the agreement signed thirty-five years ago that the consent of the UK was needed before British bases were used in an emergency. Also, by the terms of a second secret annex, the right existed for the UK to terminate the base agreement. Officials were supposed to be saying that the word 'veto' was not in the agreement, but that the use of the bases depended upon a British decision. A former Minister of Defence is reported to have said in 1983 that the successive agreements between Presidents and Prime Ministers had been kept secret partly to discourage other countries, including West Germany, from demanding similar deals. The published formula, which stated that the use of bases would be a 'matter for joint decision in the light of the circumstances prevailing at the time' was left deliberately vague, mainly to satisfy the US Congress and to avoid constitutional problems for the US President as Commander-in-Chief. However, there were expressed doubts about the status of the agreement, and its binding character in a time of crisis. Like Britain, successive US Governments have refused to clarify its nature and have denied in public that it gives the UK the right of formal veto.

The conclusion of the study of this case, following on an examination of the pattern of informal agreements and the scope of the new Official Secrets Act, is the startling one that the state practice of the UK is, in a very significant respect (i.e., the special relationship with the USA), not at present amenable to the rule of law, whether at a national or an international level. This is not to say that in the event that the UK was called before the ICJ it would hesitate to disclose the nature of its relationship with the USA or that it would conceal the facts which it considered the justification for its own conduct or for that of its ally. However, the confidence which its acceptance of the optional clause jurisdiction might inspire in the international community is not unqualified.

The History of the UK Acceptance of the Optional Clause Jurisdiction
of the ICJ and Terms for its Improvement

When the UK became the first major power to accept the optional clause in 1929 this represented a definite commitment of the new Labour Government precisely with respect to the adjudication of issues of major military and strategic significance, within the context of a now fully developed international legal structure and organisation. The history of the UK attitude to compulsory jurisdiction at the time of the Versailles Peace Conference has been covered recently. The UK did not wish to see the friction which had focused upon the interpretation of maritime belligerent rights – a crucial military question during the First World War – submitted to independent international adjudication.[29] The issue was precisely that an international court would adjudicate upon a matter at a time of 'greatest national peril' and Britain would have to choose between losing the war or defying the court.[39]

In its memorandum to Parliament in 1929 the Labour Government confronted directly the military concerns which had been expressed at the end of the war. It reasoned that article 2 of the Kellog – Briand Pact insisted exclusively on the pacific settlement of international disputes but provided no method of achieving it. So for justiciable disputes, the UK saw acceptance of the optional clause as the logical consequence of the acceptance of the Pact. If the legal renunciation of war was to be fully effective it was necessary to accompany it with definitive acts providing machinery for the pacific settlement of disputes – for all justiciable disputes. The idea of the UK initiative was to stimulate other countries, and it was noted that during the last League Assembly, Czechoslovakia, France, Italy, Latvia, Nicaragua, Peru, Siam and all the dominions had followed suit.[31]

It is clear that the Government retained the principle that only justiciable disputes should be submitted to law. The declaration of acceptance affirms that disputes which are really political in character, even if juridical in appearance, should go first to the League Council, but this is for a limit of not more than a year. A political forum might have the 'first bite', but, in the final analysis, the legal issue would have to be determined by a legal tribunal if the controversy continued. The Government was very impatient of argument about the deficiencies of international law. To say that one should postpone acceptance of the optional clause until codification removed all uncertainties in the law would be to wait for an indefinite time. In any case, codification is a continental rather than Anglo-Saxon way of developing the law. The Government believed that the method of building law by judicial decisions, as the common law has been produced, is more suitable for some branches of international law.[32]

Despite the reservations and perhaps lack of clarity about the notion of justiciable disputes and about the general state of the law, the Government dismissed as completely obsolete the unease previously felt about the belligerent maritime law. The issue could only arise if the country challenging Britain has also signed the optional clause, which would mean that it was a member of the League. There are clear disputes about the relation of belligerent to neutral rights with little prospect of codification, but this discussion supposes that war itself is legitimate as an instrument of national policy, and that a neutral is equal as to either belligerent. With the Covenant and the Pact this is no longer true. Neutrality is excluded by article 16 of the Covenant and states may not aid an offender against the Covenant. There follows an absolutely crucial assertion which demonstrates the view still held by the UK, that the World Court is a primary means for the peaceful settlement of disputes. It was considered inconceivable that the League and the Pact would fall, leaving as the only instrument binding upon the UK, the Optional Clause.[33]

Given the apparent contradictions in the UK's present attitude to the rule of law and the use of force it is thought worthwhile to note the contemporary expression of dismay which came from Prof. Pearce Higgins in Cambridge at the apparent disregard by the Government of the whole character of international law, which had not in fact changed substantially with the League and the Pact. Obligations in international law remain a matter of auto-determination. Article 16 of the Covenant still leaves it to each state to determine whether a breach of the Covenant has been committed. The Pact as well says, with respect to self-defence, that the state 'alone is competent to decide whether circumstances require recourse to war in self-defence'.[34] Higgins thought the banishment of the state's legal right to determine what its vital national interests required to be premature.

In another response to the 1929 acceptance of the Optional Clause, Fisher Williams objected as well to limits in the nature of international law. He pinpointed the reservation of the UK that a matter could, within ten days of being seized of the Court, be referred to the League Council for a period up to a year, after which it might go back to the Court.[35] This was presented by the Government as a conciliation procedure. However, Williams interprets it as an indication that the UK might feel, in a particular case, that it does not want to settle a dispute by law, that it would rather see the law changed. If the UK had just concluded a treaty it might be unwilling to admit that such was its real inclination. The issue of vital national interest has, in Williams' view, merely become represented in another form. If an interpretation of a treaty risks going in a particular direction, it could have vast consequences. It is this risk which the UK probably covers by allowing a reference to the League Council.[36] He considers the two venues incompatible (i.e. the Council and the Court) – that it makes no sense to go back from the Council to the Court. In his view, more indicative of the UK's true position was what it said contemporaneously at the Disarmament Conference: that treaties were not to be recommended which provided that if parties did not accept conciliation, the matter should be referred to the Court.[37]

In the post-war period, Britain did introduce severe restraints on consideration of issues relating to the use of force in its acceptance of the optional clause. The high water mark was 1957 and the present position was completely restored only in 1969. The 1957 declaration provided that jurisdiction was excepted, *inter alia*, with respect to disputes, hostilities, war and the state of war, belligerency or military occupation in which the UK was involved, 'or relating to any question which, in the opinion of the government of the UK, affects the national security of the UK or of its dependent territories'.[38] The declaration of 1958 dropped the reference to auto-determination of issues of national security, but continued the exceptions related to disputes arising out of or having reference to war, hostilities, etc.[39] The final reversion came with the 1969 declaration which has continued until the present and does not include any reference to exclusion of disputes, hostilities, etc.[40]

The review of British state practice by E. Lauterpacht in 1958 noted that the national security reservation ressembled the Connelly Amendment in the USA and the domestic jurisdiction reservations of France and India. The position as stated by the Foreign Secretary was that in matters of national security Britain had to reserve its own position as other countries did. When every Soviet bloc country and all Britain's allies so reserve their position, then so must the UK.[41] The general position remains the same but, nonetheless, the UK reversed this policy.

H. Lauterpacht's resistance to such a stance and his criticism of the first Optional Clause acceptance are celebrated history.[42] It might appear that he has had a determining influence upon what the UK sees as the significance of its acceptance of the Optional Clause, i.e., hostility to the subjectivity of many states' reservations to acceptances, and indeed disapproval of the general absence of acceptances, on the part of other states. When the UK introduced a subjective reservation to its Optional Clause reservation in 1957, in response to political pressure, this met with some academic disapproval. After the Norwegian Loans Case (in which Norway successfully invoked the French clause against France)[43] it was probably appreciated that the clause could be counter-productive as well as appearing disreputable.

However, the question remains, in my view, very open: which approach is to be preferred, that of Higgins and Fisher Williams or that of Lauterpacht and, for example, a more recent supporter, R. Higgins? For instance, in 1968 R. Higgins took up Lauterpacht's challenge in terms of a vindication of his view that the international legal order is sufficiently complete to allow the judiciary to meet new contingencies and crises. The general principles of law recognised by civilised nations can always be constructively developed.[44] The principles of law are admittedly very general, but the judiciary should follow a creative role, provided they do not go against an express rule. Indeed, it is the element of compulsory jurisdiction of the ICJ which is seen as a main hope for the radical development of the legal system (ibid.).

It is now fashionable, in the wake of the Nicaragua Case, to argue that military and defence questions, potentially very closely linked to the possibility of actual hostilities, are not suitable for adjudication. For instance, the deputy agent of the US at the jurisdiction phase of the case asserts that society tolerates judicial law-making only to the extent that political consensus supports it.[45] Adjudication is supposedly unsuited to the resolution of polycentred problems, i.e. multi-dimensional ones. Instead, executive discretion should be given full sway. It may lead to negotiated agreement.[46] He comments at length on the views of R. Higgins who, writing in 1968 had praised American jurists for taking a quite opposed position. She drew a distinction between conservative, English scholarship in international law, and a more policy-oriented American approach. The divide was between law as a matter of applying objective rules and law as decisions, i.e., decision-making by legally authorised persons in response to claims, etc., a matter of policy-orientation.[47] Norton argues that Higgins can be called in to support the thesis that there is no UN Charter (presumably legal) definition of either threat to the peace or of an inherent right to self-defence, that only the Security Council could define these.[49] Yet she insists in the same article that giving full competence, e.g. over the 1965 Rhodesia crisis, to the Security Council, does not mean the matter is inherently political.[48] For instance, the South West Africa question raises complex humanitarian issues. Yet it does not follow that the Trusteeship Council is better equipped to handle it.[50] A dispute is legal if resolved by authoritative legal decision.[51]

I agree with Norton's criticisms of Lauterpacht's view of the plenitude of international law, that his perspective is valid only if one is 'to regress to principles of such vagueness that law and equity are indistinguishable'.[52] However, this is not to take anything away from another central thesis of Lauterpacht's, that states can formulate every international dispute in legal terms. This is provided one understands the statement differently than Lauterpacht intended. The time to make the legal formulation is not when the dispute arises, but when the decision is taken to characterise a particular element of foreign relations. Decisively formulated obligations, i.e. with respect to the very serious matter in hand, can be effectively interpreted by the ICJ. What this calls for, in the case of the UK, is a revision of its treaty-making practice in matters of national security, defence and military affairs. This is what, in my view, has to be included in the agenda for discussions with the Soviets about broadening the function of the ICJ in peace and security aspects of international relations.

The question is whether the traditional debate about 'liberal', 'progressive' or 'dynamic' perspectives on the judicial function are sufficiently focused to resolve the issues raised by state practice in military and defence questions. In her study *Nuclear Arms Control*,[53] J. Dahlitz pinpoints the vacuousness of so much discussion as to whether the international legal order is a complete system of norms which the judges could complete by reference to analytical methods of legal interpretation. She criticises the failure of international legal theory to inquire into the legal implications of such state practice as the ongoing nuclear arms control negotiations. It does not come to grips with the fragile quality of international discourse on military matters.[54] In her discussion of how the Nuclear Tests Case might have been decided by the ICJ, she objects, as a matter of general principle, to the usual devices for constructing general customary law. It is simply spurious to argue that there is no difference between a state acting as if it is bound by a NAC treaty and giving its consent explicitly.[55] However clear the content of treaty rules may be in this area, there is never a sense of *opinio juris*, with respect to existing customary law, when states draft these treaties. They are simply devising methods and techniques for prescribing future conduct.[56] So whatever the support of theorists for a progressive judicial function, there is no compelling merit in leaving it entirely to the discretion of the judges of the ICJ as to whether France and China should have their own views of their national security needs predetermined by their being simply deemed bound by various treaties to which they are not parties. Dahlitz goes on to make the important general point that there is a discrepancy between the character of such contemporary disputes and 'the anachronistic and vague notions to be invoked in any judicial attempt to settle these disputes'.[57] She points to the contrived nature of the insistence upon treating article 38 of the Statute of the ICJ as affording the criteria for identifying the law applicable to a UN Charter concern, e.g. a matter of treaty interpretation being automatically a legal question, and, as such, a concern of the ICJ. It is technically true but is out of touch with the structure of the UN, i.e. it leaves an arbitrary choice to a few.[58] In particular, military questions and issues of national security are deliberately precise, while international law approaches to issues of aggression/defence and to military postures generally, tend to be diffuse, contradictory and *ad hoc*.[59]

This is to appear to leave little hope for the Optional Clause in the defence and military field. However it is another matter if states determine that a subject should be resolved judicially. So for instance, taking the example of the Hostages Case, it would be true that the ICJ is not suitable to adjudicate the overriding political considerations that may have prompted a party to conclude a NAC treaty, but one can say that unequivocal treaty commitments are justiciable even in complex and strategically sensitive situations.[60] So whatever the debate on justiciability in general, it is perfectly conceivable that the ICJ should be given the quite definite task of filling out the details of treaties where the parties have done everything possible to 'fill in the gaps' and where they intend that the ICJ should do the rest.

The problem of distrust of adjudication has to be faced, but not in terms of abstract speculation upon either the nature of the judiciary or upon the nature of the international legal order. Instead it is better to accept that there exists, at most, discrete clusters of density of legal normativity within which it may be possible to 'place' the ICJ. These discrete clusters have to be seen, as well, within the perspective of the state which one wishes to encourage to submit to adjudication. This is the way in which to approach concretely, and therefore effectively, the engagement of the UK in the adjudication of issues of defence and military security. Neither general UK attitudes to judicial settlement (which appear very positive), nor general UK attitudes to the application of the rule of law to these subjects (which appear starkly negative) should be taken as conclusive.

There is plenty of scope to criticise the attitude of a state to these subjects without committing oneself either to a world judicial state or to a licence for states to engage in auto-interpretation of utterly imprecise norms. In my view it is this false dichotomy which has dominated US state practice and official utterances in relation to the ICJ, as outlined in the review by Franck and Lehrman.[61] If it is abandoned, then one can treat the unwillingness of a state to submit to adjudication as an integral, but essentially consequential, measure of its commitment to juridically rigorous international legal relations. It has been the main thrust of this chapter to examine the record of the UK in this respect.

Conclusion/Postscript

A major part of this paper has concerned analysis of the formal, and speculation about the informal agreements concluded between the UK and the USA. Little has been said of the strategic military/political assumptions which underlie these arrangements. This would be properly the subject of another chapter.[62] However, it is worthwhile noting some remarks made by Dahlitz on the implications of a defence strategy which is based on reliance upon the doctrine of nuclear deterrence, a belief in the maintenance of uncertainty about one's intentions. Dahlitz deals precisely with this point in her discussion of the attempts of the non-aligned countries to obtain firm legal guarantees from nuclear powers to exclude the use of nuclear weapons against them.[63]

In the context of UN disarmament discussions in 1981/82, the non-aligned countries in effect raised the issue of the so-called 'flexible response', central to NATO's defence strategy, and strongly supported by the UK. The non-aligned countries wished to have defined exactly the limited circumstances in which nuclear weapons would be used. The UK gave an uncertain guarantee which it regarded as solemn, but not binding in the form of a treaty. It would not use nuclear weapons against a non-proliferation State, 'except in the case of an attack on the United Kingdom, its dependent territories, its armed forces or its allies by such

State in association with a nuclear-weapon State'.[64]

In other words, the uncertainties in what are not even legal commitments are rooted, so far as concerns nuclear weapons, in the initial political decision that national interest/security require reliance upon a preferably undefined capacity to deliver an equally undefined threat. In my view this is the more general and more profound reason why no major issue of nuclear 'defence' is likely to become justiciable without major changes in official UK attitudes to the problem of nuclear disarmament.

Notes

1 Case Concerning Military and Paramilitary Activities in and against Nicaragua, ICJ Rep. (1986) 14.

2 Nuclear Tests Case, ICJ Rep. (1974) 253.

3 Fisheries Jurisdiction Case, ICJ Rep. (1974) 3.

4 For instance, ICJ Y.B. 1985–1986, the 1969 Declaration of 1 January 1969.

5 United Kingdom Materials on International Law, 1986, ed. G. Marsten, 47 BYBIL (1986) 613.

6 United Kingdom Materials, 43, BYBIL (192) 497, where the Prime Minister said she would consider the possibility of reference to the ICJ very seriously, but that it is Argentina which makes the claim to the Falklands and must therefore make the first move to the Court.

7 H. Waldock, The Plea of Domestic Jurisdiction before International Legal Tribunals, 31, BYBIL (1954); and The Decline of the Optional Clause, 32 BYBIL (1955), 244; and J. Merrills, The Optional Clause Today, 50, BYBIL (1979), 87.

8 18 April 1957, ICJ YB (1957–58) 211.

9 R. Y. Jennings, Recent Cases on 'Automatic Reservations to the Optional Clause' 7, I.C.L.Q. 349 at 362.

10 The Corfu Channel Case, ICJ Rep. (1949) 4.

11 A. Aust, The Theory and Practice of Informal Agreements, 35 ICLQ (1986) 787, 812.

12 Ibid., 793.

13 UKTS (1963) no. 59 Cmnd 2108.

14 UKTS (1950) no. 13; and Exchange of Notes UK – USA Concerning a weapons production programme in accordance with the terms of the Mutual Defence Assistance Agreement of Jan. 27th 1950, UKTS (1962) no. 66.

15 Exchange of Notes on the Setting up of a Missile Defence Alarm System in the UK (1961) no. 65.

16 Exchange of Notes on Setting up of a Ballistic Missile Early Warning System in the UK, UKTS (1960) no. 24.

17 UKTS (1958) no. 41.

18 UKTS (1958) no. 14.

19 The British Strategic Nuclear Force, July 1980. Texts of Letters exchanged between the Prime Minister and the President of the USA and between the Secretary for Defence and the US Secretary of Defence, Cmnd 7979; and subsequent thereto, Exchange of Notes on the Acquisition of Trident I Weapons System under the Polaris 1963 Agreement, UKTS (1980) no. 86.

20 The Leased Bases Agreement 27 March 1941 (1941) UKTS no. 2.

21 The Official Secrets Act 1989.
22 White Paper, The Reform of Section 2 of the Official Secrets Act 1911, Cmnd 408, (1988) para. 58–61.
23 Official Secrets Act sec. 3.1.b.
24 White Paper, paras. 74–6.
25 Ibid., para. 61.
26 Ibid., para. 58.
27 The debate outline following is taken from Hansard, Parliamentary Debates, Vol. 95 Official Reports, 6th Series, commons 1985–86, April 8–18, numbered by column.
28 White Paper, paras. 34–8.
29 L. Lloyd, A Springboard for the Future: A Historical Examination of Britain's Role in Shaping the Optional Clause of the Permanent Court of International Justice, 79, AJIL (1985) 28, 36.
30 Ibid., 37.
31 Memorandum on the Optional Clause of the Statute of the P.C.I.J. (1929) Mis. no. 12 Cmnd. 3452 paras. 5–11.
32 Ibid., paras. 12–13.
33 Ibid., paras. 19–22.
34 A. P. Higgins, *British Acceptance of Compulsory Arbitration under the Optional Clause and its Implications,* Cambridge, 1929, esp. addendum.
35 J. Fisher Williams, The Optional Clause, 11 BYBIL (1930) 63, 76–77.
36 Ibid., 78.
37 Ibid., 80.
38 ICJ YB (1957–58), 211.
39 The 1957 Declaration was therefore replaced almost at once in the Declaration of 26 November 1958, ICJ YB (1962–63) 257, dropping the concluding reservation for any question which in the opinion of the UK affects national security, unless the case concerned matters arising before the date of the present declaration. The 1963 Declaration (27 November 1963), ICJ YB (1963–64) 239, continued the reference, in its par. V exception, to disputes arising out of or having reference to hostilities, war, state of war, or belligerent or military occupation in which the government of the UK is or has been involved, while dropping the time limit on the concluding subjective reservation, now completely abandoned.
40 1 January 1969, ICJ YB, (1968–1969) 71.
41 E. Lauterpacht, UK State Practice in Internatinal Law, 7 ICLQ (1958), 124.
42 See, *inter alia,* 10 Economica (1930) 137.
43 ICJ Rep. (1957) 9, esp. Lauterpacht, 43–66, questioning the compatibility of the reservation with art. 36 (6) of the Court's statute. The validity of the reservation was not questioned by the Court, which allowed Norway to invoke it against France, the originator of the reservation. After this case a number of states, including the UK, abandoned their subjective reservations; see also M. Akehurst, *A Modern Introduction to International Law,* 6th ed., London, 1987 p. 248.
44 R. Higgins, The International Judicial Process, 17 ICLQ (1968) 67–68.
45 P. M. Norton, The Nicaragua Case: Political Questions Before the

International Court of Justice, 27 Virg. JIL (1987) 459, 511.

46   Ibid., 513.
47   Higgins, The International Judicial Process, pp. 58–9.
48   Norton, The Nicaragua Case, p. 473.
49   Higgins, The International Judicial Process, p. 81.
50   Ibid., 82.
51   Ibid., 74.
52   Norton, The Nicaragua Case, 507.
53   J. Dahlitz, *Nuclear Arms Control with Effective International Agreements*, London, 1983.
54   Ibid., p. 69.
55   Ibid., p. 97.
56   Ibid., p. 106.
57   Ibid., p. 108.
58   Ibid., p. 128.
59   Ibid., p. 116.
60   Ibid., pp. 111–12.
61   T. Franck and J. Lehrman, Messianisme ou Chauvinisme: L'Engagement des États-Unis en Faveur de la Paix par le Droit, 31 AFDI (1985) 59.
62   See, e.g., T. Carty on the origins and legality of nuclear strategies in H. Davis, ed., *Ethics and Defence*, Oxford, 1986, pp. 104–54.
63   Dahlitz, *Nuclear Arms Control*, p. 61.
64   Ibid., 62, 65.

Part III
Current Controversies: Technology Transfer, Outer Space and Environment

12.

Transfer of Technology: Recent Developments

MARK M. BOGUSLAVSKY AND OLGA V. VOROBYOVA

Attempts to reform external economic relations are being made not only in the USSR but also in other Eastern bloc countries. All the states have pushed hard for change, albeit in different ways and aspects, because they associate it with the development of a new international economic order. So in this case we may be speaking about the restructuring of world economic relations in a broad sense. Central to the drive for Perestroika is transfer of technology, the point raised by A. V. Lowe in his chapter. In our chapter we would like to analyse some new Soviet - Western forms of partnership connected with technology transfer, encouraged, above all, by the current restructuring of Soviet economic management.

In the Soviet Union, reform is aimed at inspiring as many Soviet economic organisations as possible to partake in international economic, scientific and technological co-operation. It is expected not only to add a new dimension to the framework of traditional business deals but also to promote new forms of partnership as part of the drive to put the world-wide division of labour to the best possible advantage. In the Soviet - Western context, new partnerships may be based on technological co-operation, co-production arrangements and joint ventures.

It is a proven fact that new partnerships today depend entirely on the transfer of technology, so legal arrangements are crucial. In this article, we will focus on such arrangements. By technology transfer, we mean scientific and technical findings, including those (inventions) safeguarded by national legislation and international treaties, and also unprotected R&D results (know-how, design plans and specifications, instruction manuals, researchers' reports and other documents and information on research and development). The result of technological research and development, as understood by the authors, is a category common both to internal trade contracts and to arrangements involving scientific and technological co-operation with foreign countries.

'Know-how' is a universal term that may mean any technical or other information. In some instances, it may imply an actual invention which is deliberately kept in secrecy and is not patented, or part of an invention not included in instruction manuals. In other circumstances, 'know-how' may mean a scientific and technological achievement that cannot be patented because it fails to meet the requirements established by law. We consider 'know-how' first and foremost as the result of a research effort in technology, though the term is often used in areas other than technology.

Following the above introductory remarks, let us proceed to a review of the legal issues applicable to technology transfer as part of the aforesaid partnerships.

I

As a form of partnership, scientific and technological co-operation implies that the sides undertake research and development in line with a single, co-ordinated programme (often referred to as a working schedule) to achieve specific end results. Organisationally, joint R&D projects may assume two forms. Under the first arrangement, more common to deals between Soviet organisations and Western firms, each side undertakes a certain amount of work specified in the contract and then hands over the results to the other in exchange for a fixed sum. The sides exchange intermediate findings and in so doing arrive at the end result.

Under the second arrangement, the sides set up a group of scientists and specialists under the auspices of a national organisation to work on a joint project. Though the group may not have the status of a juridical person, with its members retaining a working relationship with the side that has delegated them to the group, it can nevertheless be regarded as an organised and separate entity working 'under one roof' and managed by a common authority appointed by the parties to the contract. Earlier, Soviet organisations never worked under such an arrangement with countries not belonging to the Eastern bloc. But several such groups have sprung up recently. Known as scientific and technological centres, they are still few in number, for which reason in this article we shall devote less attention to the latter form of scientific and technological partnership.

It is crucial to both sides to define clearly their rights to the results of research and development undertaken as part of a joint project. To this end, a clear line must be drawn between scientific and technological findings obtained by either of the sides before and after the joint project was launched.

The rights to the inventions, know-how, documents and other scientific and technological information transferred under the terms of the contract shall always remain with the transferring party. Such information is usually shared only for the purpose of co-operation as part of the contract and is not used widely inside the recipient country.

The rights of the sides to joint scientific and technological results pose a greater problem. Contracts for joint R&D projects more often than not envisage that the results of joint research and development shall be equally available to both sides, which can subsequently use them to their own advantage as specified by the contract. The scope and scale of the employment of such results by each side depends on how joint research and development results are interpreted in the contract.

It would be appropriate to note here that neither Soviet–Western nor other international deals offer a precise definition of a joint research and development result or a joint invention. This fact is mentioned, among other publications, by OMPI's manual for joint inventions.[1] Some interpretations are loose and imply everything developed by one or both parties to the contract. In other instances, the results are understood as joint developments by the specialists of both parties to the contract working on a joint project under the auspices of an organisation in the country of one of the partners.

A more commonly used legal framework is the one that envisages that each party to the contract reserves the rights to the results of scientific and technical research it sells to the other side on terms stipulated by the contract. So intermediate results are seen as belonging to the recipient party and are usually transferred for unlimited use on the territory of the partner-country. The latter has the exclusive right to use these results on its territory.

The end results are shared by both parties to the contract. The parties also share the rights to other results produced jointly by their specialists. So each party's share in the end result depends on the creative contribution (co-authorship) of its specialists to the joint project.

Soviet organisations and Western firms have not yet devised a standard framework to regulate such issues in projects undertaken by specially set-up research. However, both sides normally share all the results produced by such groups, for two reasons. First, the specialists of both parties work in close contact on one joint project 'under one roof'. Secondly, both parties finance the project on a joint basis, paying salaries to their specialists and providing equipment, instruments, materials, etc. The joint financing of the project is crucial to the recognition of all the results as being achieved corporately. Such an arrangement appears to us as befitting this form of partnership.

All questions connected with legal safeguards, if it is feasible to safeguard such results, and the use of joint results are resolved by agreement between the sides. This is stipulated in virtually all accords on joint R&D projects.

Most of the contracts concluded by Soviet organisations with foreign partners, irrespective of the criteria for recognising results as joint, contain a provision according to which each side shall legally safeguard joint inventions and other results that can be safeguarded at its own expense (usually in the name of both partners) and on the territory of its country, and is entitled to use these joint results on the aforesaid territory without any restrictions or commissions due to the other partner.

As for the protection of joint inventions and other protected property in third countries, the sides must agree who should carry out patent coverage in which countries, in whose name such coverage should be registered, and how they should share patenting expenses. The sides should also agree on a number of other issues related to legal safeguards in third countries.

In determining specific terms for using joint results in third countries, the sides may in particular agree either that they shall jointly share the returns on utilisation, or divide the territories among themselves, whereby each side receives the exclusive right to use joint results (with or without payment of part of the revenue to the other side), decide on the territories where they have non-exclusive rights, or arrive at other arrangements. Here utilisation means not only the transfer of results under license, but the export of products manufactured on the basis of these results.

The granting of exclusive rights to utilisation on a territory implies that the other party should not export to the territory in question products made on the basis of the joint results, or use them in any other way. If the right to utilisation is transferred to third persons, the latter should agree to abstain from exporting the products to those territories so as not to infringe upon the exclusive rights of the other side.

II

The issues concerning the protection of intellectual property in Soviet co-operation with foreign countries in fundamental research are very specific. Fundamental research produces scientific and technical results which can be referred to as inventions and know-how, and also scientific works protected by copyright laws. That is why co-operation in fundamental research should be covered adequately and effectively by legal safeguards of intellectual property developed or transferred in the course of such co-operation.

Measures to apply copyright laws to scientific works created as part of co-operation arrangements must be taken by the sides in compliance with their respective national legislations and international copyright agreements to which the USSR and the corresponding country are signatories. The Universal Copyright Convention is a case in point. Questions pertaining to publishing or any other use of rights should be decided on the basis of mutual agreement between the partners. If there is no other agreement, each side must have the right to a non-exclusive, non-revocable license, free from royalties due to the author, to translate, publish and circulate the published scientific or any other works within its country. Personal rights of authors should be provided for.

III

Non-disclosure arrangements are crucial to agreements on joint scientific and technical projects, as well as to other documents on scientific and technical co-operation. By vowing confidentiality, each side commits itself not to disclose any data, scientific and technical information, or results obtained during the course of a joint project. Under the terms of the contract, each side, as was mentioned above, reserves its rights to scientific and technical data, know-how, inventions and other similar results. Their transfer to the other side shall be linked to a specific purpose, while their transfer to third persons must be banned.

As far as the secrecy of joint results is concerned, restricted publications included, such commitments are undertaken to provide for the legal safeguard of results. For instance, if the essence of an invention is made public too early, this may prevent it from being patented. The sides can stipulate in their contract that they shall exchange scientific and technical information on the assumption that information on scientific achievements can be disclosed only after applications for patents or other documents ensuring legal safeguards have been submitted.

International scientific and technical co-operation is sometimes accomplished with the following condition: the sides commit themselves to take every precaution against premature disclosure of information about the scientific and technical results of their joint developments (by publishing, transmitting over radio and television, or exhibiting displays, etc.), to preserve the right to patent coverage of joint inventions and other industrial property.

Contracts signed by Soviet organisations with capitalist companies feature detailed confidentiality clauses. They stipulate, among other things, that the personnel employed by the two sides shall undertake not to reveal information to third persons, that the results obtained shall be made public only by mutual agreement, etc. Confidentiality obligations must be thoroughly elaborated, in order to rule out any chance of violation.

In this context, the following recommendations can be made. First, it is recommended that the contract pledge each party to keep secret the data made available by the other. This commitment should apply to every area of co-operation for a certain period of time, say ten years following the start of co-operation. The parties may extend this period if necessary.

Second, it would expedient to ensure that neither party should allow scientific or technical publications to carry the information on co-operation made available by the other party except in cases when both parties shall find this necessary. The parties' publications based on their own work must not contain information, the publication of which may violate the confidential nature of collaborative activities. Given the risk of secrets being revealed, the parties must hold consultations concerning such publication.

Third, it is possible to make the following provision: if either party obtains findings that may warrant application for inventors' certificates and finds it useful immediately to inform the other party of this in order to expedite collaborative activites, it should request the other party to confirm in writing the advisability of making these findings available. In agreeing to receive these findings, the other party shall not use them in its patent applications and shall take the appropriate measures to ensure that these findings remain confidential until publication.

Fourth, it may be agreed that if either party proposes widening co-operation to include an area which is the subject of a patent application of the other party, then the latter, upon agreement, shall pass on the necessary information contained in the patent application and in other materials. Meanwhile, the party which has received the information shall keep it secret until publication by the patent-holding party.

IV

Of special interest are legal issues relating to the transfer and use of technology in connection with the formation of joint ventures in the Soviet Union. These issues are not unknown to the Western business community, which has had experience in handling them.[2] The Soviet side, though, is taking the first steps in this area.

Soviet legislation (USSR Council of Ministers Resolution No. 49, passed 13 January 1987) on joint ventures seeks such measures as would attract advanced foreign technology, know-how, and managerial exper-tise to the Soviet economy – as one of the aims of joint ventures in the Soviet Union. Of course, the use of world scientific and technological achievements in the national economy is part of Soviet external economic strategy. But then, we should not ignore the possibility of the foreign partner being interested in pooling the scientific and technological capabilities of the Soviet and foreign partners and in using Soviet scien-tific and technological advances in a joint venture.

Such a profound form of co-operation as joint venture arrangements can go a long way towards expediting the purchasing, application and assimilation of new technology, thus improving the quality and competi-tive position of products and allowing efficient marketing. But if all these opportunities are to be turned to good account, a number of complex legal and economic issues must be sorted out in each particular case involving the establishment and operation of joint ventures.

The very first question involving technology, which arises in the course of the joint-venture drive, is about partner contributions. Under Article 11 of Resolution 49,'contributions to the statutory capital of a joint venture may include premises, structures, equipment and other material values, as well as the rights to use land, water and other natural resources, premises, structures, and equipment, and other property rights (includ-ing the rights to inventions and know-how), and cash in partners' national currencies and in convertible currencies'.

The Soviet partner's potential technological contribution may include the rights to know-how. Under some circumstances, the joint venture may receive an exclusive license to the use of know-how, or a non-exclusive license, whereby the owner of the know-how reserves the right to use it independently on the territory of the USSR. It ought to be noted that in the latter case, the Soviet partner shall, as a rule, use the know-how in its own production framework and shall not sell the right to any third party (provided, of course, that the right has not been transferred to a third party earlier).

The situation with inventions appears to be more complicated, considering the current system of authors' certificates (as of early 1989). The rights to inventions safeguarded by authors' certificates belong not only to the Soviet partner in a joint venture but also to all Soviet state-owned and co-operative enterprises and organisations, while exclusive rights to such inventions are reserved by the Soviet state. Soviet lawyers have not yet achieved a consensus on how Soviet partners to joint ventures can contribute inventions to the statutory capital, if they are not entitled to exclusive rights to the aforesaid inventions.

According to one view, draft agreements to establish joint ventures, if they regulate the transfer and use of industrial property rights, must be co-ordinated with the USSR State Committee for Science and Technlogy, or the USSR State Committee for Inventions and Discoveries. In this event, Soviet partners will not require a special permit for contributing inventions to the statutory capital[3] with the new pending legislation that will regard patents as the only legal safeguard of inventions in the USSR, this problem will no longer arise, as under the new system, Soviet enterprises participating in joint ventures will be patent holders and will therefore have the right to conclude license contracts on the use of inventions.

License arrangements will be crucial to joint ventures for which technologies will be provided by foreign partners as part of their contribution to the statutory capital. The rights to know-how and inventions may be transferred to a joint venture under license arrangements. There may be sole and non-exclusive licenses. Theoretically, if a foreign participant gets a patent for an invention in the USSR, patent rights may be fully ceded to it, but we doubt that such an arrangement will be widely practised. The value of a license to a joint venture is clear, and so its terms should be fixed either in a constitutional or special contract. It is difficult to estimate the value of such a contribution. Admittedly, in coping with the issue, one may rely on the practise of fixing a license fee.

In estimating the value of a license, one should take into consideration the value of the unit of output to be manufactured under license arrangements and the volume of output throughout the duration of the license contract. The value of the license will reflect the type of the property transferred under license arrangements and legal safeguards thereof (for example, inventions or know-how).

Other criteria used in Soviet licensing practice, such as the uniqueness of a license and its technological level, may be used for fixing the value of the technological contributions as well. It goes without saying that these questions may only be settled through negotiations.

The value of a license may be linked to a lump sum or royalties due throughout the duration of the licensed product's use. The final sum will make up the partner's contribution to the statutory capital of a joint venture.

The second issue concerning technology boils down to the fixing of the transfer terms of foreign participants' rights to scientific and technological achievements in a joint venture in operation. Arrangements of this kind should be fixed in license contracts. But such contracts should differ from conventional ones, since they will determine the framework for technology transfer from parent companies to their subsidiaries.

This in effect amounts to in-house technlogy transfer, though legally the foreign partner and the joint venture are two independent right-holders belonging to different states.

It seems, however, that in terms of the legal regulation of license operations, contracts of this kind should be regarded as applying to international technology transfer.

As regards technology transfer arrangements between a joint venture and Soviet organisations, including the participants in this venture, these are regarded in legal literature and in the Soviet legislation as internal relations regulated both by the general civil and special economic legislation.

The third question, which arises in connection with technology as regards joint ventures, is who will own the scientific and technological results produced in the course of joint venture activity, and how they can be used. Two possible answers to this question have been discussed in other works.[4] According to the first one, such property is treated as joint inventions and know-how, with all the rights resting with the constituent members of the joint venture; and the second one reserves the rights to these objects for the joint venture itself.

As per Clause 17 of Resolution No. 49, 'the rights to industrial property belonging to joint ventures are ensured by Soviet legislation, including in the form of patents. The order of transferring the rights to industrial property to the joint venture by its constituent members, as well as the commercial use of these rights and their protection abroad, shall be determined by the constitutional documents.' In our opinion, it follows from what has been said above that, first, Soviet legislation proceeds on the assumption that the rights to inventions and other objects produced by a joint venture shall rest with the joint venture itself as a juridical person, and not with its constituent members; and second, that Soviet legislation guarantees joint ventures full freedom to determine, on their own, the terms of transferring such rights to its constituent members as well as the terms for the commercial realisation of such rights.

For joint ventures likely to produce inventions and know-how, it would be feasible to regulate the entire range of issues involved in a special supplement to the constitutional documents. Special attention should be paid to the fact that a reservation was made in the regulations dealing with the operation of the system of authors' certificates in the USSR, saying that inventions produced by joint ventures can be patented. In the USSR, applications for patents are to be submitted by the author of the invention or his/her successor in interest, who should state the name of the real author (Clause 40 of the 1973 Regulations Applying to Discoveries, Inventions and Innovations). The way a joint venture can secure its own rights and interests under this regulation depends on how this problem is tackled in the constitutional documents, or in the special internal regulations governing industrial property rights adopted by the venture, or in any labour contracts the joint venture concludes with its staff. Such a contract could contain a provision specifying that the rights to inventions made by employees whilst accomplishing tasks assigned by the joint venture and related to the object of its activity are to be reserved by the joint venture.

The legal safeguards for such an invention will be different from those for inventions by the employees of Soviet state-owned enterprises, because under the current legislation (early 1989) the right to inventions shall belong to the state, whilst their authors shall be entitled to authors' certificates with all the ensuing implications.[5] Once the patent becomes the only legal instrument to protect inventions in the USSR, joint ventures will stop being an exception from the general rule for issuing patents. In our view, however, joint ventures should retain the right to use constitutional documents or house regulations, or labour contracts to deal with all issues that may arise between themselves and their employees in an invention situation.

The fourth issue to deal with, in the event of technology transfer in the setting up of a joint venture involving companies from capitalist countries on Soviet territory, is the level of technology that is turned over to the Western partner. It is a fact that licensing R&D products inevitably results in a certain lag in the technological level of the licensee. This is because most often a license is sold when the licensor has to some degree exhausted the potential of the product in question.[6] It is on the strength of this circumstance that the size of the lag acquires extreme importance. Given the pace of the modern technological advance, licensing ten-year old technology would preserve the already considerable lag of the licensee. That is why the acquisition of technology that is obsolete in terms of world standards, as part of the statutory capital of a joint venture, cannot be seen as economically effective, even if the technology transferred is more advanced than that available in the licensee country.

Mention should be made of restrictive measures being taken by Western countries with respect to technology transfer to the USSR or other Eastern bloc countries, i.e. CoCom. While in the 1970s the CoCom list banned the export of such products and technologies to the Eastern bloc that had to do with weapons, in the late seventies and early eighties the list was significantly extended to include so-called 'dual goods', or the state-of-the-art technologies available in a number of the leading industries. As of now, they incorporate all high-tech products and advanced technologies. The measures taken by CoCom have precipitated a situation whereby the Western partners not infrequently cannot transfer their most advanced technology as part of their contribution to the statutory capital of joint ventures set up on Soviet territory.[7] For their part, the Soviet partners find themselves faced with the need to be cautious with respect to the technologies that are offered by their Western counterparts. In addition, it would be expedient, in our view, for Soviet legislation to contain minimal requirements for the level of foreign-bought technologies (in particular, those contributed as part of the statutory capital), and establish effective state control.

Summing up, it should be noted that the heavy restrictions on technology transfer to the USSR and other Eastern bloc countries can in no way promote the progress of economic, scientific and technical co-operation, joint ventures included. It takes an adequate economic and legal framework to promote such co-operation, and it must be devised both by the Soviet side and the foreign partner-countries. The Soviet Union since 1986 has adopted a number of regulations as part of the drive to provide the most favourable conditions for all sorts of external economic links. In particular, all Soviet state, co-operative, public and other organisations feeling they could offer internationally competitive goods and services have been allowed to do business with foreign partners on their own. Any deals involving technlogy transfer are not an exception. Although the transfer of Soviet technology and other results of scientific and technological activity to foreign countries is to be controlled by the state through a licensing procedure in 1989–90 (meaning that each export offer requires permission from the USSR State Committee for Science and Technology), it does not imply any pre-arranged restrictions on transfer of any Soviet technologies. Also, the Soviet Union has simplified the procedure of joint-venture creation, granted companies more autonomy in organisational and economic decision-making, offered tax breaks, and is now looking for ways to overcome outstanding operational issues.[8]

By contrast, the Western nations have so far not taken any tangible steps towards encouraging co-operation with the Soviet Union, in particular, abolishing, if only partially, restrictions on advanced technology exports to the USSR. This will undoubtedly contain the opportunities inherent in expanding business links between Soviet organisations and Western firms.

Notes

1 *Manual for Joint Invention Activity*, Geneva, OMPI, 1984, paras. 24–6.

2 For recent publications see *International Joint Ventures* by J. Dobkin, I. Burt, M. Spooner and K. Krupsky, Washington, 1986.

3 For details, see 'Joint Ventures and Industrial Property' by Olga Vorobyova, in the collection of articles on *Legal Status of Joint Ventures in the USSR*, Moscow, 1988, p. 114 (in Russian). A similar approach is to be found in the article 'Safeguards for Joint Venture Industrial Property Rights – Inventions, by Zavyalova and Matveyev, 1988, No. 10, P. 14.

4 See Olga Vorobyova, ibid., p. 118.

5 See *Joint Enterprises, International Associations and Organisations on the Territory of the USSR: Normative Acts and Commentaries*, Moscow, 1988, p. 223.

6 It is, of course, not the only reason inducing the owner of advanced technology to seek an export licence. The motives and objectives of licence trading have been sufficiently described in numerous writings on licence business by economists and lawyers throughout the world.

7 The issue is analysed in more detail in the chapter by A. V. Lowe.

8 See Resolutions No. 1405 of 2 December 1988 (Collection of Soviet Government Resolutions 1989, No. 2, Article 7) and No. 203 of 7 March 1989 (*Ekonomicheskaya Gazeta*, No. 13, 1989) by the USSR Council of Ministers.

13.

Some Observations on Transfer of Technology

VAUGHAN LOWE

The chapter by Mark Bogulslavsky and Olga Vorobyova on 'Transfer of Technology: Recent Developments' gives a lucid account of the new legal mechanisms for the transfer of technology between Western firms and the USSR. The importance of technology transfer to the Soviet economy, and the reasons for which it is sought, have been discussed in detail elsewhere, and will not be treated here.[1] East – West Industrial Co-operation is not a new phenomenon, although the forms which it takes are changing.[2] It has been estimated that in the recent past over 80 per cent of industrial co-operation agreements between the USSR and the West took the form of co-production or specialisation agreements (in which each party was responsible for the manufacture of some part of the final product), or in the simple delivery of plant or equipment; licensing, joint ventures and joint products were relatively uncommon.[3] The new Soviet measures envisage a shift towards joint ventures and licensing, which is invaluable if the transfer of technology is to be enhanced.

The mere selling of advanced equipment does not transfer technology. The buyer of a sophisticated personal computer may be quite unable to take it apart and discover how it works, and even if it were possible to copy each of the components, it is a very long way from the stage of being able to copy components one at a time to being able to engage in large-scale commercial production of the whole machine. That last stage, which would permit competition with the manufacturer, depends primarily not upon knowledge of the technical specifications of the product, but rather upon know-how and experience in the manufacture of the components and the assembly and marketing of the machine. In most cases, it is this know-how and experience which converts a theoretical breakthrough into a commercially profitable innovation. This is the difference between selling or allowing others to use advanced equipment, which tends to perpetuate dependence, and, on the other hand, transferring commercially valuable technology to them, which breeds independence. While Western firms will always be pleased to sell their goods, they are less likely to want to equip others with the means of competing with them and taking customers away from them.

This is generally true even where the Western firms license a Soviet undertaking to produce goods. As Bogulslavsky and Vorobyova note, licences are often sold only when the licensor has largely exhausted his own ability to profit from the exploitation of the licenced technology by making the goods himself. Admittedly, this is not invariably the case; foreign firms may enjoy access to local resources and markets in a way which makes licensing a more profitable way of entering that market than attempts to establish a manufacturing plant in the country or to export the goods to it. There can be little doubt, for instance, that for a Western firm successfully to penetrate the Soviet market for consumer goods, collaboration with those who know and understand at first hand Soviet tastes and susceptibilities is indispensable, and licensing may be the best way of securing this collaboration. But even here the licensor may well insist that the licensee does not try to export his production of the licensed goods to markets where the licensor (or another of his licensees) is actively marketing similar products. Moreover, there is usually a premium value attaching to new technology by reason of its scarcity: for any firm possessing it, its value is likely to be greater the fewer the competitors who have access to it. This, too, will tend to lead firms to adopt a cautious licensing policy, preferring to license those who will pay most for the licence and compete least with the licensor.

The crucial importance of know-how in the commercial exploitation of new technology, noted above, means that a simple licence may be ineffective as a vehicle for the transfer of complex new technology. If the technology is to be successfully integrated into the licensee's commercial and industrial processes it may need to be accompanied by a continuing collaboration, under which the licensor assists the licensee with the training of workers and the development of the licensed technology for the licensee's particular purposes and agrees to provide the licensee with any improvements and know-how which will assist with its exploitation. The transfer of improvements and know-how may be a two-way obligation: the licensee may, through his experience of operating the new technology, himself make significant improvements of value to the licensor. The system of royalty payments encourages such a continuing relationship; when he is paid a share in the profits, the licensor has an incentive to assist the licensee in making the fullest and most profitable use of the technology.

This kind of collaborative relationship best facilitates the international transfer of commercial and industrial technology. The new measures in the USSR, which mirror the legal devices which have long operated in Western countries in order to bring together technology and capital or other prerequisites for the effective exploitation of technology,[4] should assist this process.

The acquisition of technology must be seen as only the first step in the transfer of technology, if that transfer is to realise its full potential for contributing to the economic development of the USSR. Transfer must be accompanied by the absorption of the technology by the economy, and by its diffusion throughout the economy. There is little point in acquiring the patent licences and associated know-how to engage in the commercial manufacture of semiconductor chips if the economy cannot provide skilled labour or raw materials or other components of the necessary quality and in sufficient quantities at the right times and in the right places. Like a transplanted organ rejected by the body, the technology will fail to be absorbed into the economy and will not fully serve the function for which it was acquired. Similarly, even if these needs are met and the technology is successfully absorbed and exploited by the undertaking, the social benefit of buying the technology is not fully realised unless the technology and the experience gained in using it is diffused throughout the economy. It needs to be passed on (as far as it can be, within the limits of the parties' legal obligations) to other undertakings in the State. Ensuring such diffusion of the technology is a task quite as important as its initial acquisition. When such matters are attended to, the selective importation of foreign technology can have an enormous impact upon the domestic economy. The experience of Japan, which built much of its post-war economic revival on a careful and discriminating policy of buying in Western technology, is an indication of what can be achieved in this way.

Up to this point the focus has been economic. But it is not only legal and economic obstacles which have impeded the growth of East – West trade. A major factor has been the deliberate policy of Western States of denying advanced 'strategic' technology to the USSR and its allies. This policy was initially conceived as part of the strategy of the political and economic 'containment' of the Soviet Union, proposed in the famous 'Kennan telegram' of 1946.[5] It led in 1949 to the establishment of CoCom, a secretive organisation based in the US Embassy in Paris, which co-ordinates the Western embargo on trade in strategic goods with the Eastern bloc and other countries.[6] Its aim is to prevent the acquisition by certain States of technology which might contribute to their military development in a manner adverse to the security interests of the USA and its allies. Technology, in this context, includes both technical knowledge and know-how, and goods from which such knowledge may be acquired or which might make an immediate contribution to another State's military potential.

The great difficulty which CoCom and other administrators of exports controls face is in deciding what technology is militarily valuable and what is not. During the last thirty years most of the major developments in weaponry and other military equipment have not arisen through improved explosives or other specifically military material but through developments in electronics and engineering techniques of kinds which find ready uses in civilian industries. It is not possible to draw a line between military and civilian technology, where the most advanced technology is concerned. Inevitably, there is an ever-present risk that the transfer of technology to the USSR intended for civil purposes will be prohibited, or the export of spare parts for previously exported equipment blocked, because of the military potential of the technology. The magnitude of that risk will vary to some extent according to the state of East – West relations, and in particular with the foreign policy of the USA. It will also be greatly affected by the extent to which the West believes that the USSR has already developed similar technology: there is little point in banning on security grounds technology already possessed by the USSR. But there is no foreseeable possibility of all the CoCom controls being removed.

The position is complicated by the fact that the CoCom controls are not directly operative but must be implemented in the laws of each of the Member States. Quite apart from the possibility of divergences in the detailed regulations adopted by each State, a particular problem is created by the US legislation on the matter – the Export Administration Act. That Act forbids the export of goods on security grounds, but in an exceptionally wide fashion. It applies not merely to goods, but to 'technology' including, for instance, know-how and technical data, and even the expertise of servicing engineers. Moreover, the Act applies not only to exports from the USA but also to exports from other States of goods and technology of US origin, and also to exports of embargoed goods or technology, whether or not of US origin, by any person subject to US jurisdiction. The latter phrase is interpreted so as to include foreign firms owned or controlled by a US parent company. Thus, the export of goods made in the UK by a British company, but containing a certain proportion of US components or technology, is covered by the Act, as is the export of any goods by a British subsidiary of a US company. British exporters must check that their proposed exports conform, not only with British law, but also with US law. In cases where British law allows the exports, they may nonetheless be forbidden by US law, because the US lists of embargoed goods have tended to be longer than the lists in other CoCom States. The penalties under US law are too great to be ignored; the British firms have little choice but to comply with them.[7]

This problem is exacerbated by the fact that US export controls do not provide merely for the blocking of exports on security grounds. There are in fact three grounds for the blocking of exports under the US Export Administration Act. In addition to the control of exports on security grounds, export bans may be imposed in order to stop the outflow of goods in short supply in the USA. More importantly, bans may be imposed 'to the extent necessary to further significantly the foreign policy of the United States or to fulfil its declared international relations'.[8] Thus, even goods and technology of no military importance whatsoever may be embargoed, if US foreign policy so requires.

These problems were strikingly demonstrated during the 'Pipeline' affair of 1982. After the declaration of martial law in Poland (for which the USA blamed the Soviet Union), the US authorities imposed economic sanctions on the USSR in the form of a ban on exports of a wide range of goods to the USSR. Difficulties arose when the USA tried to compel European companies to comply with the export ban, and to prevent them from fulfilling the contractual obligations which they had undertaken to deliver equipment to the USSR for use in the construction of the Siberian gas pipeline.[9] The equipment which the European companies had contracted to supply was of no military importance; the US controls were imposed on foreign policy, not security, grounds. The equipment was being exported from Europe, not from the USA, but because the companies were using US technology the exports were (in the eyes of the US authorities) subject to US law. The move aroused great indignation in the European countries concerned. It was observed that not only were the exports at all times lawful according to the laws of the European States concerned, but they were lawful under US law at the time that the contracts were made. The US was attempting to impose a retrospective ban, forcing the European companies to break their contracts with the USSR simply in order to underwrite a sanctions policy which was not even accepted by the other members of CoCom. The US action was regarded by the European governments as an exercise of exorbitant extraterritorial jurisdiction unjustifiable as a matter of international law,[10] and this is surely correct. While the CoCom bans cannot, in the absence of any legal obligation to allow free trade with other States,[11] be said to violate international law, the extrateritorial application of unilateral US measures to persons and transctions outside the USA plainly involved in at least some cases an assertion of jurisdiction to which the USA is not entitled.[12]

The US failed in this attempt to impose its laws on European businesses because of the resolute opposition of the European governments and of the EEC. Some of those governments used domestic legislation to compel their companies to disregard the US export ban and to fulfil their contractual obligations. Indeed, in the UK the startling position arose in which it was made a criminal offence for the British companies affected by the ban to comply with the US law.[13] Situations in which one NATO State makes it a criminal offence for its citizens to comply with the laws of another NATO State are unusual, and the episode highlights the persistent tension within CoCom over the proper scope of the embargo. The tensions remain. Although CoCom meetings after the 1982 'Pipeline' affair resulted in a rationalisation of the list of goods embargoed on security grounds, which is now subjected to regular revision, there is still disagreement over the proper extent of the list. Moreover, the USA still maintains its claims to regulate exports from other States, where the exports embody US technology or are made by US companies or subsidiaries. Nonetheless, the underlying policy of denying militarily valuable technology to the USSR and other States remains unchanged, and is likely to remain unchanged for the foreseeable future. Only in the case of export bans imposed on foreign policy grounds (such as the ban in the 'Pipeline' case) is there likely to be a relaxation of Western policy in the foreseeable future.

This is not a problem only for the USSR, which may find supplies blocked. It is a problem for the most willing Western exporters, since they too run the risk that they will be instructed by their own (or the United States') government to withdraw from eastern European markets. Some Western firms have decided that the administrative burden of compliance with Western export controls and the risk of trade being interrupted by revisions of the embargo lists are too great for it to be commercially practicable for them to operate in trade with the Eastern bloc. Customers, too, fear the interruption of supplies, and are turning to suppliers in States which adopt more relaxed export control policies. This imposes a real cost on Western economies. The US National Academy of Sciences estimated that the maintenance of the export controls was costing the US economy alone $9 · 3 billion and 188 000 jobs.[14] No matter how easy the new Soviet measures make it for Western firms to enter into commercial relationships with Soviet undertakings, the increased transfer of advanced technology will remain dependent to a considerable degree upon the policies of Western governments.

There are signs of enthusiasm for the opportunities which the new laws have created. At the end of 1988 at least four joint ventures with UK firms had been registered with the Soviet authorities, and around forty other British applications were in the pipeline; and the UK is regarded by the USSR as having been rather slower off the mark than other Western countries.[15] This development should be warmly welcomed. Joint ventures offer a vehicle for *detente* of almost unique importance. They establish close collaboration, where opportunities arise daily for the fulfilment of promises, or the defeat of expectations by defaulting contractors or bureaucratic obstruction. Moreover, their success can in part be measured in the precise language of profits and losses. In addition, as time goes on they should produce an increasing degree of interdependence and community of interest between East and West. Perhaps, above all, they create an opportunity for changing the perceptions of those outside the charmed circle of government, of the political situation in Europe. The Soviet measures have a great significance as far as the peoples of Eastern and Western Europe are concerned. However, the question which must be asked in the context of this collection of essays is, do the new Soviet moves amount to a restructuring of international law on technology transfer? What is their significance for the rest of the world?

However their global significance might be described, the Soviet initiatives do not amount to a restructuring of the system for the international transfer of technology. The measures do not seek to establish any novel principles or ways of securing the international transfer of technology, or of subordinating the exploitation of private technology to global social goals. From the point of view of the States of the Third World, the USSR has simply joined a club of industrialised countries, in which technology is freely exchanged and traded.[16] Indeed, the success of the Soviet initiative from the point of view of the Western partners is likely to be inversely related to its radicalness; Western firms and governments will be best pleased if technology transfer and joint ventures in the USSR turn out to operate in the same way as, say, similar transactions between the UK and the Federal Republic of Germany. Whatever dim hopes the Third World might have had of the USSR leading a campaign for new principles on technology transfer, of the kind envisaged in the New International Economic Order, must have evaporated.

For the remainder of this chapter I want to address some of the underlying issues concerning the international transfer of technology. For the sake of clarity the remarks will be directed to intellectual property rights, and chiefly to patents. They are, however, broadly applicable to all kinds of intellectual property of industrial value, and to 'know-how' which, while not amounting to property in the strict sense, achieves an analogous position by restraints upon its use secured by contractual arrangements.

Intellectual property rights are temporary monopolies granted by the State to inventors (or, more often, to their employers) in return for disclosure of the invention. The monopoly allows the proprietor, or those he has licensed to exploit it, the right to charge higher prices than would obtain under free competition, were competitors who had not incurred the development costs of the innovation allowed to exploit it freely. The monopoly is considered necessary in order to allow the inventor to recover the development costs and to make a reasonable profit, thus providing an incentive for further innovation. The patent monopoly, the temporary denial of the innovation to other users, and the higher prices which it may entail, are the price paid by society for access to the new technology, which will be freely available for use by all when the patent expires and which can be used (as long as it is not actually copied) as a basis for further, independent innovation even before the patent expires.

The system has disadvantages. For instance, two pharmaceutical manufacturers may each invest $10m in developing a new cure for AIDS, but only one can win the race to a patentable invention. Discounting any incidental benefits of the research, the $10m invested by the other is wasted, and the system in this sense is inefficient. Furthermore, the system inevitably tends to concentrate research in fields which will yield high profits – in pharmaceuticals, in the development of drugs for the treatment of high-income earners, for example – whereas a more comprehensive and explicit calculation of the benefits of innovation might seek to develop products for the advantage of social groups without high spending power. In addition, the intellectual property monopoly may be unfairly exploited, for the extraction of unconscionable profits, or even not exploited at all but used simply to deny competitors access to the innovation. This latter problem is addressed in most States by the utilisation of laws providing for compulsory licensing or for the control of unfair and anti-competitive practices.

The question is, how does this approach translate to the international plane? The first point to be made is that the system described above for the grant of intellectual property rights and for safeguards against their abuse is centred upon the social unit of a single State, its citizens and economy. The State grants and provides for the enforcement of the monopoly by the legal system; it (or rather, its citizens) pays the enhanced prices; it checks abuses by means of competition laws and compulsory licensing; it benefits from the disclosure of the innovation; it benefits from the encouragement of further innovation. The State takes the burden but also benefits from the system which it maintains. Abuses may be restrained in the interests of society as a whole. The inventor has to accept the restraints upon abuse of the monopoly as the price of protecting the invention. In international technology transfer between States of unequal economic development, this balancing of public and private interests does not function in the same way.

The developing States face a number of problems. They are compelled to offer strict protection of intellectual property if they are to be able to attract foreign investment, or even to win trade concessions in other fields. One of the most difficult issues in the current Uruguay Round negotiations in the GATT, prefigured in the negotiations in WIPO over the revision of the Paris Convention for the Protection of Intellectual Property, concerns the question of intellectual property rights. The USA has argued strongly for the strengthening of intellectual property rights and the establishment of internationally agreed procedures to secure their enforcement. But strict protection of those rights does not give these States the benefits which they need if they are to develop their economies into something more than a source of raw materials and cheap labour for the developed States. Moreover, many developing countries see the enhancement of their power to regulate the use of intellectual property rights through measures such as compulsory licensing and price controls as necessary steps towards the assertion of control over the development of their economies.

The developing States cannot compel firms to develop and patent technology of the kind most useful in a developing economy. Complex technology, which can only be utilised in the context of an already developed industrial economy, may be of little interest or use to them. They cannot compel firms to transfer even the technology which is developed. States compete for foreign investment and technology transfer, and will not get it unless they offer attractive conditions to the foreign firms. Developing States cannot simply take the technology, by searching through the patent registers of industrialised countries, because that would arouse the hostility of the patentees and their governments alike;[17] and in any event, the patent specifications would usually be of little use without access to the know-how and equipment to put the technology to commercial use. Even such technology as is imported may do little to develop the economy of the State. The manufacture under licence of consumer goods, for instance, may simply result in the treatment of the State as a passive market for the products or as a source of cheap labour. Expatriate workers may be imported to perform the most complex operations, and little effort put in to training the indigenous work-force. Indeed, where local personnel are trained, they may become (in the UNCTAD phrase) part of the 'reverse transfer of technology' if they subsequently leave the country to take up employment in the industrialised nations.

The ability of developing States to overcome these problems is limited. The battle to introduce a principle of compulsory transfer of technology into international law was fought in the Third UN Conference on the Law of the Sea in relation to technology for deep sea-bed mining. The Group of 77 sought the establishment of a system which would guarantee access by the International Sea-Bed Authority (an international organisation established to regulate the mining of the deep ocean bed) and developing States to the mining technology developed by the consortia of mining companies from the industrialised States. A watered-down provision was included in the 1982 Law of the Sea Convention, requiring the transfer of technology only by firms themselves exploiting the deep sea-bed under permits granted by the International Sea-Bed Authority, and only in cases where similar technology is not available on the open market. It also provides that any compulsory transfer should be made on fair and reasonable commercial terms, to be settled by commercial arbitration if necessary. Even the adoption of these moderate provisions was a pyrrhic victory. Primarily as a result of their inclusion the USA, the UK and the Federal Republic of Germany announced that they would not ratify the Convention. The time has not yet come where developing States can insist on the transfer of technology to them.

If a foreign firm refuses to licence technology to an enterprise in a developing State, or if a group of firms operate a cartel and refuse to supply technology except at an exorbitant price, there is nothing that the developing State can do to compel the transfer on reasonable (or indeed on any) terms. The accepted principles of international law do not permit the extraterritorial application of laws to punish such refusals to supply goods or services.[18] Even if such action were permissible, it is unlikely that any attempted action by the State would be effective. The imposition of a fine, which the firm might choose to ignore, would not secure the transfer of the technology. Indeed, it is likely to be counter-productive, since it would give the State a reputation for hostility to international business, deterring foreign investors.

The position of the developing State is little better when technology has been transferred to it. If the foreign firm has registered a patent in the State but is not exploiting it fully, the State might contemplate issuing a compulsory licence. But that may have little value if the firm will not transfer the know-how necessary for its exploitation. If the know-how is transferred, the exploitation of the technology may be limited by terms in the licensing contract. For instance, licences may include obligations not to use the technology except for the manufacture of limited categories of goods; or not to export any goods made under the licence; or to sell goods made under licence at a price fixed by the licensor; or to assign to the licensor all rights over any improvements to the technology. The government might threaten the use of regulatory laws, but the firm may respond by threatening to run down its operations and move its investment to another State. The State's laws might not even be relevant to the firm's strategy. For instance, prohibitions in a licensing contract on the export of goods by the licensee may be unlawful and unenforceable under the States' law. But the licensor does not need to seek the enforcement in the host State of such a contractual export ban. He can simply use his parallel intellectual property rights in the other States to which the goods are exported to prevent their entry into those States.

In short, as has been observed, the filing of a patent in a developing country is in effect a way of giving the proprietor the right to licence imports of the protected goods or processes into the country and to control the use of the technology there.[19] A crucial part of the public function of economic planning is usurped by private, foreign interests. But that is the reality of economic power.

That is not to say that all developing States will always be unable to regulate the exploitation of intellectual property rights. Some, notably the Latin American States, have achieved a degree of success in this regard.[20] Nonetheless, the internal logic of the system tends to work against, rather than for, the interests of developing States.

Developing States need to grant intellectual property rights in order to attract foreign investment. Those laws advance the same interests as do equivalent laws in industrialised States. They reward the inventor with the grant of a monopoly. They encourage innovation. But in the cases with which we are concerned here the inventors are not indigenous; they are foreign firms. Some or all of the rewards, depending on the nature of the State's taxation and exchange control laws, will be taken out of the economy and transferred abroad, to the industrialised homelands of the multinational firms. The social benefits which offer a justification of the intellectual property system in a national context will not necessarily go to the State which bears the burden of maintaining the system when technology transfer occurs in an international context. The further innovation which is encouraged will take place largely in those industrialised nations. The new inventions will start off the cycle once more, as the developing States ask if the firm will transfer the invention to them, and if so, on what terms?

The fundamental reason for this is simple. Within a single State the possession of property rights of all kinds is regulated by the legal system so as to ensure that the rights are exercised consistently with what is conceived as the public interest. But there is no international public interest. There is no real sense of duty towards those living in other States. In international technology transfer there is nothing but a free-for-all, where the owners of the technology may pursue their self-interest unchecked by the kind of constraints which could be applied to them within the State in which they operate.[21]

Is it acceptable for international law to allow the persistence of a vacuum, an area of unrestrained discretion lying largely in the hands of private corporations, on the subject of international technology transfer? Is it practicable to impose constraints on the use and abuse of intellectual property rights in order to advance an international public interest? And more generally, should firms be free to invest a large proportion of the industrial research and development resources of humankind in making marginal increases in the quality of life in developed States when so much of the world lacks the ability to provide basic essentials such as water, food and housing? I do not know what the answer to these questions should be. There is no point at all in subjecting research and development to a system of controls in the global social interest if the result is that market forces lead companies to abandon research and development altogether or rely upon secrecy, rather than patent rights, to protect their innovations. On the other hand, we should regard arguments based upon the inevitability of the laws of the market place with great suspicion, especially when they lead to injustice and suffering which would not be tolerated within the borders of any civilised State.

We have outgrown the view that the primary function of international law is to preserve peaceful co-existence between States. It must go further, and make that peace tolerable for those who live in them. Famine, disease, and ecological disasters are an ever-present danger; if there is a solution to these challenges, it will require the harnessing of appropriate technology. And that harnessing will require the development of new principles which can promote the development of the kind of technology which the world needs and ensure that this technology is available to enable developing economies to evolve to meet such challenges, but without making innovation uneconomic. While the experience of the drafting of the UNCTAD Code of Conduct on the Transfer of Technology is not auspicious,[22] this task should not be beyond the imagination of the world's lawyers.

In the autumn of 1988 families throughout the world sat in front of television sets watching the spectacle of Soviet and United States men and machines struggling to save whales which had become trapped in the Arctic ice as winter drew on. In an almost mythical struggle, East and

West came together, working together to safe life as the whales tried to escape from the death which was closing in around them and find a future in the warm seas just beyond the horizon. It was a parable for our times: the two greatest powers in the world coming together in a titanic effort to overcome the forces of nature. Technology fighting to save life; technology taking the pictures to humankind all over the globe; technology uniting peoples throughout the world in common concern for the lives of other animals with whom we share this planet. And this in the same globe in which men, women and children die, daily, in conditions of wretched, abject misery for want of the clean water or simple food which technology could bring them. The facilitation of trade in technology between East and West is important; but the restructuring of the principles of international technology transfer which the world needs most urgently will come only when such outrageous contrasts are consigned to history.

Notes

1 See, for example, the series of publications of the Organisation for Economic Co-operation and Development (OECD): E. Zaleski and H. Wienert, *Technology Transfer Between East and West* (OECD, 1980); M. Bornstein, *East – West Technology Transfer: The Transfer of Western Technology to the USSR* (OECD, 1985); H. Wienert and J. Salter, *East – West Technology Transfer: The Trade and Economic Aspects* (OECD, 1986).

2 See Bornstein, op. cit., n. 1, ch. 3, 'Modes of Transfer of Technology'.

3 Ibid., p. 72. The figures relate to a survey conducted in 1983.

4 See, for example, L. Eckstrom, *Licensing in Foreign and Domestic Operations* (Looseleaf); H. Hearn, *The Business of Industrial Licensing* (1986).

5 See 'X', 'The Sources of Soviet Conduct', 25 *Foreign Affairs* 566 (1947); G. Kennan, *Memoirs: 1925–1950* (1970), pp. 547–53.

6 The States members of CoCom include the USA, UK, France, Belgium, Italy, Luxembourg, the Netherlands, Canada, Denmark, the Federal Republic of Germany, Norway, Portugal, Japan, Turkey and Greece. Measures agreed within CoCom are implemented by each State through its own export control laws. The USA has persuaded other States to adopt similar measures, in at least some cases (it is said) by threatening to block exports of US goods to those States unless they co-operated with the CoCom embargo. See further, S. Macdonald, *Whisper Who Dares: Exploring the Implications of National Security Export Controls* (1989); G. Adler-Karlsson, *Western Economic Warfare 1947–67* (1968); A. F. Lowenfeld, *Trade Controls for Political Ends* (1977); K. Cahill, *Trade Wars: The High Technology Scandal of the 1980s* (1986).

7 See, e.g., Lowe, 'Export Controls: A European Viewpoint', 3 *International Journal of Technology Management* 71 (1988).

8 Section 6, Export Administration Act, 1979. See further J. P. Murphy and A. T. Downey, 'National Security, Foreign Policy and Individual Rights: The Quandary of US Export Controls', 30 *International & Comparative Law Quarterly* 791 (1981).

9 See the Symposium on the 'Pipeline' affair in 27 *German Yearbook of*

International Law 28-141 (1984); N. R. Baratyants, 'Extraterritorial Action of the US Export Legislation', *Soviet Yearbook of International Law 1986*, 258.

10 See the Comments made by the European Community to the US Department of State on 12 August 1982: reprinted in 21 *International Legal Materials* 891 (1982).

11 Attempts have been made from time to time to challenge the export control system under the GATT; but article XXI of the GATT permits controls for security purposes, and it is almost inconceivable that the CoCom measures could be proved to fall outside any reasonable interpretation of that article. Czechoslovakia has tried, more than once, to obtain a GATT ruling that the Western embargo violates the GATT, but has not succeeded.

12 See, for example, the symposium in 27 *German Yearbook of International Law* 28-142 (1984), and R. Ergec, *La compétence extraterritoriale à la lumière du contentieux sur le gazoduc Euro-Siberien* (1984), and further references therein.

13 See the *German Yearbook* symposium, loc. cit., n. 12 above, at pp. 67-70.

14 See the analysis in National Academy of Sciences, National Academy of Engineering and Institute of Medicine, *Balancing the National Interest: US National Security Export Controls and Global Economic Competition* (1987).

15 According to the International Chamber of Commerce (British branch), *Progress Letter No. 46* (December 1988), p. 25.

16 This view has been advanced in the past, see, e.g., M. Benchikh, *Droit international du sous-développement* (1983), p. 228.

17 A dispute between the USA and Brazil, arising from the imposition of 100 per cent tariffs, worth about $39m each year, by the USA on certain Brazilian goods in retaliation for Brazil's alleged failure to pay for patented pharmaceutical processes belonging to US companies, is currently before a Gatt disputes panel. One estimate of the cost to US businesses of the world-wide violation of intellectual property rights put the figure at around $43-61bn in 1986.

18 See, e.g., A. V. Lowe, 'The Problems of Extraterritorial Jurisdiction: Economic Sovereignty and the Search for a Solution', 34 *International & Comparative Law Quarterly* 724 (1985).

19 E. Gold, 'The International Transfer and Promotion of Technology', in R. St J. Macdonald, D. M. Johnston and G. L. Morris (eds.), *The International Law and Policy of Human Welfare* (1978), 549, at 556.

20 See, e.g., G. M. Corea, 'Transfer of Technology in Latin America: A Decade of Control', 15 *Journal of World Trade Law* 388 (1981); P. Nanyenya-Takirambudde, *Technology Transfer and International Law* (1980), esp. chs. 5-10.

21 The EEC experience is instructive here. The incompatibility of restrictions on the use of technology resulting from the existence of separate national intellectual laws and from contractual constraints imposed by the proprietors has been recognised by the European Commission and Court, which have declared many of the abuses described above unlawful. What the EEC has, and the world community lacks, is a conception of a European public policy prevailing throughout the EEC, to which private interests must be subordinated.

22 See, e.g., D. Thompson, 'The UNCTAD Code on Transfer of Technology', 16 *Journal of World Trade Law* 203 (1982); *The History of UNCTAD 1964–1984* (1985), 158–69; N. Horn (ed.), *Legal Problems of Codes of Conduct for Multinational Enterprises* (1980), pp. 89–99, 177–92, 210–18, and *passim.*

14.

International Space Law: New Institutional Opportunities

ELENA P. KAMENETSKAYA

The question how to develop international space co-operation has arisen since the beginning of the space era. It seems to be symbolic that the launch of the first artificial satellite was made by the Soviet Union within the framework of International Geophysical Year – an important event in the history of co-operation among states – in which about seventy countries took part. Lately co-operation in the exploration and use of outer space has reached impressive levels. Dozens of countries are involved in space co-operation. Certain inter-governmental and non-governmental organisations and programmes concerned with space have been instituted. Co-operation in this field could, however, be more efficient if it were not for the desire of some countries to turn space into a field of military confrontation and competition. After all, the level and scale of co-operation in the exploration and use of space is sensitive to the state of the international political climate. At the same time we should not overlook the fact that the space effort is in itself an important contribution to furthering mutual understanding between people.

The co-operation of States in the exploration and use of outer space is regulated by international agreements which establish the rights and obligations of the parties, the goals of space activities and the principles underlying international co-operation itself. The legal basis of such co-operation currently includes: (a) basic principles and rules of international law, including the principles of the UN Charter; (b) basic principles of international space law; (c) special norms of international space law regulating the issues concerned with international co-operation of states in space research.

The special role played by international co-operation in space research necessitates a clear understanding of the legal content of the principle of co-operation of States in the conquest of space. This principle is contained in the Outer Space Treaty as well as other basic principles of international space law. There are diametrically opposite views in the literature concerning the understanding of this very principle: from the proclamation of co-operation in space as an unconditional duty of States, to the complete negation of the legal force of this principle.

Without going into detailed analysis of this principle it is desirable to stress the following. There are good reasons to believe that the principle of the co-operation of States in the exploration and use of outer space is just one facet of the more general principle of co-operation in international law, and that international space co-operation confirms, strengthens and develops this general principle in the sphere of relations connected with space exploration. The principle of co-operation should not be considered in isolation from other key principles of international law and space law, but presupposes, above all, the duty of States to co-operate with one another in maintaining international peace and security in outer space. In other domains of space co-operation, States should promote joint programmes and experiments in accordance with international law, i.e., they should not hamper international contacts and links in the respective fields, should not raise discriminatory barriers, and should take due account of appropriate measures aimed at the development and furthering of international co-operation. The specific areas, forms and conditions of this co-operation, as well as the rights and duties of the co-operating parties, should be regulated by special agreements.

In recent decades there have grown up certain international mechanisms for co-operation in the exploration and use of outer space. In the scientific literature the problem of the development and improvement of the forms of uniting international efforts is constantly at the centre of attention. International space co-operation is mainly effected in the traditional well-known forms. It concerns mutual bilateral and multilateral activities based on the corresponding intergovernmental and non-governmental agreements. Bilateral co-operation is the most frequently used form of uniting the efforts of countries. Different States have concluded hundreds of bilateral agreements on various problems of the exploration and use of outer space. The activities of international intergovernmental organisations are a typical form of multilateral co-operation. These organisations are making a considerable contribution to the promotion of international relations in the exploration and use of outer space. A specific form of this co-operation which differs from other forms of co-operation, not only in the exploration and use of outer space, but also in different spheres, is the co-operation of socialist states within the framework of the Intercosmos programme.

At present, countries co-operate in the peaceful exploration and use of outer space both within international organisations whose terms of reference are much wider than just space issues (e.g., the United Nations Organisation and some of its specialised agencies) and within international organisations dealing specifically with international co-operation in various areas of space research and uses of space for peaceful purposes – the so-called international space organisations, the most famous of which are INMARSAT, Intersputnik, INTELSAT and the European Space Agency (ESA). An important role is also played by non-governmental space organisations such as the Committee on Space Research (COSPAR), the International Astronautical Federation (IAF), the International Academy of Astronautics (IAA), and the International Institute of Space Law (IISL). Thus, there are many international organisations related to one or another aspect of space research. But there is no specialised universal international organisation called on to promote the co-operation of states in all the main areas of space-related activities.

Beginning from 1970 in connection with the further development of space exploration we can witness the growth of interest in the improvement of mechanisms of space co-operation. The suggestions put forward in this connection can be divided into two groups. The first group was aimed at the development of the activities of the existing organisations or at the establishment of new space organisations engaged in specific space-related problems[1] (up to now international space co-operation has been developing in this particular direction). The second group was aimed at the establishment of a universal space organisation engaged in all main areas of space-related activities.

The suggestions of these two groups seem not to exclude each other and not to contradict each other. However, it should be noted that co-operation in space is not limited to particular spheres. Besides, the problems of the exploration and use of outer space have much in common and therefore the establishment of organisations according to different directions of the conquest of outer space without a permanent centre of co-operation might complicate the co-ordination of international efforts, reduce the effectiveness of co-operation and greatly increase the expenses of the states concerned.

The earliest ideas in the literature about an international space organisation date back to the late 1950s.[2] In those days space co-operation was just beginning; there was neither a system of UN organs concerned with space, nor international intergovernmental space organisations. Therefore the proposals of those days differed markedly from those made in recent years. The latter, of course, cannot but take into consideration the fact that there are now in existence a multitude of space co-operation agreements and that the United Nations and the international space organisations make a substantial contribution to co-operation in the exploration and use of outer space.

Suggestions about the establishment of this new space organisation which were made in scientific literature[3] and in the UN[4] in the course of the last ten to fifteen years were aimed at improving the forms and methods of space co-operation. The majority of them contained only a very general reference to the advisability of having such an organisation and only very few of them provided justification for the formation of a comprehensive space organisation or general ideas concerning the objectives and tasks of a future space organisation, the structure and competence of its organs. It is worth noting here that one item on the agenda of the XXth International Colloquium on the Law of Outer Space was concerned with the feasibility of the foundation of a new space organisation.[5] The reports submitted for the Colloquium and the discussion held at it showed that there were arguments both for and against this idea. In particular, there appeared some misgivings that States, in view of the specifics of space activities, would not agree to wide co-operation, that future organisations would duplicate those already existing and that it would face serious financial problems.

The year of 1985 was marked by an event which made an important contribution to the development and promotion of institutional mechanisms of co-operation among States in the exploration and use of outer space. The first official suggestion concerning the establishment of a World Space Organisation (WSO)[6] was brought to the United Nations Organisation. This initial suggestion was made by the Soviet Union and was aimed at the development of space co-operation on a qualitatively new level. This Soviet initiative was later clarified and developed in the official letter sent in 1986 to the UN General Secretary by the Soviet Premier N. Ryzhkov.[7] The idea of setting up a WSO has resulted from a new approach to the evolution of world trends as well as from a clear understanding of the interdependence and integrity of the world. It is a recognition of the increasingly clear fact that the exploration and use of outer space is one of the contemporary global problems which can be successfully settled on the basis of mutual efforts of all States in the interests of all mankind. Global problems require the internationalisation of efforts and universal mechanisms.

The non-weaponisation of outer space and worldwide peaceful co-operation on the basis of the new approaches and forms – this is the essence of the attitude to the exploration and use of outer space within the framework of new political thinking reaffirmed by M. Gorbachev in his speech in the UN in December 1988.

The Soviet suggestion of 1986 pointed out that a WSO could facilitate the solution of the global problems of space co-operation which cannot be successfully solved on a regional or bilateral level, and provide for the access of all States to the benefits and results of space activities without discrimination and on a mutually profitable basis. The new organisation would render differential assistance to developing countries in their participation in space activities. One of the main objectives of a WSO would be the verification of international agreements aimed at the prevention of an arms race in space. A WSO would not 'abolish' the existing space organisations, but on the contrary its purpose would consist in co-ordinating their activities in the peaceful exploration and use of outer space.

In June 1988 the Soviet delegation brought before the UN Committee on Outer Space a working paper entitled 'Basic Provisions of the Charter of a World Space Organisation(WSO)'.[8] This document is an important practical step on the way to the establishment of a WSO since it covers the main provisions of the activities and functions of this new organisation. The working paper is formulated as a draft charter of a WSO. It appears to be a legal document that can give a concrete and precise answer to such important questions as the status of the new organisation, its aims and functions, the structure of its organs, its financial resources, relations with other organisations, etc. At the same time it should be noted that the submission of the draft charter does not exclude the importance of further national and international research into the ways, forms and methods of international co-operation in this field. In the Soviet Union this problem is under wide consideration. It becomes more and more apparent that the general approach consists of improvement of international co-operation, the increase of efficiency and the strengthening of economic, scientific and political benefits.

First of all the working paper determines the aims and functions of a WSO. The aim of the new organisation consists in serving as a focal point for broad international co-operation for the exploration and use of outer space exclusively for peaceful purposes; in co-ordinating efforts of States and international organisations in this field; in facilitating the access of all States to participation in space activities and the benefits derived therefrom; and finally, in verifying compliance with international agreements to prevent the extension of the arms race into outer space.

The functions of a WSO determined by its aims are to encourage all forms of peaceful space activities and international co-operation; to co-ordinate international activities in this field; to elaborate and implement international co-operation projects relating to the exploration of outer space and the practical application of the results of space activities; to launch special ventures operated under the auspices of a WSO; to provide support to states in the elaboration and implementation of their national space programes taking particular account of the needs and interests of developing countries; to create a system for the collection and dissemination of information on various aspects of space activities; to assist states in training scientific and technical space specialists, taking particular account of the needs and interests of developing countries, and to help to strengthen the rule of law in space and to contribute to the progressive development of international space law.

While analysing the aims and functions of a WSO it is necessary to note the importance of detailed aims of the organisation set out in the working paper because these provisions determine the 'face' of the new organisation. They seriously undermine the statements of those who are against a WSO saying that it will have nothing to deal with and will duplicate the activities of space organisations already existing. The functions of this WSO do not repeat those of other space organisations. As it was mentioned before, those organisations co-ordinate States' efforts in particular fields (for example, communication). The European Space Agency has the widest tasks among them, but it unites rather a small group of countries of Western Europe. It is worth taking into account the experience in other fields of co-operation (for example, atomic agency and civil aviation), in which apart from regional organisations and organisations in particular directions of activities, there exist organisations universal from the point of view of their membership, tasks and functions (ICAE, IAEA). The aims and functions of the WSO are of a global character and they can be put into practice only within the framework of a worldwide organisation.

The establishment of a WSO appears to pursue two kinds of aims – co-operation and verification. It is the function of verification that distinguishes a WSO as well as the IAEA from other international organisations. This is one of the principal features which may characterise international organisations in the nuclear and space age working in fields which are of special significance for international peace and security.

The working paper gives a WSO the right to verify first of all compliance with agreements aimed at the prevention of an arms race in outer space. But at the same time a WSO may monitor compliance with other agreements on the limitation and elimination of the arms race. But in this case there must be concluded a special agreement between the United Nations and a WSO.

It is necessary to note that within the framework of a WSO verification is provided on the basis, not of a bilateral agreement, but a multilateral one. It should be regarded as a positive and important factor because it enables many countries to participate in such activities. It is worth saying that the verification system of a WSO may facilitate the establishment of the mechanism of international *detente*.

It is well known that lately there has been a tendency within the framework of the United Nations to consider the problem of an arms race in space and the legal aspects of maintaining outer space for peaceful purposes. There is a certain logic in such a division if one regards the question of the weaponisation of outer space as a part of the global disarmament problem. At the same time the artificial and non-effective character of such a division appears to be obvious. In these circumstances the problem of the co-ordination of these two main directions of space activities – that is to say 'military' and 'peaceful' – becomes of extreme importance. A WSO may contribute to such co-ordination. It is relevant to remember the experience of the IAEA which adequately combines the functions of verification and co-operation.

The description of a WSO as a focal point for peaceful space co-operation is of great importance for the status of this organisation since it determines the sphere of its functions and the role of a WSO in the system of organisations and organs connected with space co-operation. First of all, a WSO could unite the effort of States and international organisations. It would effect its activities in close contact with the UN, and for this purpose these two bodies would have to conclude agreements on co-operation and consultations. A WSO would have a specific and unique connection with the United Nations. This connection is supposed to be realised, not through the Economic and Social Council and General Assembly, as is typical for the UN specialised organs, and not through the Security Council as is done with the IAEA, but through the UN Committee on the Peaceful Uses of Outer Space and the General Assembly. Thus the UN Committee on Outer Space would not be abolished; it appears that its role and functions will be strengthened. At present it might be questionable to destroy those forms and organs of co-operation which have proved to be adequate.

A WSO would co-ordinate its activities with other space organisations and agencies on the basis of appropriate agreements. The idea of such co-ordination is to avoid the duplication of efforts and to make the most efficient use of resources. A WSO should provide for other space bodies a unified approach to the global development of international co-operation in the peaceful conquest of outer space, together with a mechanism for making the best use of the potential of these bodies in the implementation of that approach.

It is necessary to stress that there exists a certain co-ordination of the activities of international space organisations and organs (including specifically the presentation of reports and the attendance of observers). The existing co-ordination even now seems to be not as efficient as is required, and in future this situation could get worse. As proposed in the working paper a WSO would provide for new and more effective methods of co-ordination which may prove acceptable to different types of international organisations.

One of the aims of a WSO is to attract all States to space activities as well as to a practical use of benefits derived therefrom. A special attention is given to the needs and interests of developing countries. No other international space organisation would render such favourable conditions as a WSO would. The idea of using a WSO as an efficient instrument aimed at increasing considerably the particpation of developing countries in space activities is in line with the intention of the UN Committee on Outer Space to strengthen the role of these countries in this field and to extend the assistance rendered to them. The world has heard many political promises to assist developing countries, to eliminate the existing gap in the social and technological level created by the colonial system, etc. Rendering favourable conditions to developing countries within the framework of a WSO would be of practical assistance to them, a concrete step on the way to attracting them into space activities.

A specific feature of a WSO is that it could not only work out international projects, unite the efforts of States and discuss different issues, but it would also directly carry space activities. As is pointed out in the WSO proposed charter, '[it] ... may lease, acquire or develop the necessary elements of a research and production base, including space objects, equipment, launchers, ground facilities, tracking and flight control stations and laboratories'. This provision shows that a WSO is supposed to be not simply a form of co-operation for the sake of co-operation, a mere symbol of joint activities in which there prevails a political rather than a scientific motivation, but also a real instrument of co-operation.

One of the functions of a WSO consists in elaborating and implementing international co-operation projects. These projects may have different aims and financial sources. A WSO at its own expense would carry out different projects of exploration of outer space and make practical use of its results. The international projects which are carried out primarily to provide aid and assistance to developing countries would be financed by a WSO Development Fund especially created for these purposes. Under the auspices of a WSO there may be carried out projects which are of interest to a certain group of countries. In this case they would be financed by these States by means of special funds or earmarked contributions.

The modern level of science and technology allows the carrying out of certain projects on a commercial basis. And it is relevant to mention here that the problem of the commercial effect of space exploration is regarded within the framework of a WSO on a much wider scale than in other international space organisations. This approach takes into account the tendency towards the commercialisation of space activities. It seems that it is worth studying in more detail possible methods for the participation of private enterprises in WSO activities than exist in some other organisations (for exmaple, INTELSAT). At the same time it would be absolutely wrong to think that commercialisation and privatisation of space activities will result in the decrease or disappearance of space activities and co-operation in this field on the level of States. States, and consequently intergovernmental organisations, will retain their positions. As for international responsibility for national activities in outer space, it would be borne by States whether such activities are carried on by governmental agencies or by non-governmental entities (Article VI of the Outer Space Treaty).

As it is stated in the working paper, a WSO may establish special ventures operating on a fully self-financing basis or on the principle of commercial enterprise. These ventures shall operate autonomously and independently but shall be obliged to take into consideration the recommendations of a WSO. A proportion of the profits of these ventures shall be transferred to the budget of a WSO. The establishment of special ventures does not mean that all the existing international space organisations shall acquire the character of such ventures. This is a matter of mutual consent, economic benefit and rational methods of co-operation.

What is the situation with the financial resources of a WSO? According to the working paper, the financial resources of a WSO shall consist of the obligatory annual contributions of member states and a proportion of the profits of the special ventures, together with the earmarked and voluntary contributions of States, international organisations and non-governmental bodies. These resources shall be utilised for the implementation of international projects, for the establishment of a Development Fund, for shared participation in special ventures, for support for the verification system and development of technical resources of a WSO, etc.

The financial participation of member states in a Development Fund – a unique one which does not exist in any international space organisation – is based on the ideas of the Soviet proposals of 1986 in accordance with which the largest proportion of expenses is borne by space powers and other economically developed countries. It is presumed that 60 per cent of the Fund would be covered by States members of the WSO Council most actively engaged in space activities, 30 per cent by States actively engaged in the conquest of space, and the remaining 10 per cent by other States members of a WSO.

According to the working paper the structure of a WSO may include the following bodies: the Assembly – the governing body – consisting of representatives of all members; the Council – the main executive body – consisting of not more than thirty members (one-third of them shall be appointed from among members of the WSO which are most active in space activities and two-thirds shall be elected according to the principle of equitable geographical distribution); and the Secretariat headed by a Director-General.

The working paper stipulates such a procedure of voting in the Assembly and in the Council which is aimed at stimulating the most active participation of member States of a WSO and the Council in voting and at the same time prevents the adoption of decisions by a small number of countries. Thus, the decisions in the Assembly shall be taken by a three-quarters majority of votes of the member States present and voting, provided that such a majority represents the majority of member States of a WSO. Decisions in the Council shall be taken by consensus or by a three-quarters majority of votes of member states present and voting, provided that such majority includes the majority of the member States of the Council.

The idea of the establishment of a WSO has met with mixed reactions. Some have supported it, some are against it and some entertain doubts. On the whole this appears to be natural, since the problem is complicated and requires detailed consideration. Probably there are several reasons for such reserved attitudes. All of them must be analysed and discussed. However, let us offer just a few words concerning some of these reservations. It is necessary to appreciate that the Soviet working document containing the draft Charter of a WSO has not yet been practically discussed in detail either in the United Nations or in scientific conferences. It is just for this reason that the analysis of this working paper is given in such an elaborate form in this chapter. It seems that certain doubts and critical remarks expressed by those who do not support this idea might be put aside by this working paper.

It was rather easy to forsee the position of the United States. In many aspects it is determined by their general desire not to assume serious legal obligations in the sphere of the exploration and use of outer space. This behaviour of the American delegation was long ago noticed in the UN Committee on Outer Space and other organs. One should hope that in future it will become more constructive. The position of the USA in this case is also determined by the fact that that country is not willing to improve the mechanism of international co-operation in the exploration and use of outer space because the existing forms and methods of multilateral and in particular bilateral, co-operation meet with the political and commercial interests both of the country and its separate firms. The idea behind the establishment of a WSO, as a part of the so-called conception of 'star peace', seems to contrast with the 'strategic defence initiative'. This has also undoubtedly influenced the American attitude to a WSO.

It proves to be more complicated to explain the rather passive reaction of a number of developing countries, since the idea of a WSO would give them a lot of advantages, and was put forward, to a certain extent, in their interests. One of the reasons here may be insufficient promotion of the idea of a WSO at the official level and doctrinal level. In this connection, it may be noted here that the methods for the consideration of the interests of developing countries provided for in a WSO might be taken into account while discussing the new subject on the agenda of the Legal Subcommittee of the UN Committee on Outer Space connected with the 'distribution of the benefits resulting from space activities'.

Some countries are of the opinion that at present the establishment of a WSO is of no use since the existing means of co-operation meet modern requirements in this field. There exist misgivings that a WSO would duplicate the activities of the international space organisations which are in action now, or would lead to the elimination of the present forms of co-operation. For example, these views were expressed by the Netherlands on behalf of the States members of the European Community, Sweden, India, Finland and some others.[9]

It appears that in spite of the fact that the existing means of co-operation prove to be reasonably efficient, the objective situation connected with the development of space activities, the intensification of international contacts, the participation of more and more States in the exploration and use of outer space – all require new forms of co-operation. As is clear from the working paper, a WSO would hardly duplicate the activities of the existing international space organisations. Its aims, functions and financial principles are in many ways unique and do not have any analogy with others acting at present. A WSO would be a universal international organisation aimed at the solution of global problems of co-operation and verification in compliance with international agreements. This new organisation would by no means destroy the existing mechanisms. On the contrary, it is intended to perfect the whole system of co-operation and to serve as its focal point.

The advantages of a WSO are many and various. For example, this new organisation could act as the inspiration and organiser of international co-operation in the conquest of outer space and promote the conduct of activities within the framework of common human values based on true democracy and open and equitable co-operation. It could bring together in a single centre, state and private resources intended for the practical development of outer space and contribute to the implementation of commercially feasible space programmes taking into account, in particular, the needs and interests of developing countries. A WSO could promote the development of a fruitful exchange of the results of space activities in the most promising fields and from a single centre provide assistance to countries which are interested in developing national space programmes. At the same time, such a new universal organisation could carry out through inter-state mechanisms the functions of supra-national monitoring of compliance with long-term multilateral agreements on preventing an arms race in outer space and halting it on Earth.[10]

At the same time one cannot but admit that in the course of the elaboration and presentation of the concept of a WSO there have been mistakes. To some extent the appropriate time for this proposal was missed as it was particularly popular in the late 1970s. The idea of a WSO, especially as it appeared in the Soviet proposal of 1985, was directly connected with the purpose of ensuring the 'non-militarisation' of outer space. The approach was too categorical. It was remote from reality and therefore did not find great support. Also in the 1985 proposal there was some inaccuracy in the wording. Thus 'non-militarisation', according to the Soviet suggestion, was understood as the renunciation by States of the development (including research), testing and deployment of space strike weapons. In the West this term is interpreted much more widely, i.e. as forbidding any military activity. The definition given in the suggestion made in 1985 did not take this into account. These different understandings of the notions greatly complicated the acceptance of the idea of establishing a WSO.

It goes without saying that it is necessary to discuss in detail all of the questions connected with the possibility of establishing a new world organisation. Certainly there exists a variety of approaches and problems in this connection. Creativity – that is what is required now for the further elaboration and realisation of the proposal to establish a World Space Organisation. Common efforts are needed in the interests of all countries and of each individual State.

Notes

1 *International Space Law,* Moscow, 1974, p. 104; J. Kolosov, *Mass Information and International Law,* Moscow, 1974, p. 69 (in Russian); F. Brooks, 'National Control of Natural Planetary Bodies: Preliminary Considerations', *Journal of Air Law and Commerce,* vol. 3, no. 3, 1966, pp. 124, 327; A. Cocca, 'The Principle of "Common Heritage of All Mankind" as Applied to Natural Resources from Outer Space and Celestial Bodies', *Proceedings of the XVIth Colloquium on the Law of Outer Space,* California, 1974, p. 175; W. Jenks, *Space Law,* New York, 1965, p. 273; N. M. Matte, *Aerospace Law,* Toronto, 1969, p. 359.

2 *Problems of Space Law,* Moscow, 1961, p. 172 (in Russian).

3 See, for example, E. Kamenetskaya, *Outer Space and International Organisations: International Legal Problems,* Moscow, 1980, pp. 115–40; A. Piradov, *Outer Space and International Law,* Moscow, 1970, pp. 42–5; E. Vasilevskaye, *Legal Problems of Exploration and Use of the Moon,* Moscow, 1974, pp. 13, 14; V. Vereshchetin, *International Co-operation in Outer Space: Legal Questions,* Moscow, 1977, p. 129 (all in Russian). H. De Saussure, 'Evolution Towards an International Space Agency', *Proceedings of the XIXth Colloquium on the Law of Outer Space,* California, 1977, pp. 32–41; I. Diederiks-Verschoor, 'Observations on the International Civil Aviation Organisation and an International Space Agency', *Proceedings of the XXth Colloquium on the Law of Outer Space,* California, 1978, pp. 16–19; D. Myers, 'A New International Agency to Co-ordinate the Actions of States in Outer Space: Some Preliminary Suggestions', *Proceedings of the XIXth Colloquium on the Law of Outer Space,* pp. 414, 416; F. Nozari, *The Law of Outer Space,* Stockholm, 1973, pp. 242–7; *Outer Space: Prospects for Man and Society,* Columbia University, 1962, pp. 120, 121; J. Jamm, 'Should an International Outer Space Agency Be Established?', *Proceedings of the XIIIth Colloquium on the Law of Outer Space,* California, 1971, pp. 53–61.

4 UN Doc. A/AC.105/C.2/L.57 u Covr. I, 1969; UN Doc. A/AC.105/C.4/L.73, 1975.

5 *Proceedings of the XXth Colloquium on the Law of Outer Space,* pp. 1–45.

6 UN Doc. A/40/192, 16 August 1985.

7 UN Doc. A/41/470, 18 August 1986.

8 UN Doc. A/AC.105/L.171, 13 June 1988.

9 UN Doc. A/41/470, 18 August 1986. For a detailed consideration of these views see the chapter by P. Dann, this volume.

10 UN Doc. A/105/407, 16 February 1988.

15.

The Institutional Framework of International Collaboration in Space Activities

PHILLIP DANN

The United Kingdom is at present engaged in a lively debate concerning space-related research and development. Government policy is to provide only modest public funding for space programmes, whether national or international.[1] It is arguable that this policy is no different from that of successive previous governments. What is new, perhaps, is that the opposing viewpoints are so clearly articulated.

In part Government policy reflects a more general belief that private industry should contribute more and governments less to research and development in advanced technologies. It also reflects a belief that private industry can judge better than governments which projects are likely to yield the greatest scientific, technical and commercial benefits.[2] If these benefits are sufficient to justify the necessary expenditure, private industry will be willing to invest in a project; if not, the argument runs, there is no justification for the Government investing instead. Underlying this argument is a general scepticism about the practical benefits to be derived from space science and technology.

It should be understood that this policy excludes considerations of national prestige. The Soviet Union and the United States, in contrast, appear to take pride in their space-related achievements, both officially and in the popular view.[3]

Within the United Kingdom there is fierce criticism of Government policy relating to space, some from within the ruling Conservative Party. The most dramatic protest occurred in 1987:

'The [British National Space Centre] had formulated its first strategic plan only to find that the government was not yet prepared to make available public funding on the scale required even to maintain established commitments, let alone to increase Britain's space capabilities. In the process Britain was beginning to emerge as the main dragger of feet in the negotiations about ESA's long-term plans. Understandably Roy Gibson, the first Director of the BNSC and a former Director-General of ESA, decided to resign.'[4]

The critics of Government policy have adopted a variety of arguments.

It is said that space-related projects require enormous investments which a market economy cannot provide. It is also argued that such projects create benefits which may not be foreseen,[5] or which may not accrue to the entity which undertakes the project. Such benefits tend to be discounted by the private investor. In addition, Government regulation and control of space-related activities may discourage private investment.[6] For all these reasons, it is argued, major projects in space science and technology will require substantial Government funding. From this point of view, it is unthinkable that the United Kingdom should not participate in large-scale space projects such as the development of new launch systems and the European space station contribution.

The current Government policy raises particular difficulties in relation to the European Space Agency (ESA). ESA is a major source of orders for European space industry. Broadly speaking, ESA's industrial policy requires that it should place contracts with industry in Member States in proportion to the respective contributions of those Member States.[7] If, therefore, a State such as the United Kingdom reduces the level of its participation in ESA, its industry will receive fewer contracts from ESA, irrespective of the price or technical quality which may be offered. Furthermore, there is no institutional basis on which ESA could allow a private company to participate in one of its programmes in substitution for the State of that company. The problem was expressed neatly by a spokesman for British Aerospace: 'Even if the ESA did take our money, as a company we would have no influence on policy decisions'.[8]

It has also been suggested that the United Kingdom's military space programme is inadequate, being too dependent on arrangements with the United States for access to satellite-based intelligence. It is argued that the United Kingdom should investigate alternative arrangements with its European neighbours.[9] There are no proposals, however, for the United Kingdom to deploy weapon systems, whether offensive or defensive, in outer space.

In one sense, the debate within the United Kingdom is taking place on common ground: even those who advocate increased public funding for space-related activities argue their case mainly on the basis that space programmes will result eventually in practical benefits of an economic, technological or strategic nature.[10] It is acknowledged that these benefits may be hard to predict or quantify. Nevertheless, there is little attempt to justify space programmes in terms of the enhancement of national prestige. Nor, in general, is it argued that the United Kingdom should extend its international collaboration in space activities because of the general improvement in its international relations which might result.

This last point requires elaboration. There are certain space projects which are too large and complex to be carried out by one country alone. For example, it is doubtful whether any country other than the United States or the Soviet Union would have the resources to develop independently an advanced launch system such as Ariane V, Hermes or Hotol. There are also smaller projects where international collaboration is desirable in order to expose scientists and engineers to the knowledge and working-methods of colleagues in other countries. International co-operation may therefore be desirable because of the nature of a project. There are also cases, however, in which the starting-point is a desire for improved international co-operation: a space-related project is then chosen as a vehicle for that co-operation. For example, the recent US – USSR Agreement on Co-operation in the Exploration and Use of Outer Space for Peaceful Purposes[11] may be seen in one aspect as a symbol of improving relations between the superpowers. The scope and methods of co-operation are expressed in the most general terms. Although an initial list of agreed co-operative projects is appended to the Agreement, virtually no details are given of their funding, schedules or implementation. There is every suggestion that the motivation behind this Agreement on Co-operation was political as well as scientific. Of course, the United Kingdom is also conscious of the political benefits which may result from technical co-operation. Even among the so-called 'space enthusiasts', however, there is little attempt to justify international collaboration in space activities as a means to the promotion of world peace.

This may begin to explain why there has been so little enthusiasm in the United Kingdom for the Soviet proposal to establish a World Space Organisation (WSO).[12] The question is raised: what is there for such a body to do, given the large number of intergovernmental organisations already concerned with space activities? If there is no convincing answer to this question, it may be concluded that the proposal is merely a grand gesture, an attempt to create an elaborate and expensive symbol of international co-operation.

Partly in response to this question, the Soviet Union presented a working paper to the thirty-first session of the United Nations Committee on the Peaceful Uses of Outer Space (UNCOPUOUS). This working paper sets out basic provisions of the charter of a WSO.[13] It states the proposed functions of the WSO in the broadest of terms, and is therefore unsatisfactory to those who remain to be convinced of the need for such an organisation. At the same time, the Soviet proposals contain enough to cause alarm to certain other States: the view has been expressed, for example, that the proposed organisation would undermine the functions of UNCOPUOUS.[14]

It is submitted that the Soviet proposals suffer from being expressed in the form of a draft charter. Questions about the proposed activities of a WSO and its relationship to existing international organisations cannot be answered by a legal document. What is required is, first, research into existing space activities and forms of international co-operation; secondly, consideration of what further activities would be desirable; and thirdly, an analysis of how new forms of international co-operation would improve or otherwise affect such activities. In this light it can be seen that the British debate on space policy is not the parochial affair which it might at first seem. It has raised precisely those questions which need to be asked in relation to the proposal for a WSO: What is the appropriate level of space activities? Who should determine this? How are space projects to be selected? What are the criteria for selection? What level of funding is available for space activities, and who should provide that funding? Above all, who should be carrying out space activities? The role of the proposed WSO needs to be defined in relation to the activities of existing international inter-governmental organisations, such as the United Nations, International Telecommunication Union (ITU) and INTELSAT; international non-governmental organisations, such as the IAF and COSPAR; governments acting independently or under co-operation agreements; and private enterprise.

It is not possible within the scope of this chapter to present a fully-reasoned argument either for or against the idea of a WSO. It is intended, rather, to demonstrate that the case for such a body has not yet been made; and that, on first impression, there are serious doubts as to the value of such a body. For this purpose it is helpful to make frequent reference to the Report of the thirty-first session of UNCOPUOUS, at which the draft charter of a WSO was first presented.[15]

The first point to be made is that we have insufficient knowledge of existing space activities and funding to plan for a WSO. For example, the draft charter of the WSO places emphasis on the needs of developing countries. One of the functions of the Organisation would be 'to provide support to States in the elaboration and implementation of their national space programmes, taking particular account of the needs and interests of developing countries'.[16] Another would be 'To assist States in training scientific and technical space specialists, taking particular account of the needs and interests of developing countries'.[17] There is also provision for a 'WSO Development Fund' which is to be established 'for the funding of international projects designed primarily to provide aid and assistance to the developing countries in the practical applications of space science and technology'.[18] However, it has been proposed at UNCOPUOUS that the Committee should examine the amount of resources available for development assistance, the sources of those funds, their utilisation as well as the real and practical needs of the developing countries.[19] A working paper on the subject was circulated by the Government of Egypt.[20] The representative of the United States proposed in particular a review of '... (1) the actual work that is carried out by the United Nations in various outer space fields and (2) the sources of financial support for relevant United Nations operational activities for development. Put rather simply, the review would summarise what is going on and who pays for it'.[21] It does not seem to have been suggested by other representatives that such information is already available; yet it is a prerequisite for considering ambitious proposals such as the WSO Development Fund.

According to the draft charter of a WSO, one of the *aims* of the Organisation would be 'To co-ordinate efforts undertaken by States and international organisations in the context of peaceful space activities'.[22] One of its *functions* is 'To co-ordinate international activity in the exploration and peaceful uses of outer space'.[23] As this example shows, the formal distinction between the 'aims' and the 'functions' of the WSO is perhaps artificial. It is entirely correct, however, to stress the importance of co-ordinating international space activities. There are, for example, many international organisations whose functions or interests relate to space. UNCOPUOUS has been responsible for the development of a considerable body of treaty law relating to outer space, and continues to study legal questions such as the principles relevant to the use of nuclear power sources in outer space and the definition and delimitation of outer space.[24] ITU allocates radio frequencies for, *inter alia*, satellite telecommunications and radio astronomy, and establishes procedures for the equitable utilisation of the geostationary orbit. INTELSAT, INTERSPUTNIK, INMARSAT and EUTELSAT provide the space segment for various types of satellite telecommunications.

Other international organisations have a direct interest in space applications. The International Maritime Organisation (IMO) has made satellite telecommunications a central element of its Global Maritime Distress and Safety System.[25] The United Nations, the Food and Agriculture Organisation (FAO), UNESCO, the World Meteorological Organisation (WMO) and the European Space Agency (ESA) have all been involved in training programmes for remote sensing applications.[26] The International Civil Aviation Organisation (ICAO) is studying the technical and institutional aspects of satellite telecommunications in relation to future aeronautical communication and navigation systems.[27]

These examples may suggest a need for the co-ordination of international activities. It is far from clear, however, that such co-ordination is at present lacking. The thirty-first session of UNCOPUOUS was attended by observers from, *inter alia*, the International Atomic Energy Agency (IAEA), ITU, UNESCO, ESA, INTELSAT and INMARSAT.[28] The Committee noted the request of the General Assembly, contained in its resolution 42/68, to all organs, organisations and bodies of the United Nations system to co-operate in the implementation of the recommendations of the Second United Nations Conference on the Exploration and Peaceful Uses of Outer Space.[29] It was also noted that this would be one of the matters discussed by the tenth Inter-Agency Meeting on Outer Space Activities to be held in October 1988.[30]

Such co-ordination is not confined within the United Nations system. INMARSAT, not itself a United Nations body, has agreements of co-operation or memoranda of understanding with various international and regional organisations, both within and outside the United Nations system. These include IMO, ITU, ICAO, INTELSAT, INTERSPUT-

NIK and the Arab Telecommunication Union.

None of this proves, of course, that co-ordination is adequate or that it would not be improved by a WSO. What can be said is that there is already extensive co-ordination between international organisations in relation to space activities. There is no clear evidence of unnecessary duplication of activities, or of diffusion of activities, due to a lack of co-ordination. The position may be less satisfactory with respect to national space programmes; the case of remote sensing is considered below.

The draft charter makes clear that the WSO would not merely co-ordinate activities: it would also 'use its own resources to elaborate and implement international co-operation projects in various areas of space exploration and its practical applications'.[31] In order to carry out these and other tasks, '... WSO may lease, acquire or develop the necessary elements of a research and production base, including space objects, equipment, launchers, ground facilities, tracking and flight-control stations and laboratories'.[32] It is even provided that 'WSO may establish, in areas involving the practical uses of outer space, special ventures operating on a fully self-financing basis or on the principle of commercial enterprises'.[33]

It has not yet been explained what projects would be better undertaken by a WSO than under other arrangements. In the field of satellite telecommunications, for example, INTELSAT and INMARSAT operate successfully on the basis of their existing institutional arrangements and there is no reason to suppose that a WSO would improve on their performance. The draft charter states that the WSO shall co-ordinate its activities with other international organisations involved in the exploration and peaceful uses of outer space, adding that, 'Such organisations and agencies, which shall operate on a commercial basis, may obtain the status of WSO special ventures'.[34] It is difficult to see why INTELSAT, for example, should seek this status. A more practical aim would be to bring about a merger of the INTELSAT and INTERSPUTNIK organisations so as to create an international organisation for fixed satellite communications of a truly global character, as INMARSAT already is for mobile satellite communications.

Paradoxically, the proposal for a WSO comes at a time when there are pressures to increase competition and extend the role of private enterprise in international satellite telecommunications. There is already considerable participation by private exterprise in INTELSAT, INMARSAT and EUTELSAT,[35] and the scale of this participation is increasing with the privatisation of many of the PTTs which are Signatories to these organisations. There are in addition commercial enterprises seeking to compete directly with the intergovernmental organisations, for example, Panamsat with INTELSAT, Geostar with INMARSAT and the Société Européene des Satellites with EUTELSAT.[36] It does not seem politically realistic to seek to establish a new international intergovernmental organisation providing satellite telecommunications facilities.

In the case of remote sensing, once again the role of the proposed WSO is unclear. It has been noted that there are remote-sensing satellite programmes underway in the USA, France, Japan, India and the USSR and that programmes are under development in Brazil, China, Canada, the Netherlands/Indonesia and ESA.[37] The American Landsat, the French Spot and the Soviet Soyuzkarta are already marketing remote-sensing data. It has been announced that data from Japanese and Indian systems will also be made available.[38] This diversity of systems has advantages. For example, although the Land Remote-Sensing Commercialisation Act of 1984 was passed with the object of transferring Landsat to the private sector,[39] the United States Government may seek to restrict the marketing of high-resolution images by Landsat for security reasons.[40] However, such controls are unrealistic if Spot or Soyuzkarta are willing to offer such images. There have also been complaints that Soyuzkarta is failing to give non-discriminatory access to remote-sensing data.[41] If there is any truth in such complaints, potential customers can simply approach other data providers.

Of course, the present situation is far from ideal. It is not clear whether the market for remote-sensing data is large enough to support so many competing systems. At present Landsat is reported to be in severe financial difficulties, and there are rumours of a merger with Spot.[42] UNCOPUOUS has noted concerns about the commercialisation of remote-sensing activities, and suggestions that 'the prices of remote-sensing data products and access fees for data reception should be reduced significantly so as to make these affordable for the developing countries and enable them to benefit fully from the use of remote-sensing technology'.[43]

These matters may indicate a possible role for a global, inter-governmental body concerned with remote-sensing. However, the feasibility of such a body requires careful study. Would it co-ordinate existing remote-sensing programmes, absorb them, or operate its own programmes in parallel? If it operated its own remote-sensing systems, how would it reconcile the conflicting requirements of different countries? Would there by any role for private enterprise in the activities of such a body? Would it make available data for military intelligence purposes, bearing in mind that some countries at present operate mixed civil and military systems? Should such a body be concerned with space activities other than remote-sensing? The last question is of particular interest because there have been proposals to establish an international organisation or consortium dedicated to remote-sensing.[44]

This raises a general point concerning the WSO proposal. However desirable it may be to promote international collaboration in space activities, it should not be assumed *a priori* that all space activities are intimately connected and can fall conveniently within the ambit of a single organisation. Reference has been made to suggestions that INTELSAT might merge with INTERSPUTNIK, and that an international remote-sensing organisation might be established. Both would be global bodies representing a high degree of international co-operation; but there would not seem to be any merit in a merger of these bodies. Various space technologies are at different stages of maturity and have different applications. Some, like satellite telecommunications, are commercially viable. Remote-sensing is now financed by a combination of revenues and subsidies, while some space science and technology remains entirely dependent on government funding.

The mention of funding introduces one of the most problematical aspects of the WSO proposal. The draft charter provides that the resources of the WSO shall consist of 'the obligatory annual contributions of member States and a proportion of the profits of the special ventures, together with the earmarked and voluntary contributions of States, international organisations and non-governmental corporate bodies'.[45] The scale of annual contributions to the regular budget and to the Development Fund of the WSO is to be fixed by the Assembly, which also reviews and approves the budget.[46] The Assembly consists of all States members of WSO, [47] and in the Assembly each State has one vote.[48]

These proposals seem to ignore political realities. It is unlikely that the developed countries would wish to leave the size of the budget and the scale of contributions to be decided on the basis of one vote per State. Nor are they likely to accept that the Assembly would have the power on this basis to approve international co-operation projects which are to be carried out by WSO;[49] on such matters it might be expected that voting should be weighted according to financial participation.

This is not to deny the present lack of funding to assist the developing countries in the application of space science and technology. UNCOPUOUS has noted the disappointment expressed by the developing countries at the lack of financial resources to implement the recommendations of the Second United Nations Conference on the Exploration and Peaceful Uses of Outer Space.[50] Such concerns underlie the provisions in the draft charter relating to a WSO Development Fund.[51] However, it is one thing to propose new institutional arrangements: it is another to create the willingness to provide extra funding; and if the willingness exists, there is no obvious reason why the extra funding should not be channelled through existing organisations and programmes.

It remains to consider one of the most important aims of the proposed WSO: 'To verify compliance with international agreements to prevent the extension of an arms race into outer space'.[52] This relates to a long-standing difference of views within UNCOPUOUS, which may be illustrated by reference to the Report of the thirty-first session:

'Some delegations expressed the view that the Committee should complement the work being done in bilateral and multilateral forums towards the prevention of the extension of the arms race into outer space ... Other delegations expressed the view that disarmament questions did not fall within the competence of the Committee. They pointed out that the question of the prevention of an arms race in outer space was properly a matter for the First Committee of the General Assembly and for the Conference on Disarmament.'[53]

Given the restrictive attitude taken by some delegations to the role of UNCUPUOUS, there would seem to be little possibility of attracting sufficient support for the idea that a WSO should verify compliance with agreements to prevent the extension of an arms race into outer space. However, the draft charter opens up further possibilities for the WSO to perform verification functions: 'On the basis of a special agreement with the United Nations, the WSO verification system may also be used to monitor compliance with other agreements on the limitation and cessation of the arms race'.[54]

It is not clear why the WSO should in such cases be required to act on the basis of a special agreement with the United Nations, but not in the specific case of verification of compliance with agreements to prevent the extension of an arms race into outer space. However, there are obvious attractions in the establishment of joint arrangements for the monitoring of arms control agreements. Whether multilateral arrangements are necessarily preferable to bilateral ones is open to question. The reference to 'the WSO verification system' implies that the WSO would operate its own remote-sensing system. However, in the atmosphere of mutual trust and openness which would be a precondition for any joint monitoring arrangements, it might be possible to make use of existing systems.

It should be added that, in this context also, the wide-ranging nature of the WSO's activities is less attractive than its proposers must have intended. There is no reason why the function of arms control verification should be combined with international projects on space applications or with the establishment of special ventures on a commercial basis. There are, indeed, disadvantages in this arrangement. Disagreement in one area of activity may spill over into another; the monitoring of compliance with arms control agreements is a delicate enough task without such distractions.

To reiterate, therefore, the case for a WSO has not yet been made, and first impressions of the proposal are unfavourable. It is not clear exactly what activities the organisation would undertake, or why it would carry them out better than governments, existing international organisations and commercial enterprises. It has not been shown that such a wide range of activities should be entrusted to a single body on the sole basis that they all relate to space.

There is a further criticism of the proposal which, although more subjective, is perhaps the most fundamental. It has already been shown that, in the field of satellite telecommunications, private enterprise has an important and expanding role. In the field of remote-sensing, there are also moves towards privatisation and commercialisation. Industry is making direct arrangements with launch agencies to carry out experiments in outer space.[55] Michel Bourely has argued that '... the current trend, at least in market-economy countries, to what has become known as the "commercialization" or "privatization" of Space would appear to be irreversible'.[56] To note these developments is not to support the present policy of the British Government, which may well exaggerate the proper role of private enterprise in undertaking and financing space activities. However, it is paradoxical that, at a time when private enterprise is becoming more involved in space activities, there should be a proposal to create a new inter-governmental organisation to co-ordinate and carry out such activities. This is not to say that the proposal is wrong as a matter of dogma; but it clearly seeks to swim against the prevailing current.

Public international law is neutral with respect to this development. It may be agreed that, 'There are no serious grounds for the claims of some Western lawyers about an existent principle in international law providing for "freedom of private enterprise in outer space".'[57] Article VI of the Outer Space Treaty makes States Parties responsible for national activities in outer space, including the activities of 'non-governmental entities'. National activities are to be carried out in conformity with the provisions of the Treaty. The activities of non-governmental entities in outer space 'shall require authorisation and continuing supervision by the State Party to the Treaty'. However, the trend towards the 'privatisation' or 'commercialisation' of space activities is not in itself inconsistent with these principles. The issue is whether each State takes appropriate steps to control, supervise and, as necessary, direct the private commercial bodies for which it is responsible. In the United Kingdom, for example, the Outer Space Act 1986, although not yet in force, provides the national legal framework for the licensing and control of commercial space activities by United Kingdom nationals, including companies.

In spite of the various reservations which have been expressed above, it should be said that the proposal for a WSO expresses an attractive idealism with respect to international collaboration in space activities. There can be few objections to the stated aims of a WSO, even if there are doubts about the concept of a WSO as a means of achieving those aims. It is disappointing, therefore, that the only alternative which is currently proposed in UNCOPUOUS is to promote international co-operation further by revitalising the work of the Committee and its subcommittees.[58] A joint working paper on this subject has been submitted by a number of delegations, including the United States and the United

Kingdom.[59] The proposal may be of practical benefit, but it is not one to fire the imagination.

Notes

1. James Eberle and Helen Wallace, *British Space Policy and International Collaboration*, 1987, London, pp. 15–22; Geoffrey Pardoe, 'The Selling of Space', *New Scientist*, 21 January 1989, pp. 45–8.
2. See, for example, the comment in Lord Chorley, 'Economics of space and the role of government', in *Space Policy* (1988) Vol. 4, p. 180 at p. 181: 'Experience suggests that few governments are good at "picking winners", at making commercial and technical decisions; moreover it is usually sensible to avoid, if possible, blurring those types of decision by adding a political dimension'.
3. One reason why the loss of the US Space Shuttle *Challenger* in 1986 created such a reaction of horror is that considerable publicity was given in advance to the mission and its crew members, and that the tragedy was seen live on television by large numbers of people including many schoolchildren.
4. Eberle and Wallace, op. cit., p. 7.
5. UNCOPUOUS has decided to include a new item on the agenda of its next session entitled 'Spin-off benefits of space technology: review of current status': *Report of the Committee on the Peaceful Uses of Outer Space* (A/43/20), 1988, p. 18.
6. These arguments are summarised in Lord Chorley, op. cit., which also includes a well-balanced critique of such arguments.
7. Convention on the Establishment of a European Space Agency (1975), Article VII and Annex V.
8. Reported in *New Scientist*, 13 August 1987, p. 21.
9. Eberle and Wallace, op. cit., p. 48.
10. See note 6 above.
11. 26 I.L.M. 622 (1987).
12. For the nature and origins of this proposal see V. Vereschetin, E. Vasilevskaya and E. Kamenetskaya, *Outer Space: Politics and Law*, Moscow, 1987, pp. 113–5.
13. A/43/20, p. 4 and Annex II.
14. Ibid., p. 5.
15. See note 11 above.
16. Section II, para 6.
17. Section II, para. 7.
18. Section V, para. 1.
19. A/43/20, pp. 5–6.
20. Ibid., Annex IV.
21. United States Mission to the United Nations, Press Release, 15 June, 1988.
22. Section I.
23. Section II, para. 3.
24. A/43/20, pp. 14–16.
25. International Maritime Organisation, *Global Maritime Distress and Safety System*, London, 1987.
26. A/43/20, pp. 8–9.
27. See for example the Third Report of the Special Committee on Future Air Navigation Systems, November 1986, passim.

28 A/43/20, p. 2.
29 Ibid., p. 10.
30 Ibid.
31 Section III, para. 1.
32 Section II.
33 Section IV, para. 1.
34 Section IX, para. 1.
35 See, for example, W. D. von Noorden and P. J.Dann, 'Public and Private Enterprise in Satellite Telecomunications: The Example of INMARSAT', in *Proceedings of the Twenty-Ninth Colloquium on the Law of Outer Space*, New York, 1987, p. 193 at pp. 195–6.
36 For Panamsat see for example *Satellite Week*, 17 October 1988, p. 1; for Geostar see for example *Telecommunications Report*, 5 December 1988, p. 35.
37 John L. McLucas and Paul M. Maughan, 'The Case for Envirosat', in *Space Policy* (1988) Vol. 4, p. 229.
38 *Satellite Week*, 14 November 1988, p. 4.
39 15 USC Sec. 4201 *et seq.*
40 *Air & Cosmos*, 20 February 1988, p. 34.
41 See note 36 above.
42 *Air & Cosmos*, 22 April 1989, p. 46.
43 A/43/20, p. 12.
44 See McLucas and Maughan, op. cit., who propose a body called 'Envirosat' based on the model of INMARSAT.
45 Section VII, para. 1.
46 Section XI, para. A.2.
47 Section XI, para. A.1.
48 Section XI, para. A.4.
49 Section XI, para. A.2.
50 A/43/20, p. 7.
51 Section V.
52 Section I.
53 A/43/20, p. 4.
54 Section VI, para. 3.
55 It was reported, for example, that a British company called Britain In Space Ltd. was entering into an agreement with the Soviet space agency, Glavcosmos, to take a British astronaut into space to carry out various experiments: *Sunday Times*, 2 April 1989.
56 'Rules of International Law Governing the Commercialization of Space Activities', in *Proceedings of the Twenty-Ninth Colloquium on the Law of Outer Space*, New York, 1987, p. 157 at p. 160.
57 Vereschetin, Vasilevskaya and Kamenestkaya, op. cit., p. 131.
58 A/43/20, p. 5.
59 A/43/20, Annex III.

16.

International Environmental Security: The Concept and its Implementation

SERGEI V. VINOGRADOV

The last quarter of the twentieth century has challenged society with new problems which can be classified as global. These problems are common to all nations and can be solved only by their joint efforts. Within this category we can include such problems as the prevention of nuclear war, the energy crisis, the feeding of the growing world population, the supply of natural and mineral resources and environmental degradation. It can even be said that the interaction of man with the environment has become one of the most acute problems of mankind. The prophesy of the notable Russian scientist, V. I. Vernadski, that mankind will become a force of geological magnitude with the ability to change the biosphere, has become a reality. However these changes are taking place in an uncontrolled manner, and we are far from the realisation of his idea of 'perestroika of the biosphere in the interests of free thinking mankind as a whole'.[1]

Contemporary ecological problems have arisen mainly as a consequence of the inroads of man into the environment without taking into account the possible adverse consequences of human activities. Today it has become apparent for all that if we don't take urgent measures for the protection of our environment, civilisation may face destruction even if we manage to evade nuclear apocalypses. The problem of environmental protection comes second to that most important of global probems, the prevention of nuclear war. The only difference between devastation by a nuclear bomb and by an 'ecological bomb' is that the latter is not immediate, but is a continuous, imperceptible process impairing the very basis of human existence.

Under these circumstances, the inapplicability not only of the *laissez faire* concept, predominant in the not very distant past, which meant practically an unimpeded use of natural resources, but also of the already outdated approach which presupposes conservation only of one or another element of the natural environment, has become evident to many politicians, scientists and scholars. Today what we need is a new paradigm based on the understanding that the Earth's biosphere and the processes taking place in it form an indivisible whole very closely connected with the processes taking place in human society. The new approach based on the new political thinking and taking into account the priorities of universally accepted values and common interests has resulted in the appearance and promotion of the concept of global environmental security as an indivisible element of universal security.

The term 'security' has been traditionally used in political and military relations to denote a state of affairs in which there is absence of threat for a nation or group of states. Security has always been one of the main aims of foreign policy, the attainment of which was thought to be best achieved, as a general rule, by increasing the military power of a state, individually or jointly with other states. With the emergence and aggravation of global problems threatening to an equal extent all the nations of the world, the limitations of the old concepts of 'security' become more and more apparent. This has led to a deeper understanding of national and respectively of international security,[2] a logical result of which is the appearance of the concept of a universal system of international security (USIS) originally proposed by the Soviet Union in 1986 and supported by many states in the UN.

This concept has met nevertheless with a dose of scepticism from a number of Western countries in the course of deliberations in various UN organs. They rightly point out that the UN Charter is one of the most effective instruments for the consolidation of international security. However in 'defending' it from the supposed encroachments, they do not wish to recognise that the USIS concept not only does not threaten the Charter, but on the contrary, it presupposes its full utilisation and promotion in a radically changed world with new problems of a kind which could not have been anticipated by the fathers of the Charter. It is thus obvious that the Charter, a fundamental basis for the insurance of international security, remains a necessary but not an entirely sufficient instrument for the settlement of crisis situations faced by the international community today. The adoption of respective resolutions by the UN General Assembly can be regarded as proof of the acceptance of this concept by the majority of member states.

In the Report by the UN Secretary General to the 43rd Session of the General Assembly it was pointed out that the constructive discussion of this concept with the participation of Member States of the UN would help put the present practices in international relations within an overall system of international peace and security envisaged in the UN Charter. This would also stimulate a wide international dialogue as to the ways and means of achieving international security in military, political, economic, environmental, humanitarian and other spheres based on the strict observance of the Charter and augmentation of the role and efficiency of the United Nations.[3]

The inclusion of the environmental aspect of security as a distinct element within the USIS concept reflects the importance attached to it by the international community. This idea was very well formulated by M. Gorbachev in his article, 'Reality and guarantees of a secure world'.[4] There he emphasises the dangerous aspects of the interrelationship between man and his environment and the necessity to solve ecological problems on the global level. 'The problems of environmental security affect all, both rich and poor. A global strategy for the safeguarding of the environment and for the rational use of natural resources is necessary'.

The representative of Czechoslovakia in the Second Committee of the UN General Assembly declared that '... the threat to the environment is becoming a factor of disruption and a source of increasing tension in international relations. International environmental security will guarantee the right of every nation to environmentally sound development'.[5]

One year later the Soviet Foreign Minister, addressing the 43rd Session of the UN General Assembly, emphasised that 'the traditional approach to national and universal security, based primarily on military defence, has become conclusively outdated and in need of revision'.[6] He linked this assertion with the idea of establishing an international regime of environmental security. For his part, M. Gorbachev in his speech at the same session underlined the importance of formulating a definition of world ecological threat and at the same time proposed specific measures for overcoming it.[7]

We must point out that the emphasis which is placed by the present Soviet leadership on the idea of environmental security reflects the general radical change of the attitude of Soviet political and scientific circles towards environmental problems. It was not long ago that these problems were considered to be inherent in capitalist countries only, a consequence of an economy based on private ownership and production directed towards profit at any cost, even at the expense of the environment. On the other hand the planned socialist economy was looked at as free from such shortcomings and guaranteeing rational use of natural resources. Such a predominant view determined the attitude towards environmental protection both on a national and an international level. For example, the above standpoint had a certain bearing on the decision of the Soviet Union and other Eastern European countries not to participate in the 1972 Stockholm Conference on the Human Environment, although there were other serious political reasons for this.[8]

However, the situation changed towards the end of the seventies. The alarming environmental conditions in various regions of the USSR showed that the monopoly of different ministries responsible for industry turned out to be no better, if not even worse, than private monopolies more or less under the control of the state.

The realisation of the imminent danger of environmental degradation led to the adoption of a number of measures including legislative acts as well as the promotion of international co-operation on universal and regional levels. Thus the USSR became one of the initiators of the 1979

Long Range Transboundary Air Pollution Convention. It was also an active participant in the elaboration of the provisions on the protection of the marine environment in the UN Law of the Sea Convention.

However, the single most powerful factor for the upsurge of public and institutional awareness of environmental questions was the Chernobyl catastrophe, which exposed the integral character of the biosphere and the risks of beneficial but potentially hazardous activities.

Thus the interest manifested towards the concept of environmental security in present day Soviet legal writing is not accidental. It reflects a very important change in the attitude of researchers in the field of international law and international relations towards the very notion of international security and its components.[9]

It must be noted that such close attention towards the concept of international environmental security is characteristic not only of the political leaders and scholars from the socialist countries. The necessity of establishing a completely new system of relations in the use of the environment and natural resources is becoming widely acknowledged.These ideas penetrate such studies as the report, 'Our Common Future', prepared by the World Commission on Environment and Development (The Brundtland Commission),[10] the UNEP document, 'Environmental Perspectives to the Year 2000 and Beyond'.[11] They have also been reflected in the conclusion of the International Conference on the Interrelation of Disarmament and Development that security includes not only military but also political, economic, social, humanitarian, environmental connotations as well as the human rights aspect.[12]

The concept of environmental security is also supported by legal doctrine.[13] Very characteristic is the opinion of the Indian law professor R. P. Dhokalia. He writes: 'The ecological crisis is a crisis of priorities in human development and is a potential and powerful agent of social change in the sense that a new concept of ecological security may emerge on the wake of a major eco-disaster'.[14]

What exactly is the concept of international environmental security and what is its legal content? According to the Soviet professor O. Kolbasov it can be defined as 'a system of measures eliminating the danger of mass extermination of human beings as a result of such adverse anthropogenic environmental changes that lead to conditions under which humans as a biological species are deprived of the ability to continue their existence...'[15] It is our opinion that the proposed definition clearly does not embrace the whole spectrum of problems connected with environmental security. Only the most important aspects are covered. The threat to the stability of the environment of a particular State, region or the international community as a whole should not be equated solely to that as defined by the author, but should include threats of a lesser magnitude as well. On the other hand security should be looked at, not so much as a system of measures, but rather as a desired target to which such legal measures (regime) should contribute.

It would be more appropriate to consider a definition in terms of the Statement of the Member States of the Warsaw Treaty entitled, 'The Consequences of the Arms Race for the Environment and Other Aspects of Environmental Security'.[16] It asserts that 'international environmental security which is called upon to promote a sustainable and secure development of all states and the establishment of appropriate conditions for the existence of each nation and each and every individual, presupposes such a state of international relations which guarantees conservation, rational use, reproduction and improvement of the quality of the environment'. Factors leading to environmental instability are also analysed in the Statement. The arms race is among the foremost. It is not coincidental that the USIS concept ties together the ecological and the military and political elements. Disarmament will significantly diminish environmental harm from military activities and release huge financial, natural and human resources which could be used for the improvement of the environment both at a regional and a global level.

On the other hand, a no less important factor of environmental instability is the conduct of everyday industrial and agricultural activity with a disregard for ecological requirements. Activities of this kind lead to such negative consequences as pollution of the world ocean and atmosphere, changes in the climate patterns as a result of the 'greenhouse effect', destruction of the ozone layer, desertification and deforestation, trans-boundary pollution and a number of other detrimental phenomena and processes.

A threat to environmental security can also arise out of an unjust economic policy towards less developed countries. Their natural environment is subjected to special danger owing to the export of polluting technologies, the dumping of toxic wastes on their territories and the over-exploitation of natural resources.

Thus, environmental degradation, being a product of industrialisation in some countries, and a consequence of underdevelopment, population boom and poverty in others, has become a challenge to the human race and a test of mankind's ability to cope with this crisis and to provide for the wellbeing of present and future generations. Under these circumstances the achievement of environmental security for each and all depends on the united efforts of the whole international community.

The present system of international environmental relations can be characterised by a lack of security, stability or balance. What we need, by contrast, is a system of international environmental security designed to prevent, rather than abate the adverse effects of present-day and future activities. Such a system should take into account the individual and collective interests of states and have as its components duly co-ordinated and mutually accepted mechanisms that include principles, rules and institutions, both existing and those that will be created in the future.

In Soviet legal doctrine, an attempt was made to define the main features of a system of international environmental security. In the opinion of Dr. A. Timoshenko, it must be universal and equitable for all participants in international relations, embracing within its sphere of action areas beyond the limits of national jurisdiction; it must be closely tied up with military, political and economic security; it must be founded on the principle of the inalienable sovereignty of States over their natural resources; it should envisage the protection of the State's environment against trans-frontier pollution, any trans-boundary movement of dangerous wastes and the transfer of ecologically hazardous technologies; it should envisage co-ordinated action by States for the protection of areas and natural resources beyond national jurisdiction, including those defined as the 'common heritage of mankind'; it should be based on equal and mutually beneficial co-operation; it should be regulated by appropriate national and international legal and institutional mechanisms.[17]

The progressive development of the norms of international law is the most important instrument in the 'perestroika' of the structure of international environmental relations directed towards the establishment of a new international environmental order. It is well known that the legal order in any society is established on the foundations of existing legal norms and reflects the values and priorities dominant in it. The essence of a legal order is its embodiment of both particular social goals and its being the result of a process of legal regulation.[18] That is why environmental security, which can be viewed as a desired target of the new international environmental order, requires not simply the further development of international law, but also such development as includes a review of the fundamental concepts underlying it.

Despite the deficiencies and limitations of international law it can nevertheless be used as a basis for a new international environmental order. At present a considerable body of norms and regulations have been enacted in this sphere. It is incorporated in a vast quantity of universal, regional and bilateral treaties, resolutions and recommendations of intergovernmental organisations and conferences, international judicial and arbitral decisions. We could mention: the Convention for the Protection of the World Cultural and Natural Heritage (1972); the Convention on the Prohibition of Military or Other Hostile Uses of Environmental Modification Techniques (1978); the UN Law of the Sea Convention (1982), and others. The Vienna Convention for the Protection of the Ozone Layer (1985) and its Montreal Protocol (1987) could be pointed out as good examples of an adequate response to a problem in need of quick solution. Other such instruments include: the Stockholm Declaration on the Human Environment (1972) and the Helsinki Final Act (1975).

The creation of a new international environmental order requires the accomplishment of a dual task. On the one hand what is needed is the working out, systematisation and thereafter codification of the fundamental principles and norms underlying the behaviour of States, oriented towards safeguarding the environment. This would allow not only a maximum utilisation of their potential by improving their interaction, but would bring out the existing loopholes in the law requiring the adoption of new legal rules or mechanisms. On the other hand, there is a task which is considerably harder to achieve – the radical improvement of environmental protection measures and stricter compliance with the norms of international environmental law.

Speaking of the role of international law for the realisation of environmental security, A. Timoshenko proposes the drawing up of special principles by the transformation of the future USIS principles and through integration of norms of international environmental law. Amongst such special principles he includes: the principle of equal and matching ecological security; the principle of the prohibition of environmental aggression (ecocide); the principle of regular information exchange on the environmental situation both on the national and regional level; the principle of control for the compliance with agreed standards of environmental protection; the principle of the prevention of environmental harm; the principle of co-operation in environmental emergencies; the principle of peaceful settlement of trans-boundary environmental disputes; the principle of science and technology co-operation; the principle of international liability for trans-boundary damage, and finally, the principle of the right to a sound environment. The author of the above proposals considers it appropriate that a draft of the principles of environmental security should be drawn up and embodied in the form of a Declaration to be adopted at the Second Stockholm Conference on the Human Environment to be followed by a universal convention.

Despite the possible appeal of such a proposal, it is in need of further deliberation. Today the USIS principles themselves have not as yet found legal embodiment in a universally accepted international instrument, not to mention that the concept itself has met unfortunately with reserve on the part of a number of States. The principles of universal security are for the time being themselves the object of legal discussion and therefore cannot serve as a legal basis for the creation of other norms. However, this does not exclude the possibility of them becoming in the future the basis of a code of environmental conduct for States, which makes it even more desirable to defend the necessity of their conversion into legally binding norms.

At the same time today there is a real opportunity for a rapid codification of existing principles of international environmental law. Such proposals and a programme of action are contained in the report, 'Our Common Future'. A set of legal principles drafted by a group of international legal experts are included. Besides legal principles of a general character, such as the fundamental human right to an environment adequate for health and well-being, the obligation to conserve and use the environment and natural resources for the benefit of present and future generations, the obligation to maintain ecosystems and to observe the principle of sustainable use of living natural resources, etc., principles, rights, and obligations concerning trans-boundary natural resources and environmental interferences are also included in the draft.[19] Most of the above-mentioned principles already function within the framework of various international instruments which regulate different spheres of interstate relations in the field of environmental protection.

A specific feature of this document is that the principles laid down by it put an obligation on States not only *vis-a-vis* one another, but also *vis-a-vis* their own nationals and even present and future generations. These obligations reflect the imperative character of ecological requirements which through the legal normative process acquire a binding character.

It may be argued that today we are witnessing, not only the formation of a separate and rather complex system of legal regulation, but also a new fundamental principle of general international law – the principle obliging States to protect their environment, both within and beyond the limits of their jurisdiction.[20] It can be anticipated that very soon, if not already, it will join other fundamental and universally recognised principles of international law such as: the principles of sovereign equality, non-use of force or threat of force, non-interference in the internal affairs of other States, fulfilment in good faith of international obligations and the peaceful settlement of international disputes.

It is clear that without compliance with environmental requirements embodied in legal norms it is impossible to realise the rights stemming from State sovereignty. Further, the concept of sovereignty itself is today in a process of change. The general obligation to protect the environment has become a criterion of the lawfulness of any State action relevant to the environment.

The creation of the legal foundations of a new international environmental order is a matter which should not be stalled. Impending environmental crises, threatening our future, leave us no time. That is why, parallel with the development of a framework convention of universal character, a package of international legal instruments on the most acute environmental problems must also be adopted on a global as well as a regional level. These instruments must regulate the production, use, transportation and disposal of dangerous and toxic wastes; the prevention of man-made global climatic changes; the conservation of biological and genetic diversity; the prevention of industrial catastrophies and the elimination of their consequences.

A positive contribution to this law-making process should come from the implementation of the 1989 Final Document of the Vienna Meeting (the Helsinki Process).[21] It envisages the adoption of an umbrella treaty on the protection of international waterways and lakes, the adoption of measures designed to alleviate the consequences of industrial accidents which could cause trans-boundary environmental damage, as well as the study of the question of liability and compensation for damages arising from the above.

To be effective the system of principles, rules, standards and procedures requires strict observance and compliance with the existing obligations of States as well as a maximal widening of the number of states covered by the above legal framework. The present situation falls far short of what is desired. Unfortunately we have to note the imperfection of the system of legal regulation in this field. Many countries which cause pollution are not parties to relevant legal instruments or do not strictly abide by them. This situation calls for a radical improvement in the existing international legal mechanism so that they can effectively control and stimulate the participation of all States and even force them to comply with the regulations when necessary.

Thus it is clear that the system of international environmental security cannot do without appropriate institutional mechanisms on a global and regional level. It is natural that in such a framework the leading role should belong to the UN system which is to the greatest extent suited to fulfil it. Today the special responsibility of the UN as centre of international co-operation in different spheres has acquired new dimensions. This is emphasised also in the report of the World Commission on Environment and Development: 'The United Nations, as the only intergovernmental organisation with universal membership, should clearly be the locus for new institutional initiatives of a global character'.[22]

In the past the UN has not always been effective enough in the solution of problems affecting vital State interests and international security. Today the organisation is on the upsurge. It can be said that the new political thinking of the present Soviet leadership plays a definite part in this process.

The contribution of the UN towards the creation of a system of international environmental security could include the systematisation and subsequent institutionalisation of measures undertaken by the international community. Such a task presupposes the exercise of certain presently existing functions as well as the acquisition of new ones. Amongst these are: monitoring, evaluation and assessment of the environment including the identification of destabilising factors or imminent environmental dangers; a law-making and regulatory function; an emergency function for the relief of crisis situations through the creation of appropriate international mechanisms and procedures; control of the implementation by States of international instruments and agreed measures.

With time, there could arise a need to endow the UN with functions similar to those given to it at present by the Charter only in cases of threats to international peace and security, in order to be able to cope with situations endangering environmental security. Such situations could be the consequence, for example, of the acts of ecocide, mass pollution of the atmosphere or the marine environment.[23] There is a question whether certain activities of States with grave environmental consequences can be qualified as a threat to peace and security, thus giving the Security Council the right to intervene with measures provided for in Chapter VII of the Charter. This question should be the object of further study, but in any case a positive or negative answer will allow us to reach a conclusion as to whether the Charter provisions are adequate or in need of change to be able to deal with such environmentally dangerous situations.

Taking into consideration the serious consequences for international security and the legal order of possible inter-state conflicts arising from trans-boundary pollution or other environmental harm, the widening of the jurisdiction of the International Court of Justice can be also proposed. One can go even further and suggest the creation of a special Chamber for the settlement of environmental disputes.[24]

The implementation of the above-mentioned proposals may necessitate a redistribution of rights and responsbilities among existing institutional mechanisms (bodies and organisations) both global and regional within the UN system and the creation of new ones. The last two or three years have witnessed numerous proposals by Soviet representatives directed at improved structures and the clarification of the functions of UN bodies. For example, it was proposed to reinforce and extend the catalytic and co-ordinating role of UNEP in the UN system with a particular focus on: developing, testing and helping to apply methodology for environmental assessment of projects at the national level; extending international agreements (such as on chemicals and hazardous wastes) more widely; extending the Regional Seas Programme; developing a similar programme for international river basins, etc.[25]

Among tasks which are proposed to be assigned to UNEP within the framework of an international environmental order, are: the organisation of regular international symposia and meetings of experts for discussion and evaluation of environmental measures; the dissemination of information on the participation of States in the various international agreements and programmes; the encouragement of mutual assistance among States, and the support of international organisations working on the solution of specific problems of environmental security.[26]

At the 43rd session of the UN General Assembly, the Soviet Foreign Minister submitted a wide programme of extraordinary measures for the linking of efforts in the sphere of environmental security. Included are three high-level meetings on environmental problems, one of which is the Second UN Conference on the Problems of the Human Environment to be convened in 1992 or earlier.

In his speech he also stressed that it is precisely within the UN that an international mechanism for the solution of urgent global problems, primarily economic and environmental, should be established. In connection with this he suggested discussing the question of the transformation of UNEP into an environmental council having the ability to adopt effective decisions for the achievement of environmental security.

The latest proposal concerns the creation of a Centre for Emergency Environmental Assistance within the UN system.[27] The principal task of such a centre would be the organisation of international co-operation in emergency environmental situations in one or other country or region. The main function could be the sending of international groups of experts to such regions for assessment of the situation and the working out of recommendations on the limitation and liquidation of adverse environmental consequences. The centre could also engage in the development of procedures for technical assistance to affected countries. Should such a centre be created and prove to be effective, the establishment in future of special task forces for emergency environmental operations could be considered. These actions and measures, if implemented, will become an integral part of a global strategy for the protection of the environment and the rational use of natural resources.

In our opinion the proposed measures are sound and should be looked into very closely. It is clear that some will be more easy to implement than others and will meet with the approval of Member States. Others, however, requiring changes in the UN system and even possible modification of the UN Charter, might face objections and therefore it can be questioned whether they would be attainable under present circumstances in a world still to undergo its 'perestroika'. Such 'perestroika' will have to take place as humanity has no other choice if it is to survive. 'In the geological history of the biosphere man has a bright future if only he understands it and uses his mind and industry towards this end and not for his self-destruction'.[28]

Notes

1 V. I. Vernadski, *Philosophical Thoughts of a Natural Scientist*, Moscow, 1988, p. 509 (in Russian).
2 See M. Simai. 'The Comprehensive System: the Different Dimensions and Levels of Security in the World of the 1980s and Beyond'. Hungarian Academy of Sciences; prepared for the 1987 Convention of the International Studies Association; R. H. Ullman, 'Redefining Security', *International Security*, Summer 1986.
3 *Pravda*, 29 October 1988.
4 *Pravda*, 17 September 1987; see also: UN Doc. A/42/574, S/19143, 18 September 1987.
5 UN Doc. A/C.2/42/SR.21, p. 12, 1987.
6 *Pravda*, 28 September 1988.
7 *Pravda*, 8 December 1988.
8 The USSR motivated its decision not to participate by the fact that the GDR was not invited.

9 See O. Kolbasov, 'The Concept of Environmental Security (Legal Aspects)', *Soviet State and Law*, 1988, No. 12; A. Timoshenko, 'The Global Environmental Security: International Legal Aspects', *Soviet State and Law*, 1989, No. 1; M. Mitrofanov, 'International Environmental Security in the Legal System of USIS', in *Universal System of International Security and Law*, Moscow, 1987 (all in Russian).
10 'Our Common Future', *World Commission on Environment and Development*, Oxford and New York, 1987.
11 Official Records of the General Assembly, Forty-second Session, Suppl. No. 25 (A/42/25 and Corr. 1), annex II.
12 UN Doc. A/Conf. 130/21, para. 14.
13 I. Seidel-Hohenveldern, 'Transfrontier Pollution Control and Criminal Law', *Law and State*, 1977, No. 16; W. Ophuls, *Ecology and Politics of Scarcity*, San Francisco, 1977; N. Myers, 'The Environmental Dimension to Security Issues', *The Environmentalist*, Winter, 1986.
14 R. P. Dhokalia, 'The Challenges to Contemporary International Law in an Integrated Global System'. Paper prepared for the Fifth Indo-Soviet Seminar on International Law, Moscow, 30 September – 8 October 1987, p. 15.
15 O. Kolbasov, op. cit., p. 48.
16 *Pravda*, 17 July 1988.
17 A. Timoshenko, op. cit.
18 See A. Vasiliev, *Legal Categories*, Moscow, 1976, p. 181 (in Russian).
19 See 'Our Common Future', pp. 352–5.
20 In the Law of the Sea this principle has been unequivocally expressed in the UN LOS Convention, art. 192: 'States shall protect and preserve the marine environment'.
21 *Pravda*, 26 January 1989.
22 'Our Common Future', pp. 316–7.
23 The UN International Law Commission has qualified such actions as international crimes. *Report of the International Law Commission: 28th session*, New York, 1977, Ch. 3, Art. 19.
24 Such practice is envisaged in the UN Law of the Sea Convention of 1982 which provides for the establishment of a special Chamber for sea-bed disputes within the Law of the Sea Tribunal.
25 'Our Common Future', p. 321.
26 O. Kolbasov, op. cit., p. 54.
27 The idea to create such a centre was first proposed in the speech of M. Gorbachev at the 43rd Session of the UN General Assembly. (*Pravda*, 8 December 1988) and further elaborated in a letter of the Minister of Foreign Affairs of the USSR addressed to the UN General Secretary (*Pravda*, 4 May 1989).
28 V. I. Vernadski, op. cit., p. 508.

17.

International Law, Nuclear Pollution and the Environment: The United Kingdom Experience

JOHN WOODLIFFE

The United Kingdom has always been in the forefront of the development of nuclear power for civil purposes. In October 1956, the world's first commercial nuclear power station began generating electricity at Calder Hall in Cumbria. The UK is one of only two countries in the Western world to undertake the reprocessing of spent fuel on a commercial basis. As of 31 December 1987, 38 out of the 417 nuclear power plants in operation worldwide were located in the UK,[1] accounting for 19 per cent of its total electricity requirements. In terms of the world's total installed nuclear generating capacity the UK occupies eighth place.[2] Geophysical factors have significantly shaped UK policy on the siting of nuclear plant; lacking rivers of a size adequate to cool large nuclear stations it has opted, in the main, for coastal sites.

At the same time, the UK has recognised the international dimension, implicit in the nuclear fuel cycle, to the commercial development of peaceful nuclear relations between states.[3] It is a founder member of the International Atomic Energy Agency (IAEA). Since 1973, the UK has been subject to the authority of the European Atomic Energy Community (EURATOM). The UK is also a member of the Nuclear Energy Agency (NEA) of the Orgnisation for Economic Co-operation and Development (OECD). The Statute of the NEA, while lacking the supra-national character of the Euratom Treaty, seeks, by means of harmonisation of measures taken at national level to promote, *inter alia*, 'the preservation of the environment'.[4] For most people in the United Kingdom, as elsewhere, it is the environmental issues associated with the use of nuclear energy that arouse greatest concern, in particular, the effects of exposure to releases of radioactivity, whether controlled or uncontrolled and whether local or transnational in origin.

Sellafield

Sellafield, situated on the Cumbrian coast and dubbed by its critics as 'nuclear dustbin to the world',[5] is the largest nuclear complex in the UK. It has been an integral part of the British nuclear industry – for civil as well as military purposes – since the end of the Second World War.[6] The main activities on site are associated with the storage and reprocessing of irradiated nuclear fuel. It receives for storage in cooling ponds used fuel from several types of reactor at both home and abroad. British Nuclear Fuels plc, a state-owned company, is the site operator. Its chief role is to provide fuel cycle services for UK nuclear power stations. It has also signed contracts for storage and reprocessing of spent nuclear fuel with thirty four overseas customers;[7] to this end a new thermal oxide reprocessing plant (THORP) is currently under construction at Sellafield and is due to start up in 1992. Sellafield accounts for the great proportion of both liquid and gaseous radioactive waste discharges from UK sources, making it the world's largest recorded source of radioactive discharges.[8] Each day, some 4·5m litres of treated liquid are pumped through pipelines into the Irish Sea, earning it the title of 'the most radioactive sea in the world'.[9] In terms of the toxicity of the substances emitted, Sellafield is claimed to be responsible for 90 per cent of the radioactive discharges in Europe,[10] and globally for 80 per cent.[11] As will be discussed later, the volume and content of radioactivity discharged into the Irish Sea has led to complaints by the Irish Government and calls from the European and Irish Parliaments for the closure of the plant.

Much of the pollution of the Irish Sea has resulted not from the normal operation of the plant but from numerous 'incidents'.[12] Over the period October 1950 – February 1986[13] some 300 such incidents were documented. The most significant incident in terms of trans-boundary effects and the most serious in terms of the volume of radioactivity released, occurred at Windscale on 8 October 1957.[14] A fire in the core of the No. 1 Pile released a substantial cloud of radioactivity which is now known to have led to increased radioactivity in several European and Scandinavian countries;[15] at the time, however, these countries were not told about the accident.[16]

This is the essential background to the two main concerns of the remainder of this chapter: a case-study of UK practice relating to the operational disposal and discharge of radioactive waste; and an assessment of that experience in terms of whether it discloses evidence of obligatory international standards of conduct. This is prefaced by a brief description of the technical substratum of waste disposal operations in the civil nuclear industry.

What is nuclear pollution?

Adapting the definition of the term used in numerous environmental protection treaties,[17] pollution is the introduction by man of substances or energy to the environment resulting in deleterious effects such as hazards to human health, harm to living resources and to ecosystems and material property, and impairment of amenities.

A method of operating nuclear power stations that does not entail the release of radioactive substances to the environment has yet to be found. The UK nuclear industry and government departments associated with its regulation, strive assiduously to avoid the term 'pollution' – preferring the more sanitised terminology of 'discharge', 'management' and 'disposal' of 'radioactive waste' – a dissociation that it is not always possible to sustain.[18] In similar vein, information literature produced for the public by the nuclear industry and government departments stress that, on average, only 0 · 1 per cent of all radiation to which the public is exposed is attributable to waste discharges from nuclear stations in the UK.

Types of radioactive waste[19]

(a) Contained waste

Radioactive waste can be classified into two basic categories: 'contained' waste and 'discharged' waste. The former arises mostly in solid form or is transferred into solid form for long-term storage.[20] Contained waste constitutes a substantial proportion of the total waste produced by the nuclear fuel cycle. The general philosophy for dealing with these wastes is one of isolation from the environment by techniques known as 'concentration and containment' and 'delay and decay'. The classification of solid wastes is broadly determined by their level of radioactivity; this in turn conditions the mode of treatment and storage, and the disposal route. High level waste (HLW) derives exclusively from the reprocessing of spent fuel and is liquid in form. Eventually, the liquids will be solidified by vitrification or encapsulation and then stored for fifty years at least, prior to final disposal. At present, the UK does not regard spent fuel as waste, but as a resource, since reprocessing extracts uranium that can be used to fuel reactors.

Intermediate level waste (ILW) consists of material which requires handling by remote control and shielding. It includes the metal fuel cladding and used reactor components. At present ILW arising from the UK civil nuclear programme is held in concrete stores awaiting the development of treatment techniques that will render the waste capable of final disposal.

Low level waste (LLW) – 12 per cent of which comes from defence, medical and industrial uses of nuclear energy – includes contaminated refuse such as protective clothing, laboratory equipment and sludges produced from treatment processes. About 20,000 tons of LLW are produced annually. UK policy hitherto has been to bury LLW in shallow trenches at Drigg, Cumbria. A second, much smaller site at Dounreay, in Caithness, takes LLW packed into steel drums which are then stored in a deep trench adjacent to the shoreline. In 1988, a start was made on making the disposal of LLW much safer by means of concrete-lined vaults into which waste compacted into drums or concrete boxes will be placed. Prior to 1983, the UK also disposed of solid LLW and ILW at sea in a defined area of the North Atlantic ocean. The legal aspects of this policy, on which the UK is said to be 'virtually isolated internationally', are dealt with below.

The Nuclear Industry Radioactive Waste Executive (NIREX)

The pressure on existing LLW and ILW storage sites resulted in the setting up in July 1982, of NIREX, which in 1985 was incorporated as UK Nirex Ltd. The Directorate of the Executive consists of all the major players on the British nuclear stage: British Nuclear Fuels plc (BNFL); the Central Electricity Generating Board (CEGB); the South of Scotland Electricity Board (SSEB); and the United Kingdom Atomic Energy Authority (UKAEA). In addition, two directors are appointed by the Government who holds one 'golden share'. Among NIREX's functions are: the selection and provision of sites suitable for repositories for LLW and ILW, together with the management, construction and operation of the sites. The work of NIREX is complementary to that of the Radioactive Waste Management Advisory Committee (RWMAC), a technical committee set up in 1978 to advise and report annually on, *inter alia*, the environmental aspects of handling and treating wastes. In 1987, NIREX issued a public discussion document, *The Way Forward*.[21] This sought to promote public understanding and discussion. The document sets out three options for a deep disposal facility for LLW and ILW: (1) under land accessed from a land base; (2) under the seabed, accessed from a coastal land base; (3) under the seabed, accessed from an offshore structure. The responses to the document were independently collated and published in November 1988.[22] The main findings revealed safety to be the paramount factor for all consultees. Monitoring and recoverability of wastes was considered to be important, and there was virtually no support for a seabed accessed offshore repository; in addition, there was general concern that radioactive contamination of the sea should be avoided. The document refers to the view of the Norwegian Environment Ministry that a precautionary approach should govern any proposal for an offshore repository, and quotes from the submission made by the Ministry: 'a guarantee against marine pollution is imperative'.[23] In its response to the NIREX document, RWMAC expressed strong reservations about an offshore repository. It also stressed that the fullest possible scientific assessments should be made available to neighbouring countries.[24] In March 1989, NIREX announced that it was recommending exploration of sites at Sellafield and Dounreay to gauge their suitability as a deep repository for LLW and ILW. The Government has accepted the recommendation.[25]

(b) Discharged waste

The approach to gaseous wastes emitted from chimney stacks and low level liquid waste discharged from pipelines into the sea or inland waters, lakes and rivers, is very different to that governing contained waste. Here, the technique is one of 'dilution and disposal' into the environment. The underlying *premiss* is that the release of wastes in such a way that they are immediately dispersed and sufficiently diluted in water or air poses no appreciable risk to human health and the environment. It is these direct discharges into the environment, particularly of liquids, that 'cause the greatest anxiety'.[26]

The principles of control[27]

The basic principle of control adopted in the UK, and indeed in the great majority of States with a civil nuclear power capability, requires that operational discharges and disposals of radioactive waste – whether solid, liquid or gaseous – are regulated by a system of authorisation that is independent of the nuclear plant's management. In the UK, no discharge to the environment may be made unless authorised by the Department of the Environment (DOE), in conjunction with the Ministry of Agriculture, Fisheries and Food (MAFF).[28]

The authorisations will include such conditions as the authorising department deems appropriate in the circumstances of each plant. Authorisations issued to the plant operator invariably include: (1) numerical limits on the amounts of radioactivity that may be discharged over specified periods of time; (2) the use by the operator of the 'best practicable means' to limit the radioactivity of the waste discharged; (3) control of the forms of radioactivity ('particulates') which may be discharged; (4) control over the manner in which the latter may be discharged; (5) measurement, monitoring and recording of the quantum and radioactive content of material discharged, especially in the immediate environment.[29]

Current UK practice for determining the conditions of an authorisation appertaining to protection of the public against radiation hazards follows the guidelines drawn up by the International Commission on Radiological Protection (ICRP) in 1977.[30] The standards of radiological protection recommended by the ICRP have acquired international acceptance and provide the basis of European Community measures on radiological safety standards.[31]

The ICRP guidelines that underpin UK law and policy are threefold. First, the principle of dose limitation ensures that, irrespective of cost, no member of the public receives per annum more than the recommended ICRP dose limits for the whole body.[32] As even strict adherence to these limits may be inadequate – there being a possibility of harm even from extremely low doses of radiation – the dose limitation principle is reinforced by two further principles, namely: no practice involving radiation exposure may be employed unless it produces a net positive benefit; and the ICRP individual and collective dose limits are to be reduced to levels which are as low as reasonably achievable, economic and social factors being taken into account. The last principle is known as the ALARA principle. In practical terms it imposes on the site operator an obligation to act 'to reduce radiation exposures until the costs of further action become grossly disproportionate in the estimated reduction in residual risk.'[33]

The ALARA principle in a nuclear context

While the philosophy of 'ALARA' is to be found in the regulatory systems of all states with civil nuclear power status, it may be premature to confer on it the character of a legally binding international norm (an issue considered in the concluding section). Some of the difficulties attaching to the concept were highlighted in the recent report on radioactive waste by the House of Lords Select Committee on the European Communities.[34] The Committee found evidence of a widespread lack of uniformity among states, including Member States of the European Community, in the application of the principle. This assumed critical importance where discharges crossed national boundaries and affected populations in other States.[35]

Unlike some countries, where ALARA is applied with reference to prescribed criteria, in the UK it is applied on a case-by-case basis.[36] In the view of the Select Committee, ALARA has effectively become equivalent to what is called ALATA – as low as technically achievable – but within the constraints of economic justification.[37] In contrast, the UK Government's officially held view is that there is not even a generally accepted definition of ALARA and that unless qualified, for example, by the costs factor, 'the concept is neither quantifiable nor enforceable'.[38]

At European Community level, Article 37 of EURATOM provides the Commission with a means of achieving some element of a common approach to the definition of 'reasonable' in the ALARA principle. Article 37 requires Member States to provide the Commission 'with such general data relating to any plan for the disposal of radioactive waste in whatever form as will make it possible to determine whether the implementation of such plan is liable to result in the radioactive contamination of the water, soil or airspace of another Member State ...'.[39] The Commission must deliver its Opinion on the plan within six months. This enables the Commission to evaluate and comment on the proposed discharge authorisation and thereby to individualise the application of the ALARA principle. An illustration is the Opinion of the Commission on the Heysham No. 2 nuclear power station in Lancashire, published on 26 February 1987. The Opinion stated that while the discharges envisaged would not result in a significant hazard to the health of the population, water, soil or airspace of the nearest Member State, namely, Ireland, the limits for liquid effluents were 'unnecessarily high'. The Opinion accordingly recommended they 'be fixed at levels taking into account the ALARA principle'.[40]

The Commission, in a report on the application of Article 37 for the period 1975–86,[41] noted that several Opinions urged national authorities to ensure that the discharge limits finally adopted took full account of the ALARA principle. While the Opinions are not legally binding on Member States, they nevertheless 'add to the moral pressure on any government to consider whether the proposals are in accord with the ALARA principle'.[42] Although the timing of the notification requirement under Article 37 has been strengthened by a recent ruling of the European Court,[43] its practical impact remains weak. It would appear, therefore, that the ALARA principle is far from satisfactory in practice. Several proposals have been put forward to improve the situation. First, in 1984 a Private Members' Bill was unsuccessfully introduced into the UK Parliament to enshrine the ALATA principle in law by statutorily fixing discharges of liquid waste into the sea.[44] The Bill was directed primarily at the Sellafield plant, where it was claimed discharge limits were markedly above those operated at comparable plants elsewhere. Secondly, the House of Commons Environment Committee's report on radioactive waste[45] suggested that drastically lower numerical limits for gaseous and liquid discharges should be set for all nuclear plant in the UK. By giving the new limits the status of fixed emission limits, all reference to the ALARA principle would be dispensed with. In addition, the Committee's proposal for a review of authorisations every three years would exert a constant downward pressure on the overall level of discharges. These recommendations were rejected by the Government on the grounds that they would encourage operators to regard the limits as targets and act as a disincentive to use the best practicable means to improve performance further.[46] Thirdly, in a European Community context, support has been expressed for the establishment of a Community nuclear inspectorate, based within the Commission, with powers to investigate situations at nuclear plants independently of national inspection and to monitor the enforcement of environmental safety standards.[47]

Case study: the Cumbrian beaches incident 1983[48]

Over a period of six days in November 1983, a series of abnormal liquid discharges were made from the Sellafield plant by pipeline to the sea. This followed cleaning out of the reprocessing plant during annual maintenance. Due to management error and defective record keeping, radioactive liquids destined for transfer to a storage tank were pumped into the sea. The public subsequently were advised to avoid 'unnecessary use' of the beaches ten miles on either side of the pipeline and to refrain from handling objects washed up by the sea. This effectively closed the stretch of beach for several months.[49] Following investigation of the incident by the DOE Radiochemical Inspectorate and the HSE Nuclear Installations Inspectorate,[50] BNFL introduced a number of short-term safety measures. Both reports raised the possibility of a failure by the site management to meet the ALARA principle.[51] In October 1984, criminal proceedings were instituted against BNFL by the Director of Public Prosecutions. The charges were brought under the Radioactive Substances Act 1960 and the Nuclear Installations Act 1965. BNFL was charged with, *inter alia:* (1) discharging highly radioactive matter and liquids into the sea 'to such amount and at such a rate that radiation exposure ... was not as low as was reasonably achievable', (2) failing to ensure 'that any person in the vicinity of the end of the discharge pipe or using adjacent waters knew of the risk' and hence 'failing to take all reasonable steps to minimise the exposure to persons of radiation'. These two charges were viewed as testing the practicability of ALARA as a workable legal principle.[52] The Crown Court trial lasted seven weeks and BNFL were convicted and fined £5 000 and £2 500 respectively on the abovementioned counts. The trial judge indicated that the sentence had taken into account: (a) that the discharge to sea had been within authorised limits; (b) the absence of harm or risk of harm to the public, and (c) the record of the company in conscientiously adhering to the ALARA principle.[53]

During a highly critical debate on the Sellafield plant incident in the European Parliament, Mr. Clinton Davies, then the Commissioner reponsible for environmental matters, pointed out that the plant had never – including the instant case – exceeded the maximum permissible levels of discharge under Community law, since it was set up in 1950. His main concern, however, focused on the verdict in the Crown Court proceedings that the ALARA principle had been broken; this still left several questions unanswered, for example: the way in which the offences had come to light;[54] whether the release was accidental or intentional;[55] whether the discharge could have been avoided;[56] how much radioactivity was released into the sea,[57] and whether the warning to the public was sufficiently prompt.[58]

Subsequent developments

The 1983 incident, together with the long history of high levels of discharge relative to comparable nuclear plants elsewhere, intensified the Irish Government's concern about the long-term effects of the radioactive discharges from Sellafield into the Irish Sea. The total amount of plutonium so far discharged is estimated at 200 kg. In addition, a report of Irish medical experts indicated abnormally high cancer clusters among children living on the east coast of Ireland. This anxiety was compounded by disclosures about the 1957 Windscale fire that had only come to light through documents released from the Public Record Office thirty years later. [59]

Formal representations are reported to have been made to the British Government in February 1984.[60] Shortly afterwards, arrangements were made for officials from both States to meet regularly and for joint monitoring of the Irish Sea. In June 1984, the Paris Commission (whose membership includes the UK and Ireland) established under the 1974 Convention on Marine Pollution from Land-Based Sources,[61] adopted a recommendation put forward by the Nordic States, that all Contracting Parties 'take account of the best available technology at existing and planned nuclear reprocessing plants in order to minimise radioactive discharges to the marine environment'. In what represented a significant change in policy, the UK agreed to the recommendation;[62] it regards the programme for reducing discharges from Sellafield (outlined below) as complying with the recommendation.

Following a further incident in 1986, in which 440 kg of uranium were discharged into the Irish Sea,[63] the pressure grew on the UK Government to take drastic remedial action. First, the UK Prime Minister, Mrs. Thatcher, in the course of a meeting in February 1986 with the *Taoiseach*, Dr. Fitzgerald, undertook to forward to the Irish Government detailed information about 'incidents at Sellafield and radiation pollution in and around Ireland'; the UK reply blamed pollution fears on media exaggeration.[64] Secondly, the Irish Energy Minister called for an international campaign for the closure of the Sellafield plant, the existence of which was tantamount to 'invading our sovereignty and undermining our integrity as a nation'.[65] On 3 December 1986, the *Dail* passed a resolution calling for the closure of the plant.[66] According to the UK Secretary of State for the Environment, Mr. Ridley, this action was 'misconceived'; radioactive discharges to the environment were one-sixth of their 1979 levels and there was 'no appreciable evidence that the Irish Sea has suffered from Sellafield'.[67]

At the meeting of the Paris Commission held in Lisbon in June 1988, Ireland sought the adoption of a recommendation calling for the closure of Sellafield but it failed to secure the necessary majority.[68] From 1984 onwards, BNFL invested heavily in new treatment plants aimed at substantial reductions in discharges.[69] These developments, which have reduced discharge levels to well below the peak levels of the mid-seventies, are reckoned to bring Sellafield into line with those of the major French reprocessing plant at *La Hague*; nor will these lower levels be affected by the coming on stream of THORP in 1992.[70] The new authorisation regulating discharges came into force on 1 July 1986. In addition to the quantitative and temporal limits on discharge of specific radionuclides, BNFL is instructed to employ the best practicable means to limit discharges.[71] In stating that reliance on the 'dilute and dispose' policy is no longer prudent, the BNFL management has declared its intention to 'invest heavily to reduce discharge levels below those set by the new authorisation'.[72] The report of the House of Lords European Communites Committee emphasised that the marked improvement in the situation at Sellafield must be sustained;[73] but it was satisfied that 'general pollution by radioactive effluent is now both low and strictly controlled'.[74]

Despite the improved position at Sellafield, the Irish Government is not satisfied and is understood to be actively reviewing the options open to it for taking legal action.[75] The most likely option is at European Community level; on the international claims level, legal action in respect of an area that is *res extra commercium* would have to contend with the problem of *locus standi*.

Dumping of nuclear waste at sea[76]

Historically, sea disposal has been the UK's favoured option for the management of low and intermediate level radioactive waste. From 1949–79, the UK dumped an estimated 67 000 metric tonnes of radioactive waste, 70 per cent of which comprised concrete and steel packaging.[77] The main dumping area, of some 16 000 square miles, is in the North Atlantic ocean some 900 kms SSW off Land's End. The depth of the superadjacent waters is 4 500 metres.[78] Criteria governing ocean dumping are laid down by the IAEA[79] and national authorities invariably impose a licensing requirement.[80] Early on, the practice developed of an annual dumping operation in which the UK joined other European States. From 1967, the Nuclear Energy Agency of the OECD assumed responsiblity for the conduct and control of the operation.[81] By 1971, the North Atlantic site had become the world's sole authorised nuclear waste sea-dump site. By 1982, only the UK, Belgium and Switzerland continued to use the site, the UK accounting for 92 per cent of the total waste dumped.[82] Prompted by a growing international concern about the long-term pollution hazards of ocean dumping, a majority of the parties to the 1972 Convention on the Prevention of Marine Pollution by Dumping of Waste and Other Matter[83] (better known as the London Dumping Convention) agreed, at a consultative meeting in February 1983, to a two-year moratorium on ocean dumping of radioactive waste, pending the outcome of various international scientific reviews.[84] The UK opposed the suspension on both scientific and legal grounds.[85] In July 1983, the UK Government publicly stated its intention to license the dumping of 3 500 tonnes of nuclear waste at the North Atlantic dump site.[86] The plan was abandoned as a result of the campaign by the National Union of Seamen, supported by other trades unions, to refuse to handle any radioactive waste intended for dumping at sea.[87] This impasse led the Government and the Trades Union Congress to agree jointly to the setting up of an independent panel of scientists, chaired by Prof. F. G. T. Holliday, 'to review the scientific evidence, including the environmental implications relevant to the safety of disposal of radioactive waste at the designated North Atlantic site'. The Holliday Report,[88] while recognising the depth of feeling against 'using the seas as a rubbish tip for radioactive waste', concluded that the risks from sea dumping were very small. Nevertheless, the Report recommended a continuation of the moratorium until current international reviews were completed and a comparative assessment had been undertaken of all disposal and storage options with a view to establishing the 'best practicable environmental option' for each type of waste.[89]

In 1985, a meeting of the parties to the London Dumping Convention adopted a stronger resolution than that in 1983, and agreed to an indefinite moratorium, international scientific reviews notwithstanding. It is apparent that the UK is keen to keep the option of sea dumping available.[90] Unless, however, it is able to convince other nations, the UK will remain internationally isolated on this issue and its stance will serve only to obscure the need to find land-based disposal sites.[91] More recently, UK Government statements indicate that, while there will be no resumption of sea-dumping of drummed radioactive waste, it is UK policy to keep open the possibility of sea disposal for large items arising from decommissioning of nuclear plants.[92]

Conclusion

The UK experience has been chiefly that of a perpetrator rather than of a victim of nuclear pollution. Moreover, because of the UK's position as a major civil nuclear power, its practice *prima facie* carries some degree of weight and significance in the process of formation of customary norms of conduct. This process has been described as one 'through which political discretion of states gradually narrows down into progressively restrictive, unavoidable and firmly obligatory patterns'.[93] The present case-study confirms this view of the indivisibility of law and politics in the evolution of customary rules of state conduct. To apply a traditional sovereignty-based approach to the operation of civil nuclear plant has two unsatisfactory consequences: first, such activity is viewed as essentially an internal matter for the State which has licensed it; secondly, the approach presumptively imposes on other States the burden of proving the existence of customary rules of international law which restrict the licensing State's freedom of action. Over the last decade, there has been a discernible shift towards the position that civil nuclear power operations are of 'legitimate concern for neighbouring states and for the international community'.[94] As the margin of discretion becomes ever narrower, so the point is reached at which *opinio juris* is established. The survey of practice in this paper in respect of the Sellafield plant is material evidence of these changes. The exact moment, however, at which a norm of conduct 'suddenly bursts into its legal existence',[95] is not easy to capture. The UK has tried to keep the debate with other States over liquid radioactive discharges to the sea at a technical, rather than a legal level, resisting attempts to make ALARA a legally quantifiable and enforceable principle; in this way, it has given itself flexibility of manoeuvre. In contrast, where the dumping of containerised radioactive waste at sea is concerned, the UK, while agreeing reluctantly to the moratorium recommended by the Paris Commission, has firmly reserved its legal position; in this instance, the practice has not been accompanied by *opinio juris*. The ALARA principle has proved to be a useful stick with which to beat recalcitrant governments; the latter cannot turn a blind eye to state-of-the-art technology. In the realm of civil nuclear power there is arguably now a duty on States to keep up with the best available practice. The contemporary formulation of the ALARA principle thus combines the exigencies of economic practicability with technological advance; it also serves to reinforce the current downward trend in discharges of radioactivity to the environment.

This survey of the UK's experience regarding the disposal and discharge of radioactive waste points to limitations on the efficacy of the juridical norm, whether of the 'hard' or 'soft' variety, as a regulator of state conduct in the environmental arena. At the same time it suggests that the cumulative pressure exerted on an unco-operative state by neighbouring states, non-governmental environmental organisations and bureaucratic-intrusive international and regional bodies, provides in the long term a more effective spur to remedial action.

Notes

1 *Nuclear Power Reactors in the World*, IAEA, 1988.

2 IAEA. Power Reactor Information System.

3 *The Regulation of Nuclear Trade: Non-proliferation, Supply, Safety. Vol. I International Aspects*, OECD, 1988.

4 See Articles 1, 8, Statute of the OECD Nuclear Energy Agency 1957, as amended in 1978.

5 Judith Cook, *Red Alert*, New English Library, 1986, ch. 5. Until 1981, Sellafield was known as Windscale.

6 See *The Development of Atomic Energy 1939–1984: Chronolgy of Events* (2nd ed., 1984), UKAEA.

7 H. C. Deb. V. 146 c. 694,8 February 1989.

8 *First Report from the House of Commons Environment Committee: Radioactive Waste* (Session 1985–86), Vol. I HCP 191, paras. 116, 118ff.

9 Ibid., para. 116. The volume of discharges from a reprocessing plant is much greater than from an ordinary reactor.

10 O. J. Deb. Eur. Parl. Doc. No. 2–329/12, 9 September 1985.

11 *Nature*, BBC 2, transmitted on 23 February 1989.

12 The nuclear industry prefers to use this term rather than 'accident'.

13 Advertisement placed by Friends of the Earth in the *Guardian* (24 February 1986); reproduced in Cook, *supra*, n. 5, Appendix 1. Several of the major incidents are reported ibid., ch. 5. In contrast, BNFL have recorded only fourteen accidents as involving 'abnormal release of radioactivity to the environment': *Investigation of the possible increased incidence of cancer in West Cumbria: Report of the Independent Advisory Group* (the Black Report), HMSO, 1984, para. 4. 17.

14 Cook, loc. cit., p. 140; R. Pocock, *Nuclear Power: Its Development in the U.K.*, 1977, ch. 4.

15 J. Blok, 7 *Applied Sci. Res.* 150 (1958); National Radiological Protection Board, *An Assessment of the Radiological Impact of the Windscale Reactor Fire*, October 1957, HMSO, 1983.

16 See 'The Windscale Fire 1957: a bibliography of publicly available material', *Atom* No. 372, pp. 27–9 (October 1987).

17 For example, Article 1, Convention on Long-Range Trans-boundary Air Pollution 1979 (text in 18 ILM 1442, 1979). The term 'environmental interference' is used in the Legal Principles for Environmental Protection and Sustainable Development drawn up by the experts group on environmental law of the World Commission on Environment and Development. The Legal Principles are reproduced in J. Lammers and R. Munro, *Environmental Protection and Sustainable Development*, Nijhoff/Graham & Trotman, 1987.

18 e.g., The Control of Pollution (Radioactive Waste Regulations) 1985 S.I.708. The body responsible in England and Wales for setting discharge limits for all forms of radioactive waste is called Her Majesty's Inspectorate of Pollution; the Sixth Report of the Royal Commission on Environmental Pollution in 1976 concerns the subject of nuclear power and the environment. Cmnd 6618 (hereinafter the Flowers Report).

19 Nineteenth Report of the House of Lords Select Committee on the European Communities: *Radioactive Waste Management* (Session 1987–88) 2 Vols. HLP 99. Part 3; First Report from the House of Commons Environment Committee: *Radioactive Waste* (Session 1985–1986) 2 Vols. HCP 191 chs 2 and 6; debated in H. C. Deb. V. 139 c 578, 28 October 1988.

20 Nuclear waste dumped at sea is 'contained' waste: see *infra*.

21 *The Way Forward*, 1987. Some 50,000 copies of this and a summary document were distributed throughout the U.K.

22 *Responses to the Way Forward*, Environmental Risk Assessment Unit, University of East Anglia, November 1988.

23 Ibid., p. 22.

24 Radioactive Waste Management Advisory Committee, *Report of Subgroup on the Nirex Proposals for Deep Site Investigations*, H.M.S.O., 1988., paras. 3, 8.

25 *Guardian*, 22 March 1989; H. C. Deb. V.149 c.505, 21 March 1989.

26 HCP 191-I *supra*, n. 8, para. 116.

27 See The Flowers Report, *supra*, n. 18, ch. V.

28 Sections 6 and 7, Radioactive Substances Act 1960.

29 See *Monitoring of Radioactivity in the UK Environment*, HMSO, 1988, p. 1. This report describes the programme of environmental monitoring for each nuclear site operator as well as the programmes carried out by government and other independent organisations.

30 Set out in ICRP Publication 26 and subsequent explanatory statements by ICRP in 1985 and 1987.

31 Dir. 80/836 EURATOM, OJ L246, 17 September 1980, p. 1.; Dir 84/467 EURATOM, OJ L265, 5 October 1984, p. 4.

32 UK indivudal dose limits are appreciably below the ICRP recommended levels.

33 Loc. cit., *supra*, n. 19, at para. 37.

34 Ibid., paras. 76, 77.

35 Ibid., para. 76.

36 Ibid., para. 37.

37 Ibid.

38 The Government's Response to the Environment Committee's Report on Radioactive Waste, Cmnd 9852, July 1986, para. 58.

39 The data submitted should follow the scheme set out in Recommendation 82/181 EURATOM, OJ L83/15, 29 March 1982. For a list of the submissions made by the UK Government pursuant to Article 37 over the period 1974–87 see H. C. Deb. V. 127 c. 461, 15 February 1988; updated to December 1988, H. C. Deb. V. 144 c. 51, 19 December 1988.

40 Opinion 87/170 EURATOM, L68/33, 12 March 1987.

41 COM (88) 109 FINAL.

42 HLP 99, *supra*, n. 19, para. 78.

43 Case 187/87, *Saarland & Others* v. *Minister for Industry Posts, and Telecommunications*, [1989] 1 CMLR 529.

44 Discharge of Radioactive Material (Control) Bill (Bill 161), sponsored by Mr. D. N. Campbell-Savours, MP, H. C. Deb. V. 58 c. 754, 25 April 1984.

45 HCP 191, *supra* n. 8, Recommendation 14.

46 Cmnd 9852, *supra*, n. 38 para. 66.

47 HLP 99, *supra*, n. 19, para. 76; Deb. Eur. Parl. No. 2 329/13/23, 9 September 1985; communication to author from Irish Embassy, London, 5 April 1989.

48 Cook, *supra*, n. 5 at p. 150ff.

49 Statement by the Secretary of State for the Environment, H. C. Deb. V. 51 c. 429, 21 December 1983.

50 *An incident leading to contamination of the beaches near the British Nuclear Fuels Windscale and Calder Works, Sellafield, November 1983*, DOE, 1984; *The Contamination of the Beach Incident at British Nuclear Fuels Ltd, Sellafield, November 1983*, HSE, 1984.

51 See statement by Secretary of State for the Environment. H. C. Deb. V. 54 c. 131, 14 February 1984.

52 D. Fishlock, 'Pollution control principle faces legal test', *Financial Times*, 5 June 1985.

53 *Atom*, No. 347, p. 76, September 1985.

54 The discharge was first detected by a Greenpeace vessel, purely coincidentally, in the course of action by Greenpeace taken as part of a general campaign against discharges from Sellafield to block the pipe outlet to the sea: Cook, *supra*, n. 5, p. 151. Greenpeace was later fined £50 000 for refusing to comply with an injunction not to interfere with the pipe: *Guardian*, 2 December 1983.

55 The Commissioner felt that the release was 'at least in part . . . deliberate': Deb. Eur. Parl. No. 2 – 329/22, 9 September 1985.

56 This was answered in the affirmative at the trial; ibid.

57 It was established that 4 500 curies were released from the reprocessing plant into the sea tank; the inadequacy of the records meant that there was no means of quantifying what part of this was pumped into the sea; ibid.

58 That this was not the case is implicit in the jury's verdict of guilty; ibid.

59 See R. Norton-Taylor, 'Chain reaction of errors in Windscale Fire', *Guardian*, 2 January 1988.

60 Speech of Mrs Banotti, Irish MEP. Deb. Eur. Parl. No. 2–329/14, 9 September 1985; 'Dublin demands Sellafield action'; *Guardian*, 18 February 1984.

61 Text in 13 ILM 352 (1974).

62 *Atom*, No. 335, p. 17, September 1984.

63 H. C. Deb. V. 90 c. 650, 31 January 1986; Cook, *supra*, n. 5, p. 155ff.

64 Quoted in, 'Thatcher backs Sellafield waste plant safety record as "excellent"', *Guardian*, 8 March 1986.

65 Speech reported in *Guardian*, 29 November 1986.

66 In 1986, the European Parliament was unsuccessfully called upon to recommend the closure of Sellafield; a similar call was made by the Manx Parliament, Tynwald: *Guardian*, 21 August 1986.

67 H. C. Deb. V. 107 c. 1192, 17 December 1986.

68 H. C. Deb. V. 137 c. 702, 20 July 1988; Tenth Annual Report of the Paris Commission, 1989, para 43.

69 They include: a Site Ion Exchange Effluent Treatment Plant (SIXET); a new Salt Evaporator; and an Enhanced Actinide Removal Plant (EARP).

70 HLP 99, *supra*, n. 19, paras. 69–70.

71 H. C. Deb. V. 144 c. 578, 10 January 1989. The new authorisations are printed in full in the BNFL evidence submitted to the House of Lords Select Committee, *supra*, n. 19, Vol. II, pp. 86–92.

72 HLP 99, para. 75. For discharge figures covering 1974–1987, see H. C. Deb. V. 143 c. 50, 5 December 1988 (reductions of alpha emissions from 170 Tbq to $2 \cdot 2$ Tbq; beta from 7 200 Tbq to 89 Tbq).

73 Ibid., para. 199.

74 Para. 219.

75 Communication to author from Irish Embassy, London, 5 April 1989.

76 For a full account of UK practice, see the Holliday Report, *infra*, n. 88, ch. 3.

77 Cook, *supra*, n. 5, p. 62.

78 Flowers Report, *supra*, n. 18, paras. 369ff.

79 The IAEA has the responsibility for providing technical guidance on radioactive materials to the Contracting Parties to the London Dumping Convention, *infra*, n. 83.

80 In the UK, under the Radioactive Substances Act 1960 and Part II of the Food and Environment Protection Act 1985.

81 See later guidelines adopted in 1977 by Decision of OECD establishing a multilateral consultation and surveillance mechanism for sea dumping of radioactive waste: 18 ILM 445 (1979).

82 R. B. Clark, *The Waters Around the British Isles: Their Conflicting Uses*, 1987, OUP, p. 235.

83 11 ILM 1291 (1972). The UK ratified the Convention in 1975.

84 HCP 191, *supra* n. 19. Minutes of Evidence, Vol. II, p. 410ff.

85 H. C. Deb. V. 37 c. 428, 22 February 1983; V. 46 c. 36, 18 July 1983.

86 H. C. Deb. V. 46 c. 248, 22 July 1983.

87 Memo. of National Union of Seamen, *loc. cit. supra*, n. 84 at p. 411.

88 *Report of the Independent Review of Disposal of Radioactive Waste in the North East Atlantic*, HMSO, 1984.

89 Paras. 9.1, 9.2. See *Assessment of best practicable environmental options for management of low and intermediate level radioactive waste*, HMSO, 1986.

90 Cmnd 9852, *supra*, n. 38, paras. 37–38, 47.

91 Ibid., para. 80.
92 H. C. Deb. V. 139 c. 397, 27 October 1988.
93 Slouka, *International Custom and the Continental Shelf*, 1968, p. 4.
94 P. Sands, *Chernobyl: Law and Communication*, 1988, at p. 49.
95 Slouka, *supra*, n. 93, ibid.

Index